IMAGES
of America

BARTLETT

OUR PAST AND OUR PROGRESS

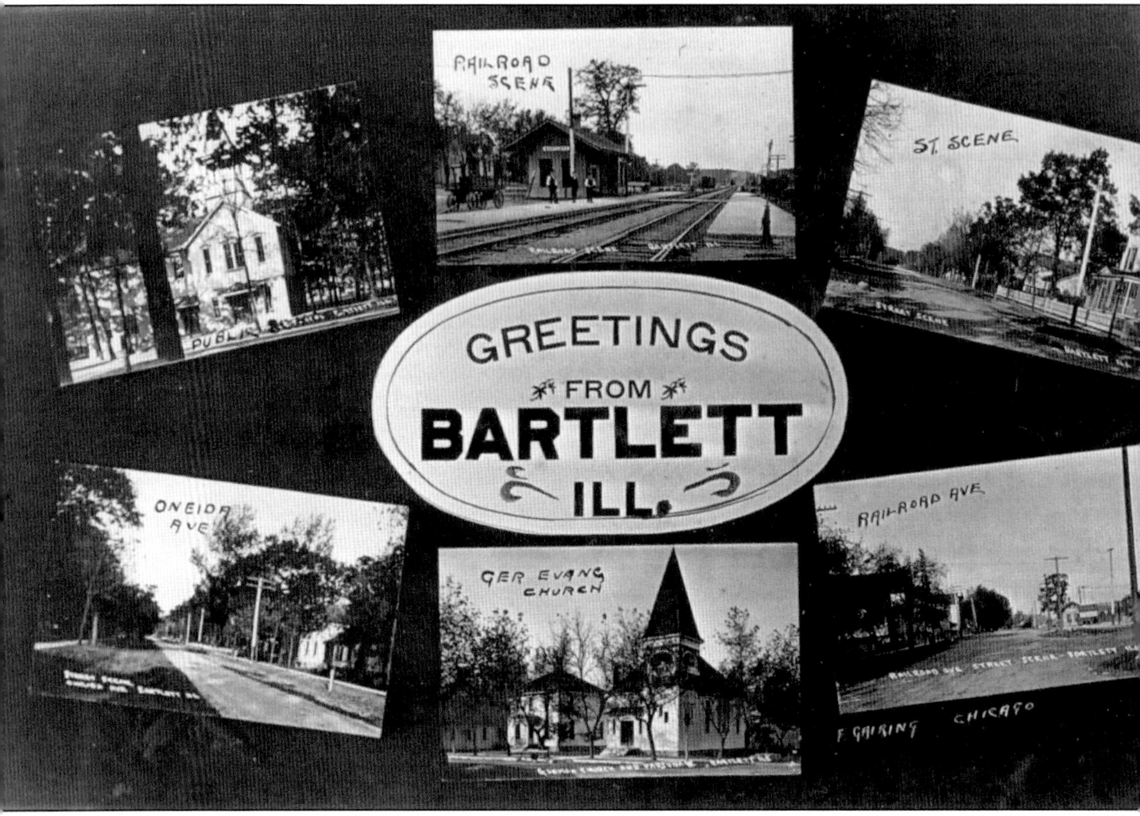

Cover Image: In 1873, the Chicago and Pacific Railroad began building a rail line from Chicago to Elgin. Luther Bartlett donated 40 acres of land and named his station stop "Bartlett." With a $300 donation from Luther, construction on the depot began in June of that year. The train depot was the first building constructed in the Village of Bartlett, is the only original station left on the Milwaukee West Line, and is also the third oldest station in the Chicago area.

IMAGES
of America

BARTLETT

OUR PAST AND OUR PROGRESS

Pamela Rohleder and Gabrielle Infusino

ARCADIA
PUBLISHING

ISBN 978-0-7385-2328-6

Published by Arcadia Publishing
Charleston, South Carolina

Printed in the United States of America

Library of Congress Catalog Card Number: 2003102286

For all general information contact Arcadia Publishing at:
Telephone 843-853-2070
Fax 843-853-0044
E-mail sales@arcadiapublishing.com
For customer service and orders:
Toll-Free 1-888-313-2665

Visit us on the Internet at www.arcadiapublishing.com

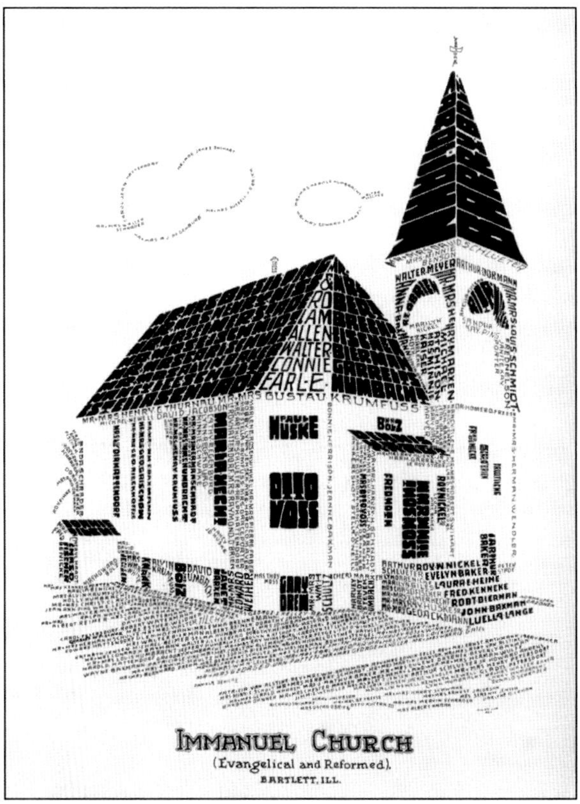

Holding true to the belief that a church is not the brick and stone of the structure but is truly its individual members, Adolph Link penned this ink drawing of Immanuel Church in 1952 using the names of the persons and families that made up the congregation.

Contents

ACKNOWLEDGMENTS

This book could not have been written without the inspiration from all of the photographs and mementos that have been shared by past and present residents with the Bartlett History Museum, throughout the years and specifically for this project. Although this book is by no means meant to be a comprehensive history, and to the regret of the authors, many wonderful pictures could not be included, we wish to thank everyone who generously lent us their family albums and scrapbooks, shared with us a nearly forgotten Bartlett anecdote or clarified a historical fact. It is mainly through these precious photos, stories and keepsakes that the fleeting moments of Bartlett's history are captured and kept, so that the next generations can always retrace the roots from which this community grew.

In putting together this book, we also relied on and benefited from many groups, individuals, and historical sources, including: The Bartlett Volunteer Fire Department; the Bartlett Fire Protection District Museum; Paul Kuester and the Bartlett Public Works Department; Ruth Norris and the Bartlett Police Department; Immanuel United Church of Christ; St. Peter Damian Catholic Parish; Immanuel Evangelical Lutheran Church; the many Bartlett civic groups; *Hanover Township: Rural Past to Urban Present* by E.C. Alft; and especially the Bartlett Centennial Commission and the Bartlett 1891-1991 Centennial Book, which was an invaluable resource for us.

Special thanks to Hoosier Grove Museum Manager Nancy Gher for making the introduction to Arcadia and whose own book *Hanover Harvesters* served as a model for this work.

Finally the authors would like to recognize the Village of Bartlett, including Village President Catherine Melchert, the Board of Trustees and Village Administrator Valerie Salmons for their support and their ongoing commitment to the preservation of local history. We also offer our appreciation to administrative staff members Karen Mich and Elizabeth McCormack for their patient tolerance of our sometimes rambunctious writing sessions. And special gratitude is extended to Assistant Village Administrator Paula Schumacher who allowed us the time and space to complete this book and never failed to cheer us on during the duration of the project.

INTRODUCTION

In its earliest incarnations, the Village of Bartlett, Illinois was an old-time camping and hunting ground for the Potawatomi, Ottawa, Miami, and Cherokee Indians. At various other times in the past, Spain, France, Virginia, England, the Northwest Territory, and Indiana also staked their claim to Bartlett. In fact, if not for the fortuitous intersection of the Chicago and Pacific Railway and 40 acres of land belonging to farmer Luther Bartlett, the Village of Bartlett, as we know it today, might never have come to pass.

The opening of the Erie Canal in 1825 opened the way for the western migration of New Yorkers and New Englanders to the Midwest. Luther Bartlett, born in 1817 in Conway, Massachusetts, made his way to Michigan in 1842 and moved to Illinois the following year. Luther and his physician brother Lyman bought 320 acres of farmland in Wayne Township in 1844 and another 345 acres the following year. Luther first tried his hand at sheep farming, but abandoned this when the price of wool went down. He then planted wheat. Luther lived on the farm with his wife Sophia and their 11 children until his death in 1882. Another brother, Edwin, established Ontarioville to the east, which was later incorporated into Hanover Park.

In 1873, when many a town lived or died according to its proximity to a railroad line, Colonel Roselle M. Hough, president of The Chicago and Pacific, began building a route west to Elgin, Illinois, to challenge the Chicago and Northwestern Railroad. People donating land for depots along the right-of-way were allowed to name the villages that were formed. Luther Bartlett donated a 40-acre "woodlot," the source of the Bartlett family's lumber and firewood, and named the town Bartlett. The original train depot still stands today and continues to serve as the heart of downtown.

The railroad was a vital link between the dairy farmers in the area and the city. The old Set-Screw factory, which stood next to the railroad line until just recently, was formerly the Huntley Dairy. It wasn't long before the area around the Bartlett train depot was found to be a hospitable home for the factories, stores, saloons, and houses being built by the large number of German immigrants who settled the area.

Adorning their storefronts and homesteads with names like Schick and Struckman, Schultz and Thurnau, Krumfuss, and Niewisch, it is these founding families of Bartlett that laid the tracks for growth. They founded Immanuel United Church of Christ, which was first built to serve the local German-speaking population and is now Bartlett's oldest continuing congregation. In the 1880s, they built Bartlett School, which has at various times served children in kindergarten through high school and has always served as a civic and social hub for the Bartlett community. These first families also spearheaded the incorporation of the Village and served as the first civic leaders.

The Village of Bartlett got its official start on Feb. 11, 1891 when the petition for incorporation was filed in Springfield, Illinois. The election for incorporation was held in Herman Niewisch's Hall on Feb. 28, 1891, and it resulted in a 49-0 vote in favor of the motion. George Struckman, a 2nd Lieutenant in the Civil War and a Springfield legislator in the 1880s, was elected as the first Village President on March 24, 1891. In that same election, Louis Stumpf became the Village Clerk, and John Carr, Jacob Schmidt, August Schick, Herman Niewisch, Charles F. Schultz, and Henry Waterman were chosen as Village Trustees.

The new century brought growth, progress, and modern issues to Bartlett. In 1901, the Village Board approved a franchise for two telephone companies, which eventually merged and became Illinois Bell Telephone Co. The first automobile arrived in the Village in 1908 and several homes were constructed in the new Schnadt subdivision in 1909. By 1910, the Village had a population of 408, and there were 200 phones in town. An ordinance to adopt the first speed limits in the Village was passed in 1915. Cars were barred from going faster than 15 miles per hour on straight roads and 10 miles per hour when turning.

In 1920s Bartlett as today, the social event of every year was the Fourth of July Parade. There was 100% participation. Patriotic residents were either in the parade or served as enthusiastic spectators. During the Great Depression, residents found some cheer by coming downtown to watch free outdoor movies. They would sit on long benches not far from the train station. The movie would be stopped briefly whenever a train came through. In the 1940s, America joined the war effort and so did Bartlett. A local chapter of the National Defense Council was organized, citizens were instructed in the handling of incendiary bombs and Victory Gardens were planted throughout the town. It wasn't until the 1950s that the Village experienced its first round of incredible growth. The 1960 census showed a population of 2,291 people, a 220% increase in just 10 years time and an auspicious foreshadowing of the booming suburban community of 37,000 that Bartlett is today.

It is our hope that this book takes you on a pleasing historical walk through the Village that existed in the years that straddled the turn of the century to the Bartlett of the mid-1960s. It is meant to show the progress of a community whose roots are European but which has grown to epitomize the all-American town. It includes images of many of Bartlett's important firsts, as well as photos of its ongoing traditions.

Finally, a pictorial history of Bartlett would be no story at all if it did not include the many wonderful pictures of its residents. From the schoolchildren of the 1920s to the firemen of the 1950s, from the shopkeepers and baseball players of the early 1900s to Bartlett's World War II generation, these photos have been saved in the care-worn albums handed down from one Bartlett generation to another and are willingly shared with the Bartlett History Museum so this story could be told.

One

FAMILY AND FRIENDS

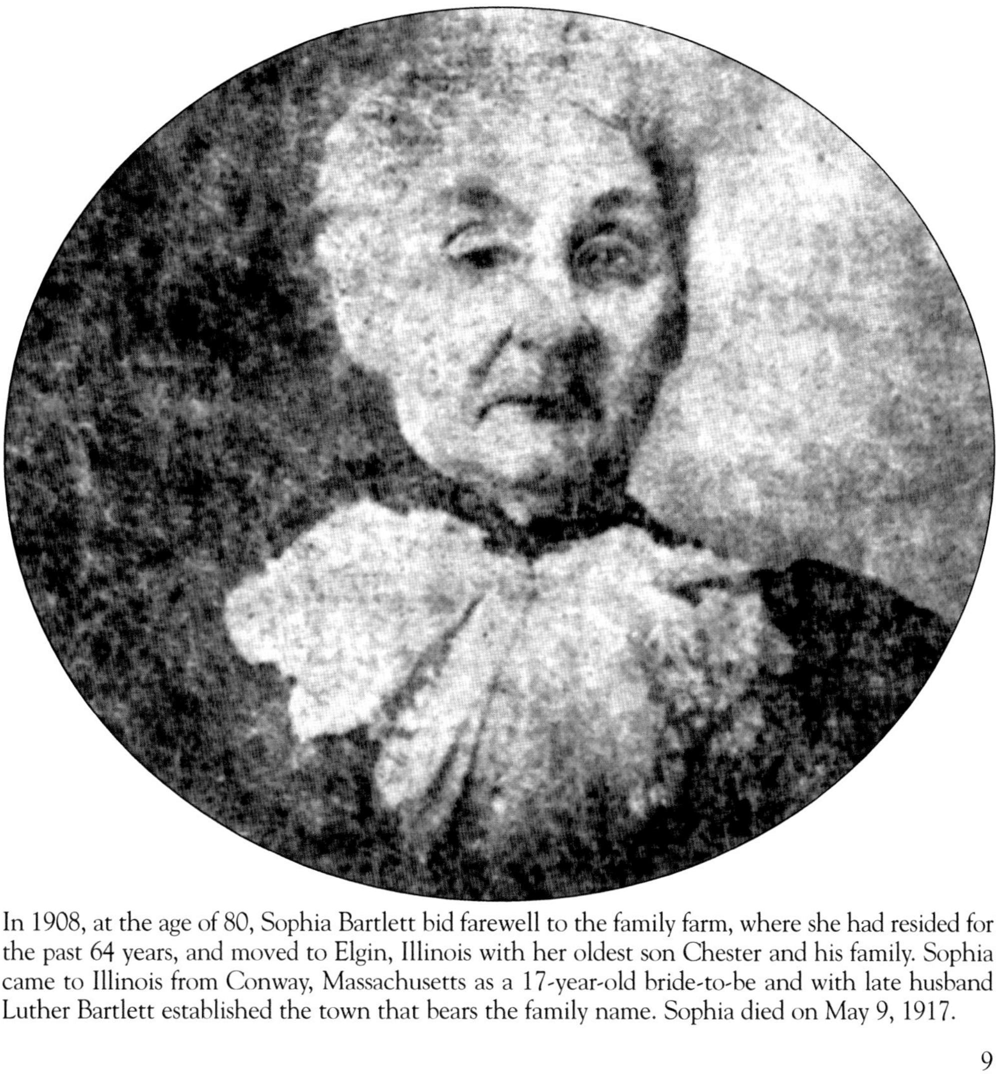

In 1908, at the age of 80, Sophia Bartlett bid farewell to the family farm, where she had resided for the past 64 years, and moved to Elgin, Illinois with her oldest son Chester and his family. Sophia came to Illinois from Conway, Massachusetts as a 17-year-old bride-to-be and with late husband Luther Bartlett established the town that bears the family name. Sophia died on May 9, 1917.

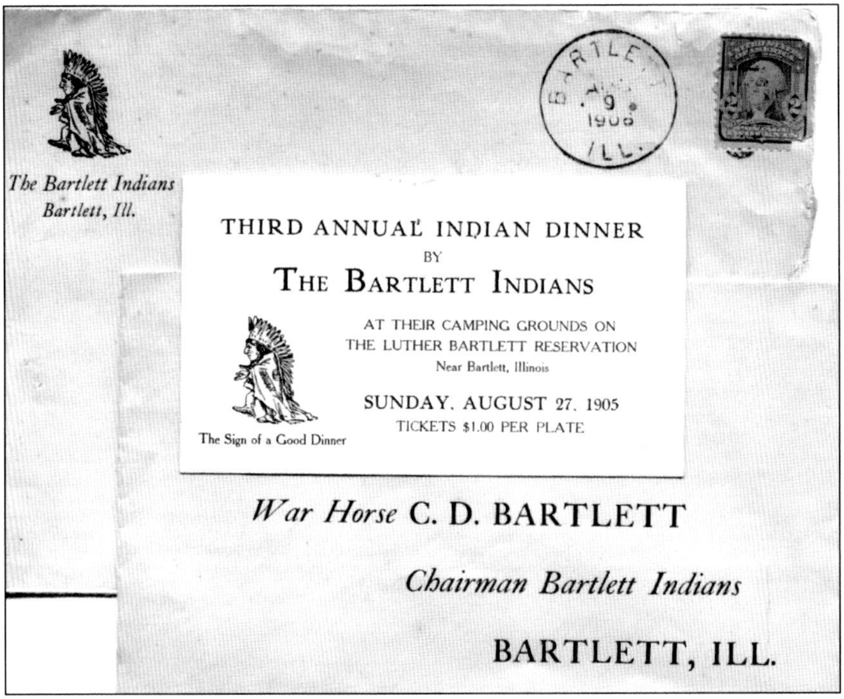

In its earliest incarnations Bartlett was an old-time camping and hunting ground for a number of Native American tribes. In fact, because a portion of the Bartlett farm sat on the trail used by soldiers traveling to the Black Hawk wars, the family had been dubbed the "Bartlett Braves." In the early 1900s, the Bartletts hosted an annual "Indian" dinner on the "Luther Bartlett reservation." The last gathering was held on August 25, 1907.

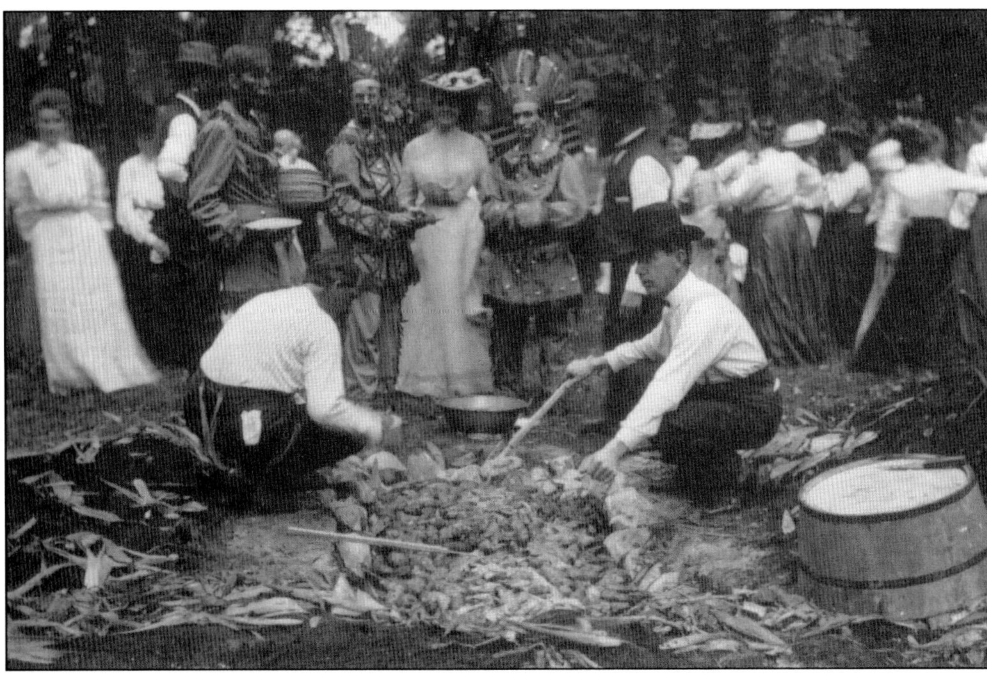

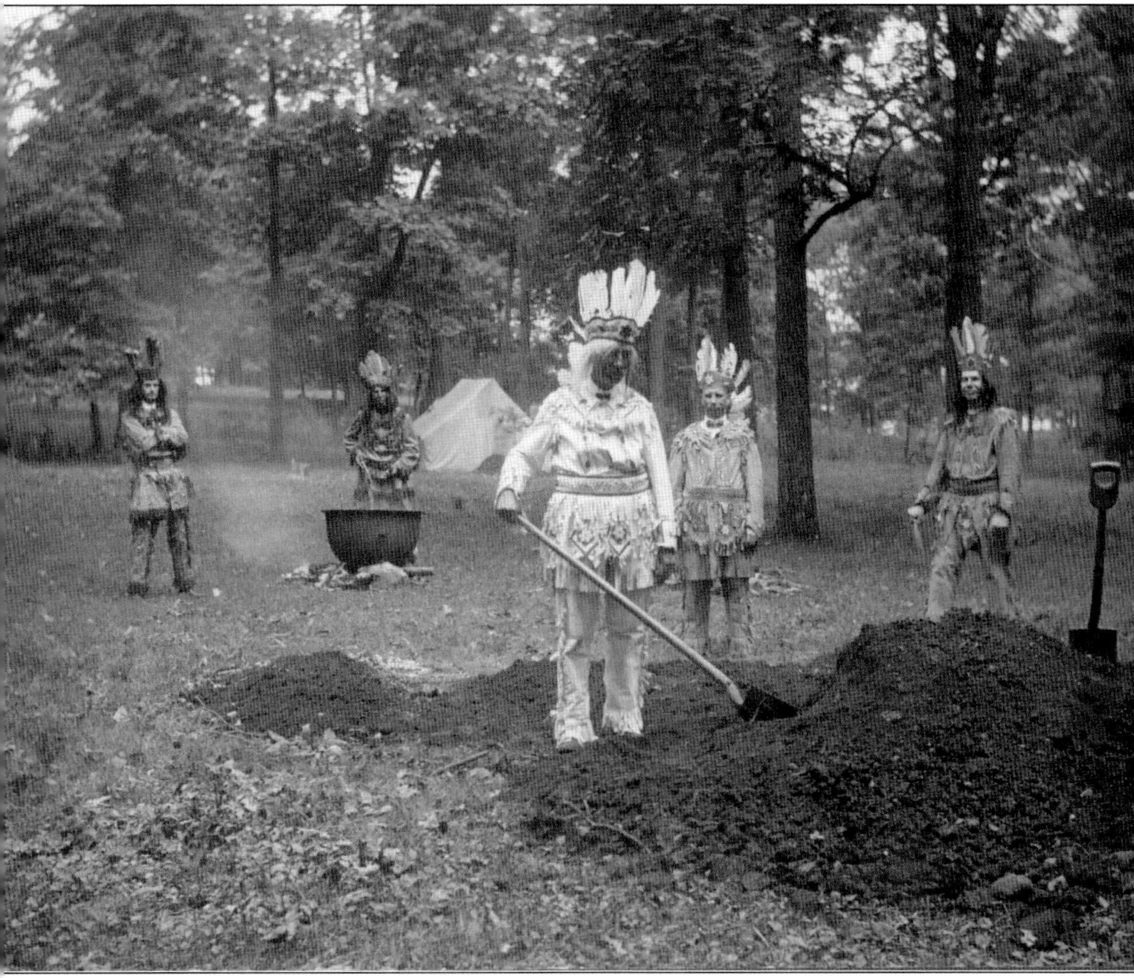

Grand Ol' War Horse Chester Bartlett in full "Indian" regalia presided over the campfires at the annual powwows. The yearly "war whoop" drew up to 300 neighbors and friends from throughout the surrounding counties to the Bartlett farm, at what is today the southeast corner of Stearns and South Bartlett Road. The Inter Ocean Magazine of 1908 described the farm as, "built on a knoll in the midst of a small forest of oak trees....The house was solidly built to withstand the winds and big storms which occasionally pass over the region, and it is apparently as staunch and solid today as it was when it was built." In 1908, Chester accepted a lucrative business offer in Elgin and sold the farm. According to Inter Ocean, "to the people of DuPage County, it meant severing the ties of more than half a century, for the Bartletts have been prominent in the affairs of the County during all that time."

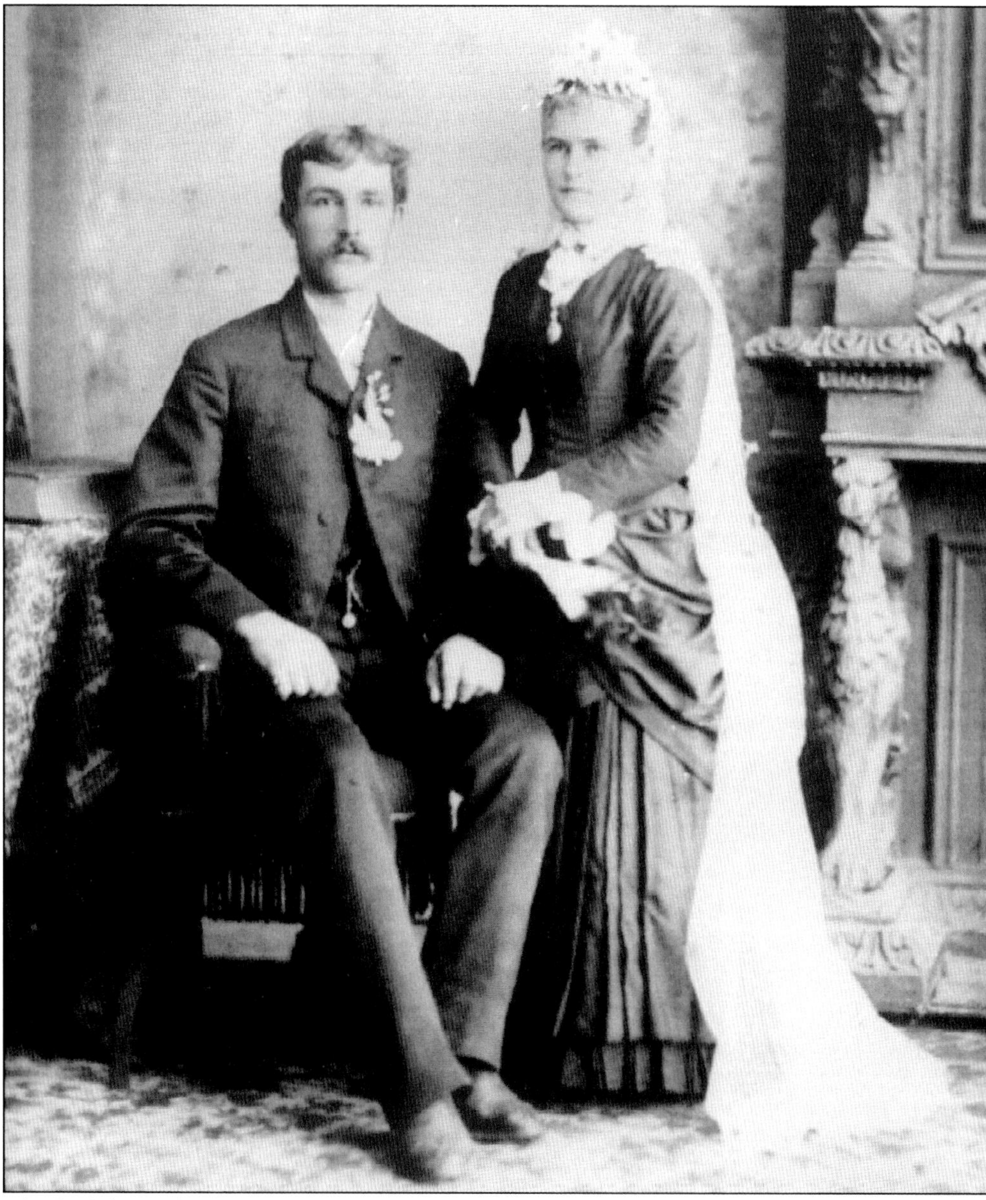

The bridal couple shown here, Fredrick and the diminutive Sophie Harmening Schick, was married in a double wedding with Sophie's brother Henry Harmening and Carolyn Hecht in 1883. Over 1,000 guests attended the reception at the Harmening Farm, which is now the Mueller Sod Farm on Route 20. Guests dined in the orchard, danced all night, and were served homemade sausage for breakfast prior to departing in the morning.

The couple settled on the Schick family farm purchased in 1865 by Fred's parents Gottlieb and Christina. Fred soon gained prominence as a successful farmer, business owner, and postmaster. In 1900, he built a new home on the property and established a general store and post office in the residence. A small portion of the Schick farm was purchased by the Illinois Central Railroad for use as a railroad stop. The stop came to be known as Schick's Crossing and was used for many years by farmers shipping milk and cattle. The farm property at 28 W 218 Schick Road remained in the family until 1998 and the adjacent road still bears the Schick family name.

The German migration of the mid-1800s brought many prominent families to Bartlett, including farmer and cattle dealer Louis Humbracht Sr. who arrived as a 2-year-old in 1852. Louis married Minnie Schuneman, an area native, in 1874. They built the home that still stands today at 102 S. Oak. Louis' farm holdings were so extensive that he gave each of his five sons a farm and his two daughters houses in Bartlett.

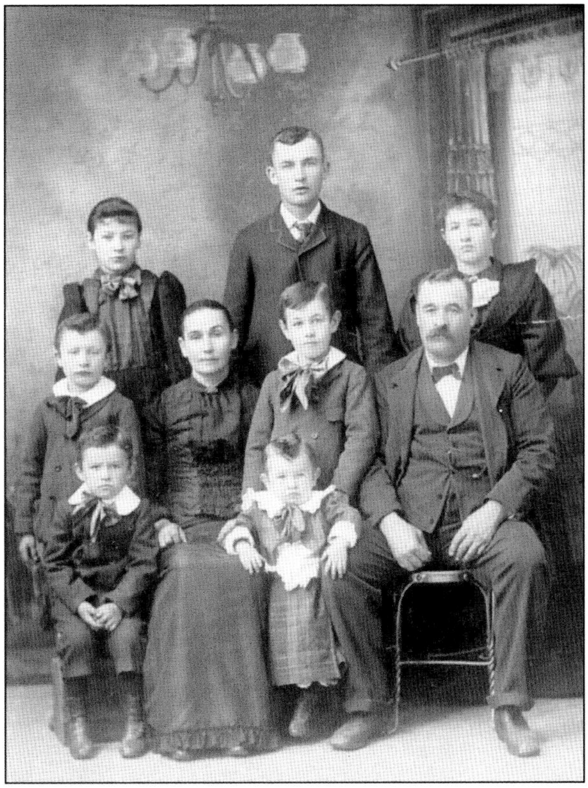

According to the 1880 census, Friedrich (Fred) C. Watermann was a carpenter and built many of the houses and barns in and near Bartlett. He is pictured here with his wife Marie Ebeling Watermann and their children, from left to right: (standing) Clara, Fred Jr., and Sophie; (seated) Martha, Alma, Esther, and Marie Sophie.

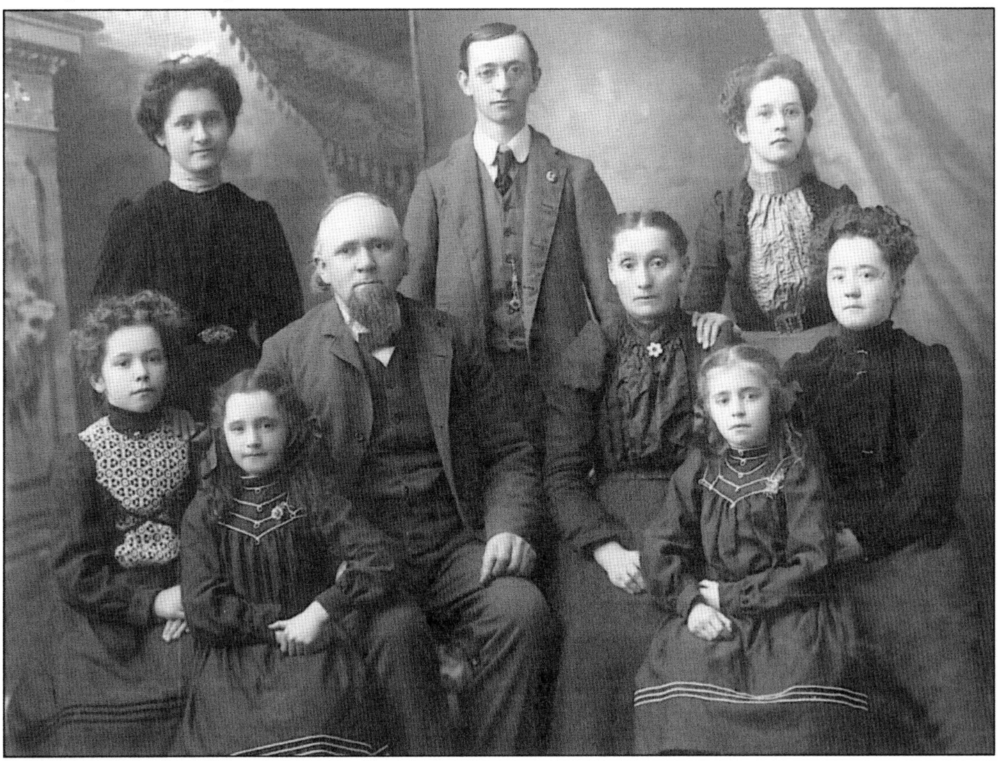

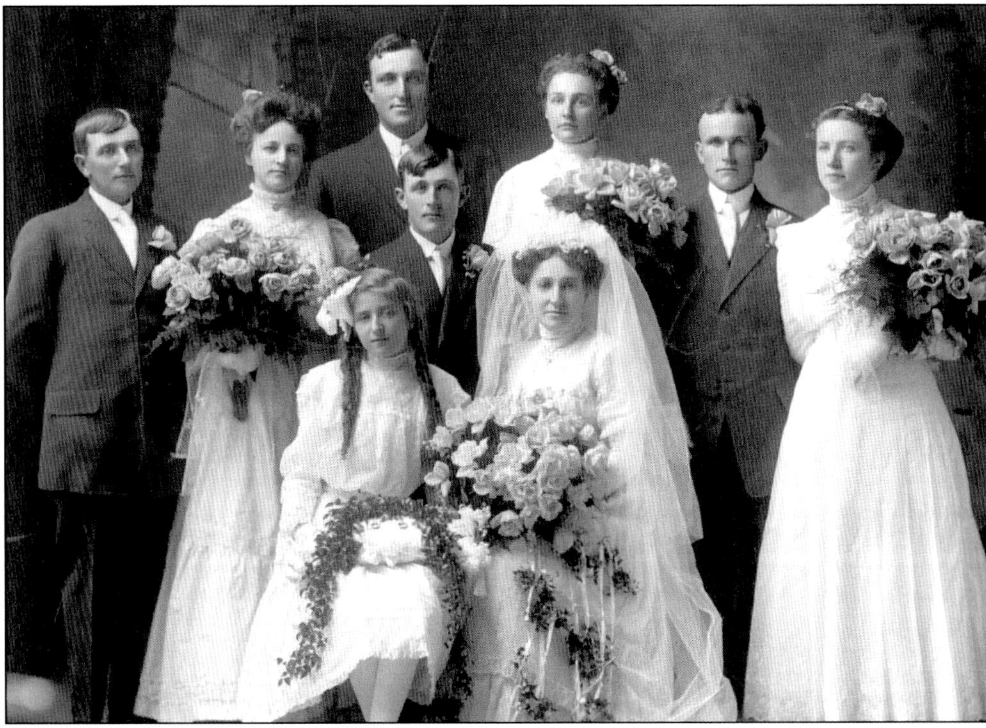

William Harmening married Ella Ahlgrim, his sweetheart from a neighboring farm, on May 25, 1910. The young couple moved to Chicago to start a dairy, but William and his daughter Ruth returned to hometown Bartlett in 1927 after Ella's death. The wedding photo includes (from top left) Henry Harmening Jr., Eva McChesney, Ernest Ahlgrim, the groom, Carrie Schultz, Fred Schick, Emma Harmening, and Mathilda Harmening, seated to the left of the bride.

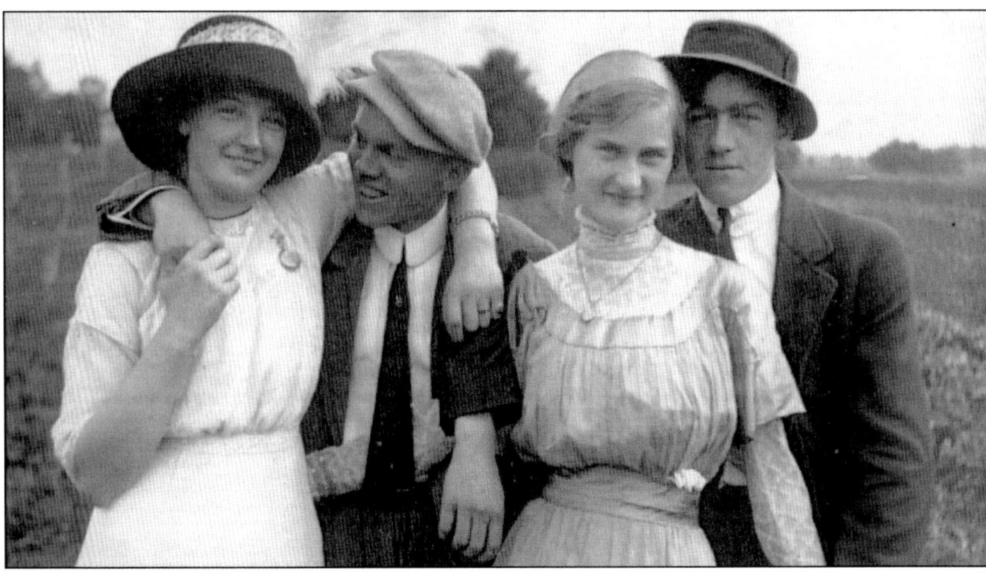

It was summertime and the strawberries were ripe for picking on the Krumfuss Berry Farm. Pals Ida Schneiel, Willie Dralle, Milly Krumfuss, and Carl Markel enjoyed a day of fun and camaraderie. The caption under this early 1900s shot in Milly's photo album reads "snookie ogums."

Bartlett fraus Stella and Magie Feurhaken would never go visiting without a pocketbook full of proper calling cards. The custom of carrying calling cards began in France in the early 1800s and became vastly popular in the United States at the turn of the century. Both gentlemen and proper ladies would leave the cards on silver "receiver trays" at the homes of family and friends whenever they went calling.

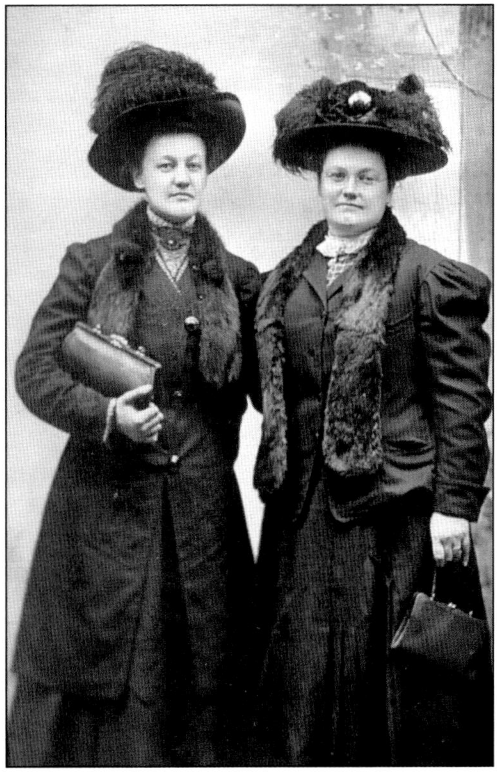

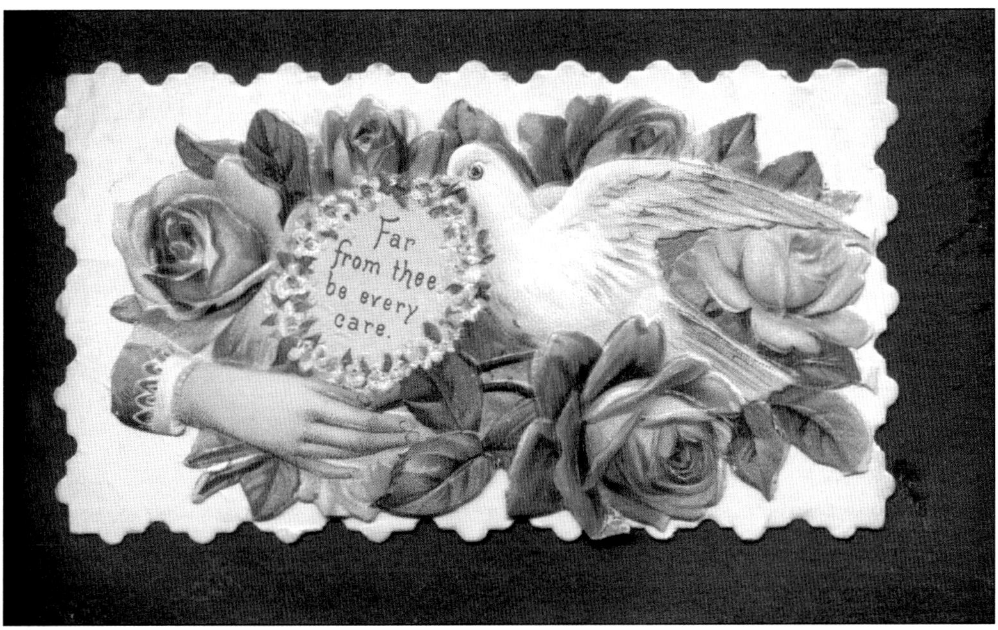

The cards were elaborately embellished with gilded edges, fan cuts, scallops, and decorated with colorful hearts, doves, scrolls, and flowers. Particular designs, styles and even border colors held special significance for the receiver. William Schick's calling card, shown here, is an example of a "hidden name" design, where the receiver would lift a "scrap" to reveal the visitor's name. With the advent of penny post cards, the formal calling card became less popular.

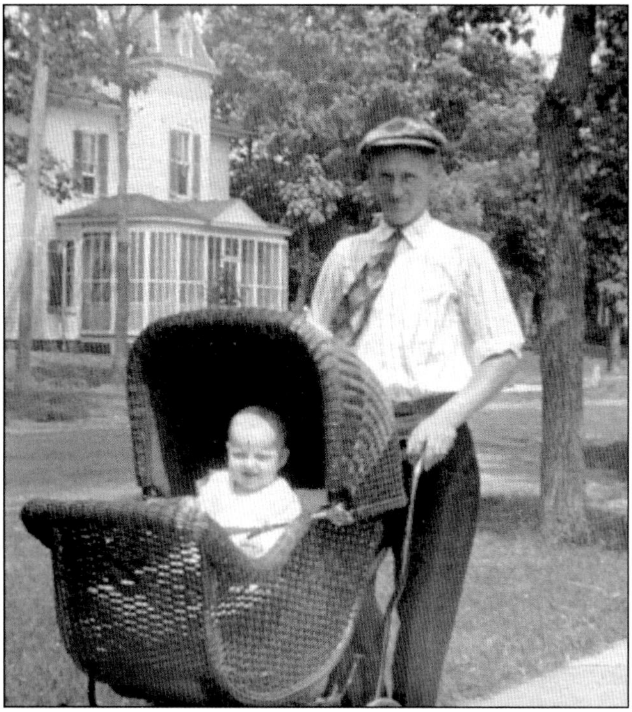

Lifelong Bartlett resident Gustav (Gus) Krumfuss strolls down Oneida Avenue with his baby daughter Ruth Ann in the summer of 1918. Gus was devoted to family and community, was a one-time Village of Bartlett trustee, and was a telephone linesman for Illinois Bell. The home in the background is that of first Village President George Struckman.

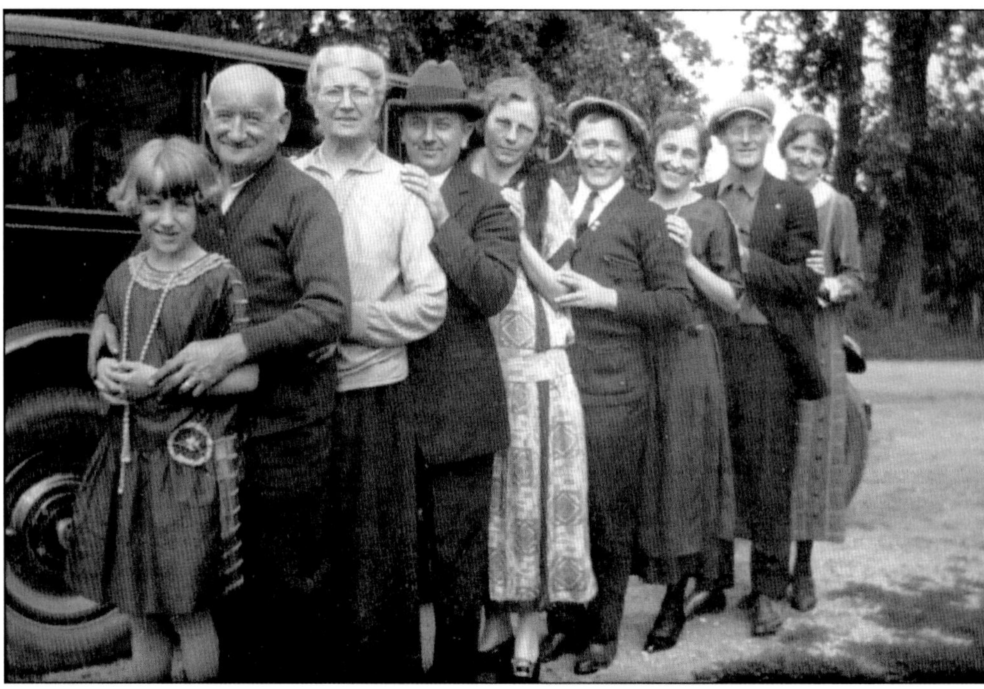

The Henry Harmening family stands beside their brand spanking new Buick on September 14, 1924. Showing off the purchase are, from left to right, Ruth Harmening, Henry Sr., Henry's wife Caroline, Henry Jr., his wife Martha, William and Ella Harmening, Malcolm Alsworth, and his wife Mathilda Harmening Alsworth. To this day, Ruth Harmening Giles fondly recalls the giant wad of bubblegum nestled in her cheek when this picture was taken.

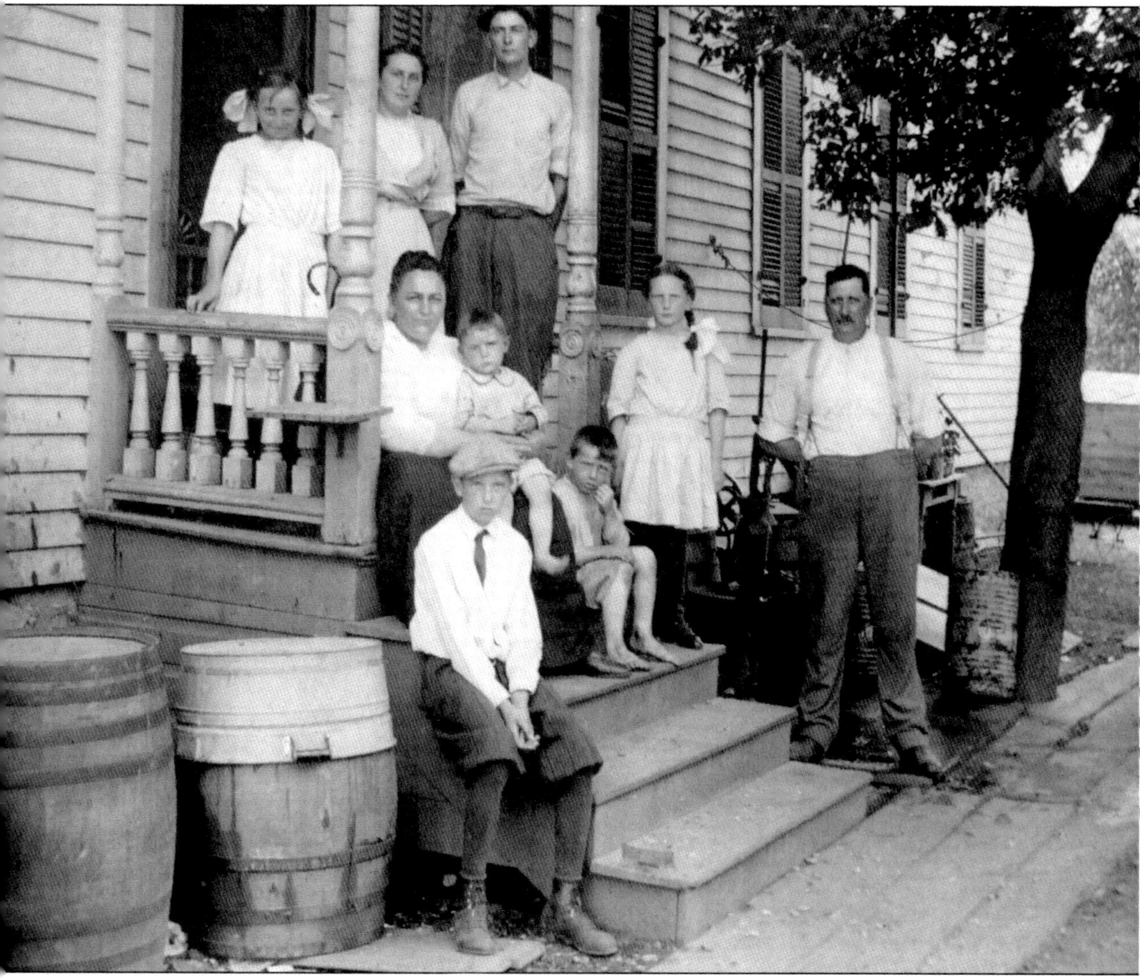

In 1905, Mr. Herman Schnadt purchased the Bartlett Tavern and moved his wife and children to the residence at the rear of the building. For many years the Schnadt family was active in the community. They participated in business, sports, music, and their church. In addition to owning the Tavern for 37 years, Herman was an auctioneer clerk, real estate and insurance agent, and was one of the founders of the Bartlett State Bank in 1910. He also served as a Village trustee and school board member. Mrs. Schnadt was involved in her church's Ladies Aid Society. By 1912, after two new additions to the family, the Schnadts relocated their household to a new home at the southeast corner of Oak and Morse. The house still stands today. A portion of the Schnadt property was always used by the community for ball games and other recreation and was eventually developed into the Village's first park, Bartlett Park. Pictured front and center is Herb; (second row) Caroline, Ray, Harvey, Estella, and Herman; (back row) Luella, Lydia, and Sam (Erwin).

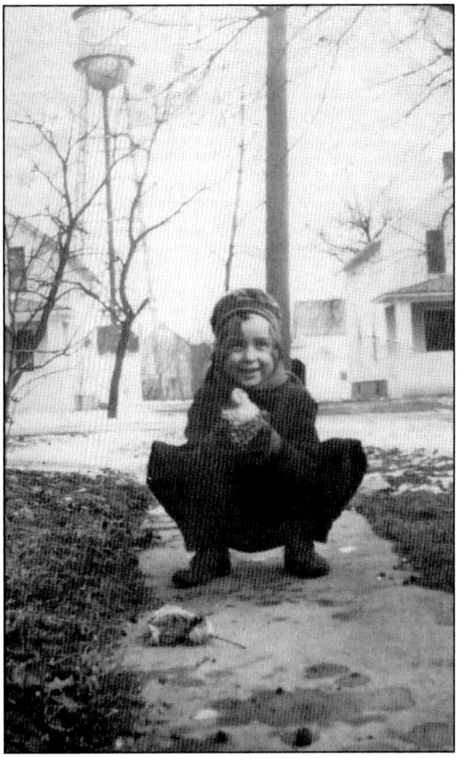

Little Joanne Whitmer, daughter of Tony and Zalia, enjoys the crisp autumn afternoon outside her home at 226 S. Oak Avenue. Behind her to the left is the Meyer home and barn where Dick Meyer raised racing pigeons. The Meyer home and the Regenburg home on the right were both razed for the expansion of Village Hall in 1993.

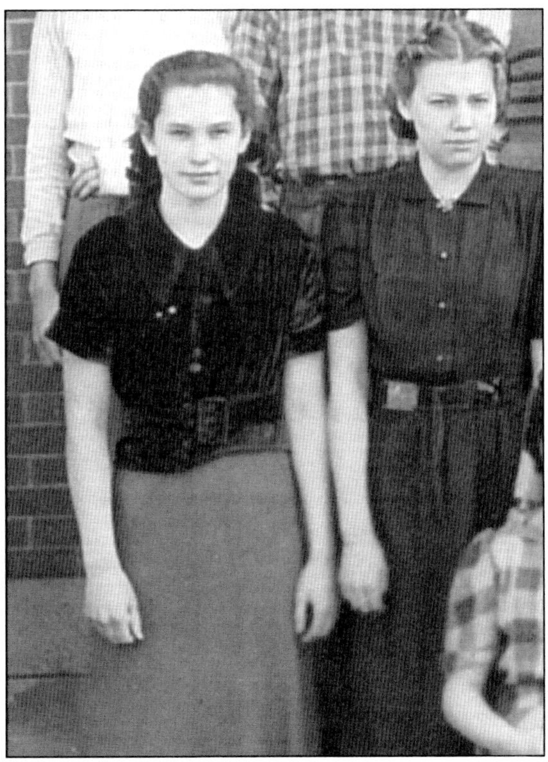

Farmer's daughter Jane Ping and "town girl" Elaine Jensen met as gap-toothed first graders at Bartlett Elementary in 1930 and quickly bridged their different upbringings to form a lifelong friendship. Jane recalls envying Elaine for her "modern mom," while Elaine enjoyed the old-fashioned farmhouse that was Mrs. Ping's domain. When it came time to marry, both girls wed the new boys in town and still live within walking distance of each other.

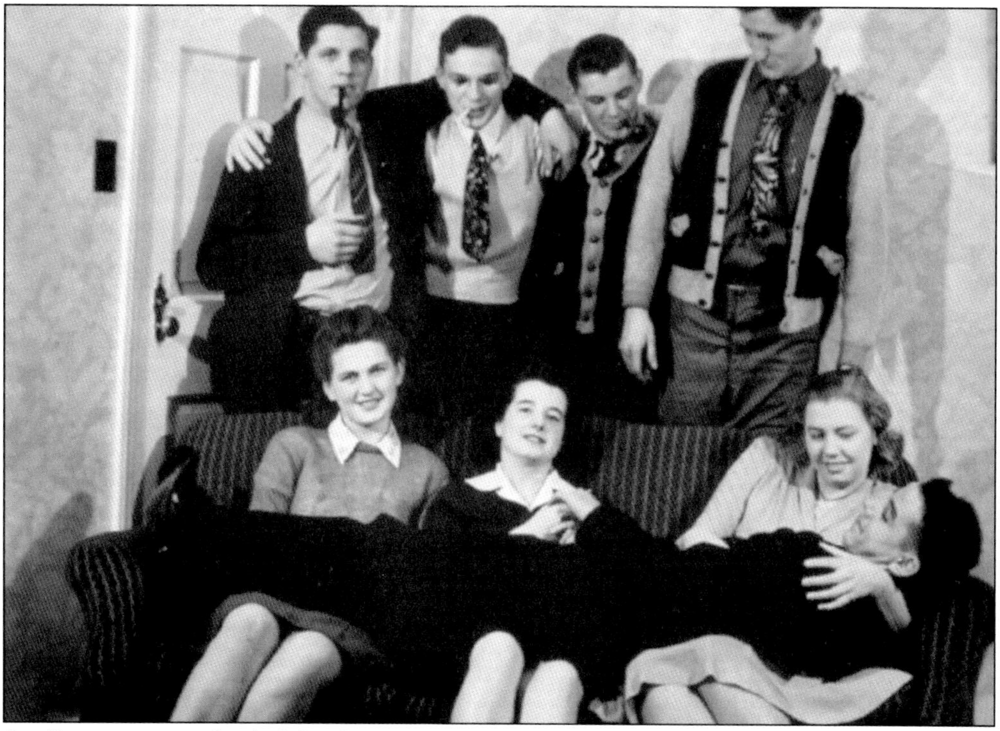

Small town guys and gals didn't have to stray far from their own backyard to find their lifelong mates. School chums Mickey Thruman, Marion Atchison, Elaine Jensen, Melbourne Atchison, Bill Jervey, Howard Gronemeier, George Vlasak, and Paul O'Brien share some fun at the Atchison home while Mel is home on leave in 1943. It was only a matter of years before Mickey married Bill, Marion wed Howard, and Elaine took Mel's last name.

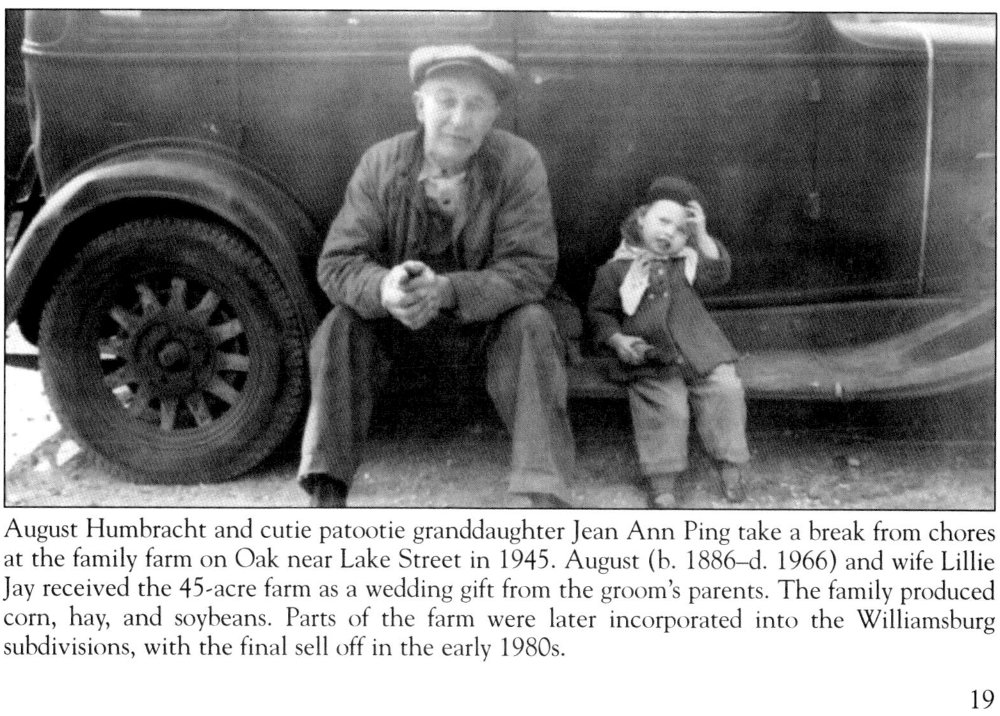

August Humbracht and cutie patootie granddaughter Jean Ann Ping take a break from chores at the family farm on Oak near Lake Street in 1945. August (b. 1886–d. 1966) and wife Lillie Jay received the 45-acre farm as a wedding gift from the groom's parents. The family produced corn, hay, and soybeans. Parts of the farm were later incorporated into the Williamsburg subdivisions, with the final sell off in the early 1980s.

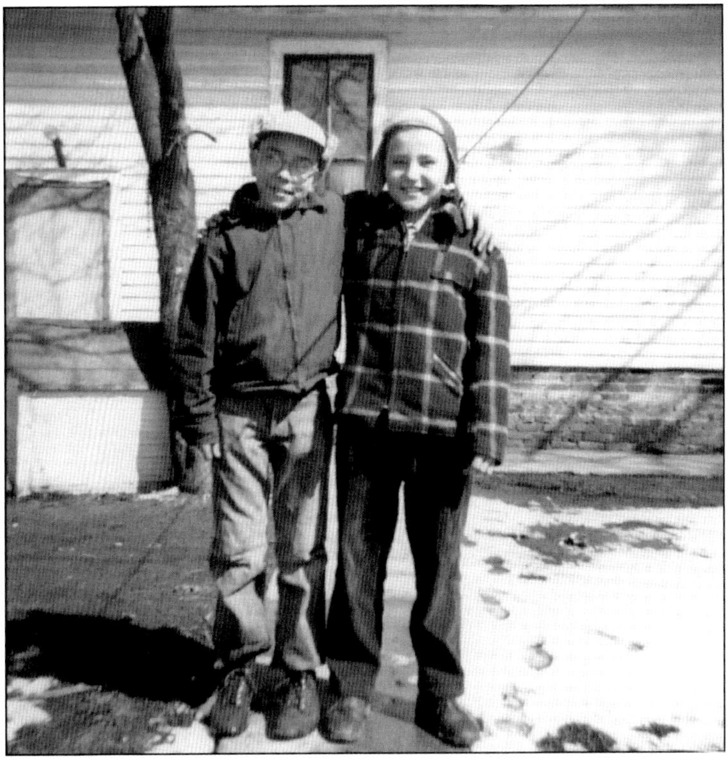

Kickin' around the neighborhood was always better when you had your best friend by your side. John Whitmer and Glen Koehler grew up just a street apart and shared one of those old-fashioned, small town friendships that lasted more than 50 years. As adults, John was one of Bartlett's first mail carriers and Glen was an insurance agent and also the 12th Village president, following in the footsteps of his grandfather Alfred Sodman who served the Village from 1933 to 1944.

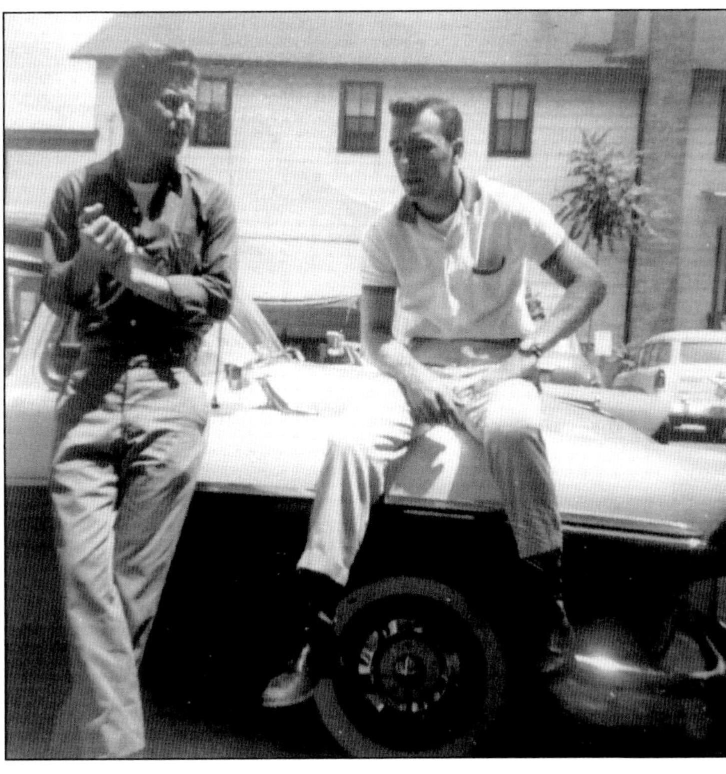

Summertime and the livin' was easy. As a teen, John Whitmer, right, and a buddy hang out on Oak Avenue, across the street from Baxmann's General Store. A jukebox with the latest rock 'n roll 45s stacked on the needle made Baxmann's a popular gathering spot for Bartlett teens in the 1950s.

Justice of the Peace Puffer married Violet Jensen to Eugene Haase on April 12, 1948 in the living room of the couple's new apartment. When Violet met Gene at Bartlett Elementary, she told her mother he'd be her future husband. Their reception was held at the family owned Bartlett Tavern where the bride and mother Serena put out a spread of sandwiches and side dishes on the tablecloth covered pool table.

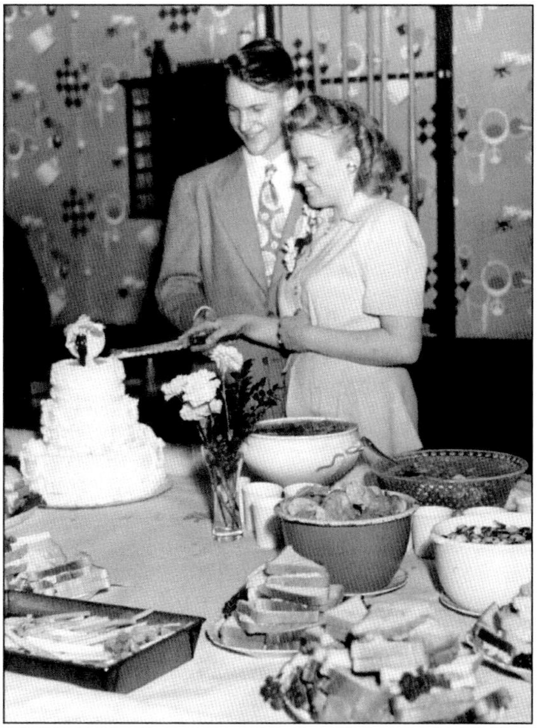

The Bartlett Tavern was closed again in 1948 for the Thanksgiving holiday, but that didn't mean that owners Ed and Serena Jensen got the day off from cooking. On this occasion it was the Jensens' extended family, rather than patrons, who feasted on food and drinks at the neighborhood bar.

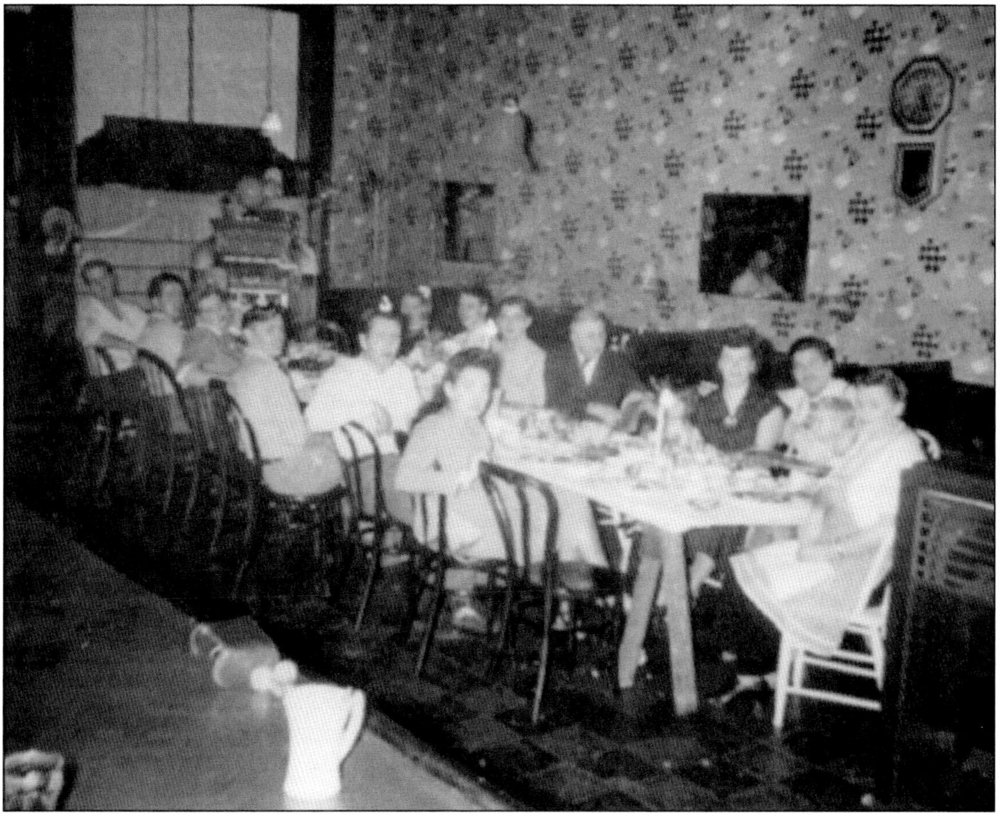

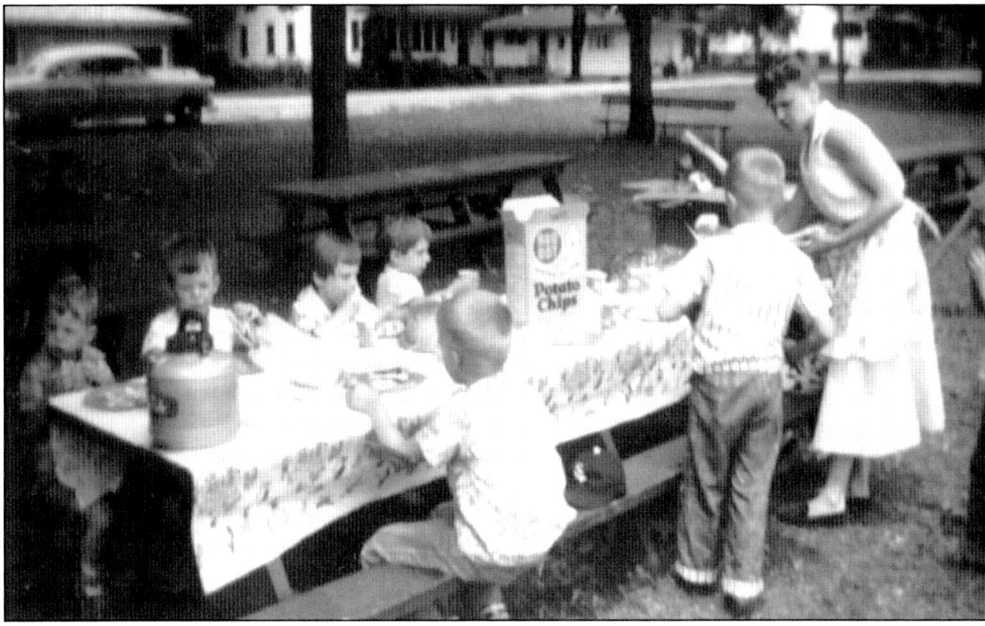

"Happy Birthday" was the song of the day in Bartlett Park on July 8, 1956, when young Bill Peterson celebrated his seventh birthday with friends. Bill (second from left, facing the camera) munches on the celebratory lunch of hotdogs and Red Dot potato chips. Bill is flanked by younger brother Paul and good friends the Giese twins. Buddies Bruce Jervey and Dave Thrun have their backs to the camera.

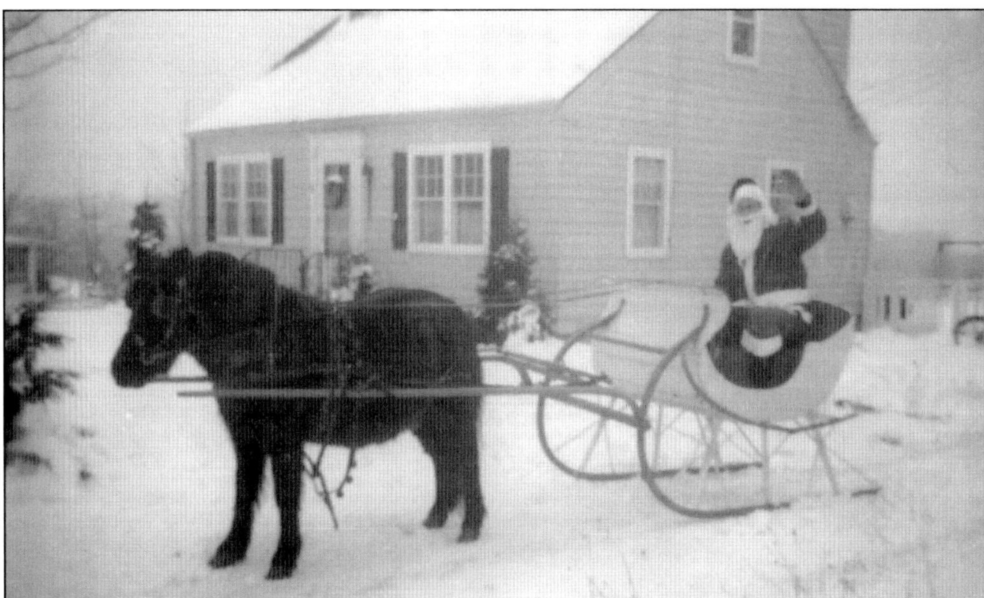

Ho! Ho! Ho! Sleigh bells are ringing and Santa's on his way to Bartlett, Illinois. Rodger Peterson, aka Santa Claus, and his pony Gunsmoke (Smokey) are outside the Peterson home on Oak Avenue getting ready to make their 1959 Christmas morning delivery of good cheer and best wishes. Peterson served as a Village trustee in the 1950s and has been a Lions Club member for almost 50 years.

Two

Public Safety and Service

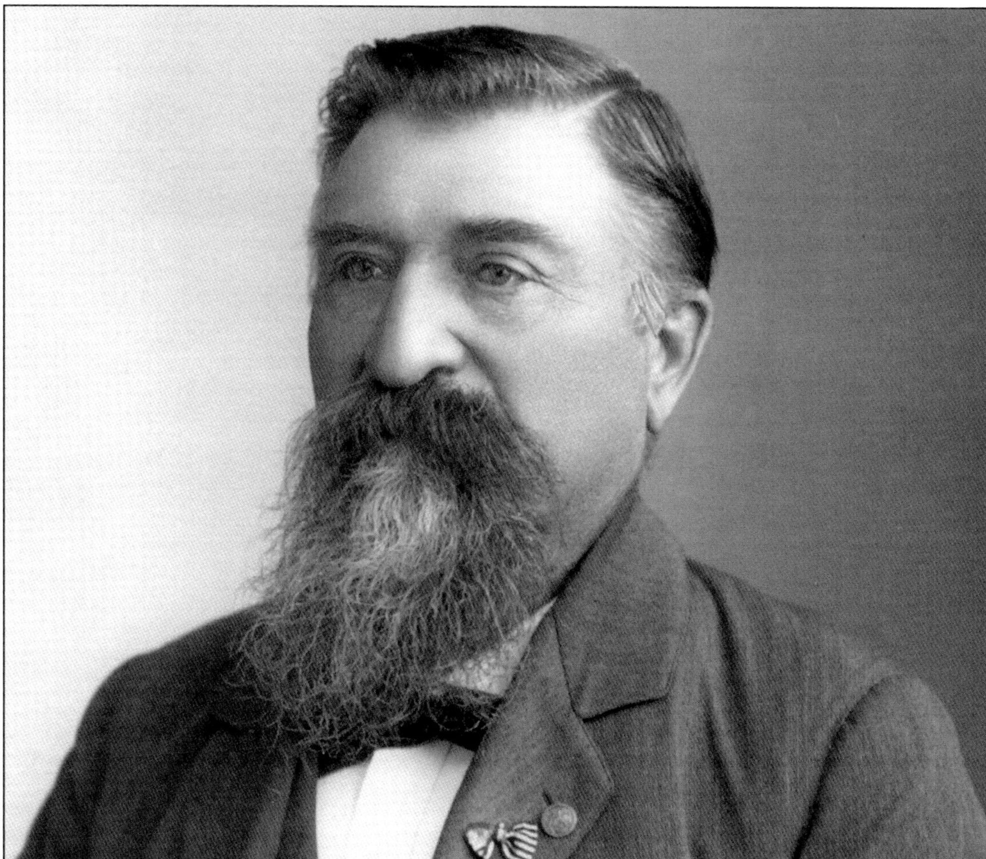

George Struckman was Bartlett's first Village President serving from 1891 to 1898 and again in 1901 to 1910. Born in Germany, he immigrated to Hanover Township in 1850. A 2nd Lieutenant in the Civil War, Struckman was one of the initial "movers and shakers" in the fledgling village. He served as Hanover Township Supervisor, Assessor, and School Trustee. Struckman was elected to the State Legislature twice. He died in 1920 and is buried in Bartlett Cemetery.

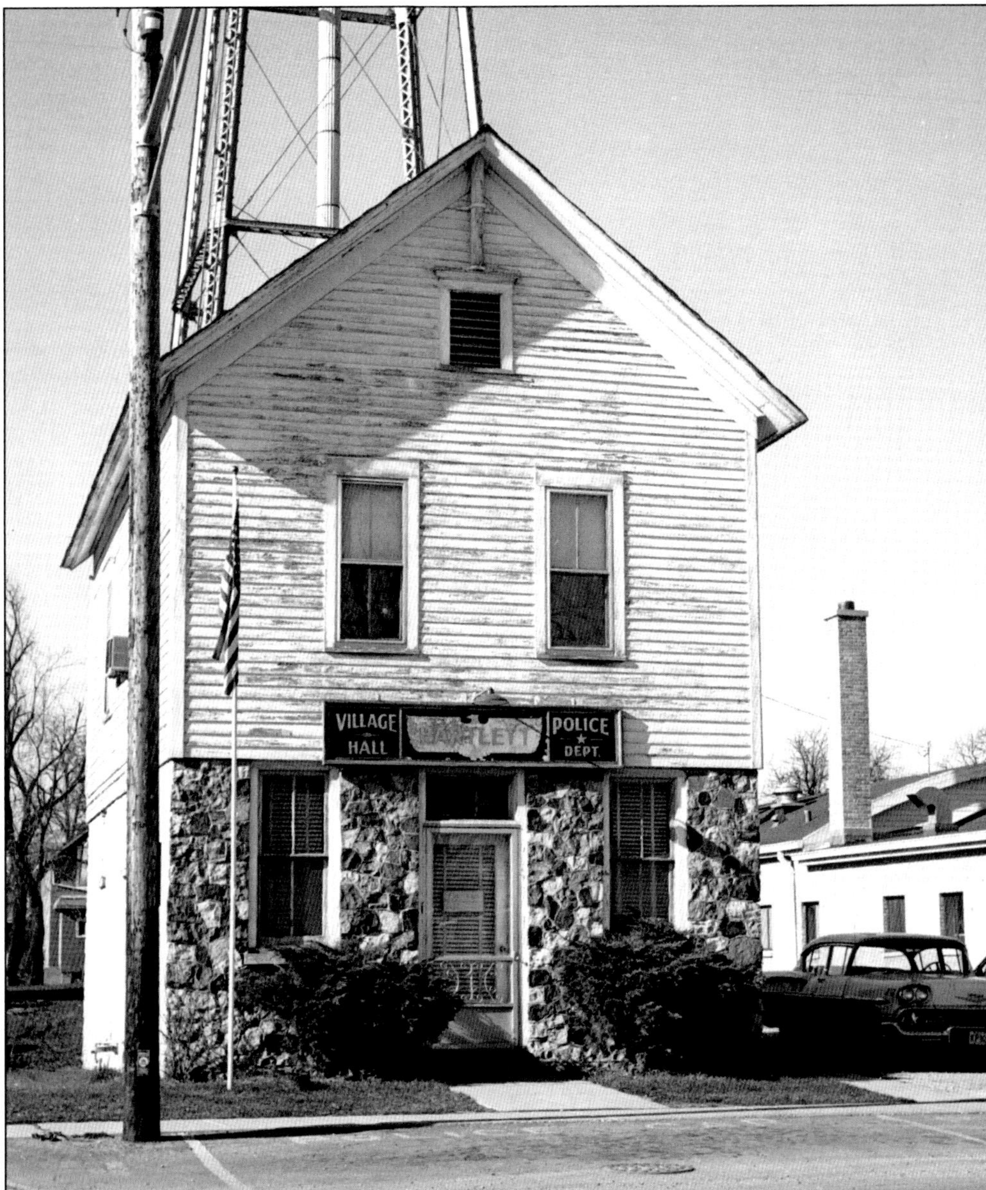

The first Village Hall was built in 1894 on Main Street in front of today's municipal building. The land was purchased from Henry Schultz for $125. The original one-story building cost $78 and was made possible by donations of materials and labor. The second story was added later for a cost of $238. The Police Department and calaboose or jail were located on the first floor and housed two iron cells, 6-foot by 8-foot by 7-foot each. Nearby residents would frequently hear the singing of unruly drunks spending the night in the lockup. The Council Chambers was located upstairs. It was not until July 1962, when an office clerk was hired, that regular business hours were kept in the facility. Bartlett's first Village Hall served residents for more than 70 years before the state fire marshal condemned it as a public meeting place in 1966. The age of the building, lack of second-floor council room exits, the chamber's inadequate size, and the heating system were the reasons for the condemnation. The building was razed in 1968.

Prior to Bartlett's 1891 incorporation, the prevailing form of government was the local township. Established in 1850, Hanover Township provided representation closer to home than Chicago, the county seat. Once Bartlett's Village Hall was built, it served as the official polling place for both municipal and township elections. Leaving no room for dimpled ballots or hanging chads, citizens used pen and ink to cast their vote and the results were hand tallied.

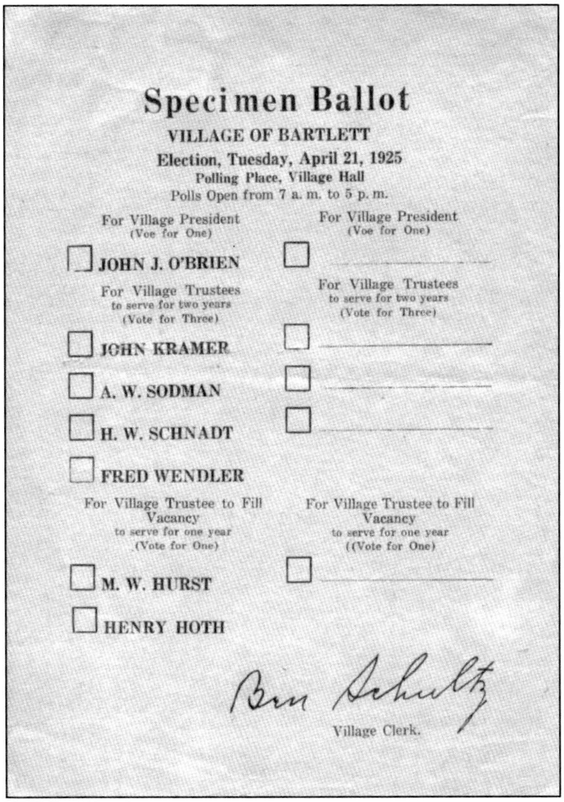

Specimen Ballot

VILLAGE OF BARTLETT

Election, Tuesday, April 21, 1925

Polling Place, Village Hall

Polls Open from 7 a. m. to 5 p. m.

For Village President (Voe for One)	For Village President (Voe for One)
☐ JOHN J. O'BRIEN	☐ ________
For Village Trustees to serve for two years (Vote for Three)	**For Village Trustees** to serve for two years (Vote for Three)
☐ JOHN KRAMER	☐ ________
☐ A. W. SODMAN	☐ ________
☐ H. W. SCHNADT	☐ ________
☐ FRED WENDLER	
For Village Trustee to Fill Vacancy to serve for one year (Vote for One)	**For Village Trustee to Fill Vacancy** to serve for one year ((Vote for One)
☐ M. W. HURST	☐ ________
☐ HENRY HOTH	

Ben Schultz

Village Clerk.

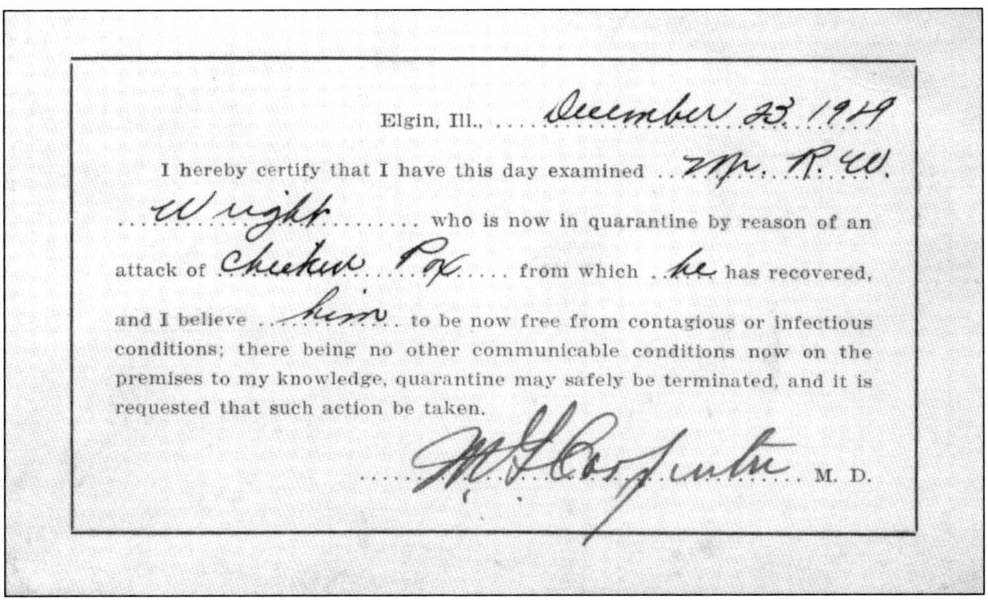

Elgin, Ill., December 23 1919

I hereby certify that I have this day examined Mr. R. W. Wright who is now in quarantine by reason of an attack of Chicken Pox from which he has recovered, and I believe him to be now free from contagious or infectious conditions; there being no other communicable conditions now on the premises to my knowledge, quarantine may safely be terminated, and it is requested that such action be taken.

M. D.

"Whenever any physician is called to attend any person in the Village of Bartlett who has cholera, smallpox, diphtheria, scarlet fever, or other dangerous contagious diseases, he shall at once notify the Village President or the Health Commissioner," so said an early Bartlett ordinance. Area doctors commonly used printed posters and quarantine cards to notify the public of the presence of these diseases in the community and to prescribe the necessary precautions.

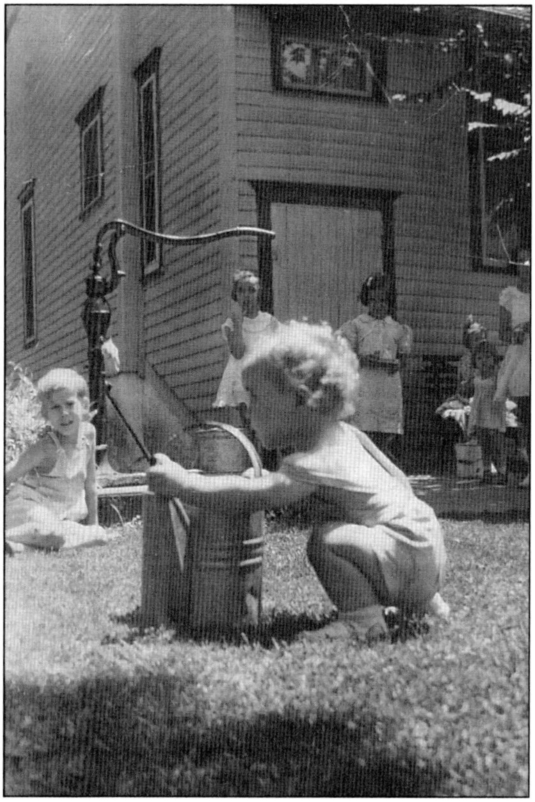

It wasn't long into the 1900s when public utilities and municipal services opened the door to the 20th century conveniences that eventually urbanized rural Bartlett. In addition to the telephone's entrance into town in 1901, gas lines for light, heat, and power were laid in 1916 and electrical energy arrived in 1922 courtesy of the Interurban Public Service Corporation. By July 1925, Bartlett residents, such as the Whitmers, began giving up their backyard wells and pumps in favor of the Village's new public water system.

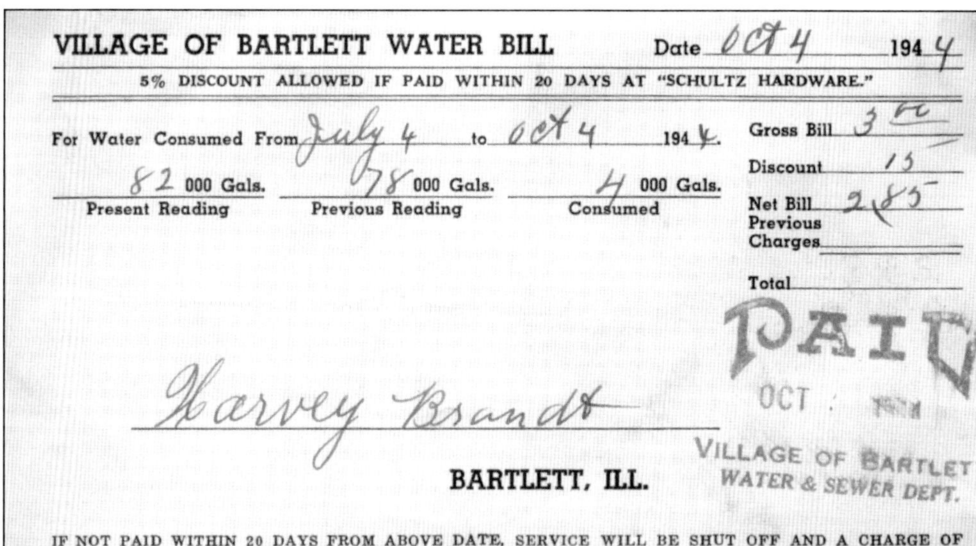

VILLAGE OF BARTLETT WATER BILL Date Oct 4 1944

5% DISCOUNT ALLOWED IF PAID WITHIN 20 DAYS AT "SCHULTZ HARDWARE."

For Water Consumed From July 4 to Oct 4 1944.

82 000 Gals. Present Reading

78 000 Gals. Previous Reading

4 000 Gals. Consumed

Gross Bill 3 00
Discount 15
Net Bill 2.85
Previous Charges
Total

PAID
OCT
VILLAGE OF BARTLETT
WATER & SEWER DEPT.

Harvey Brandt

BARTLETT, ILL.

IF NOT PAID WITHIN 20 DAYS FROM ABOVE DATE, SERVICE WILL BE SHUT OFF AND A CHARGE OF $1.50 WILL BE MADE FOR TURNING ON THE WATER.

Bartlett was soon pumping an average of 4,000 gallons per day to approximately 160 villagers. In 1944, the Brandt family alone was using 4,000 gallons of water over a three-month period for a total quarterly cost of $3.

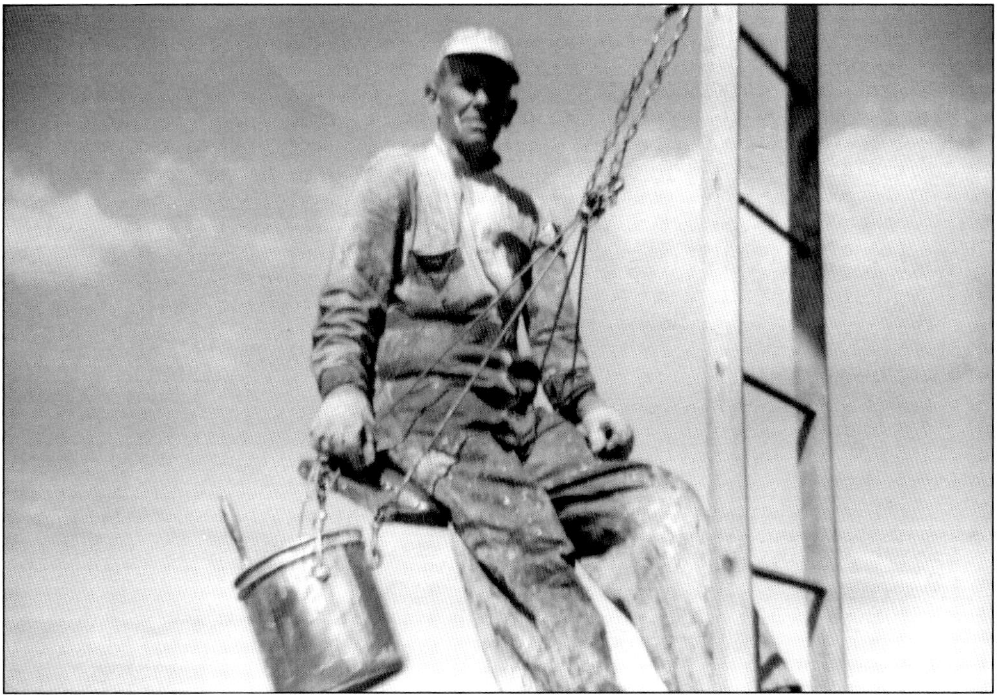

The Village's Public Works Department was responsible for the maintenance of Bartlett's streets and the smooth operation of its water and sewer systems. Keeping the 40,000-gallon, 100-foot high steel water tank in good repair was an essential task, but not one that the public works supervisor would assign to someone with acrophobia.

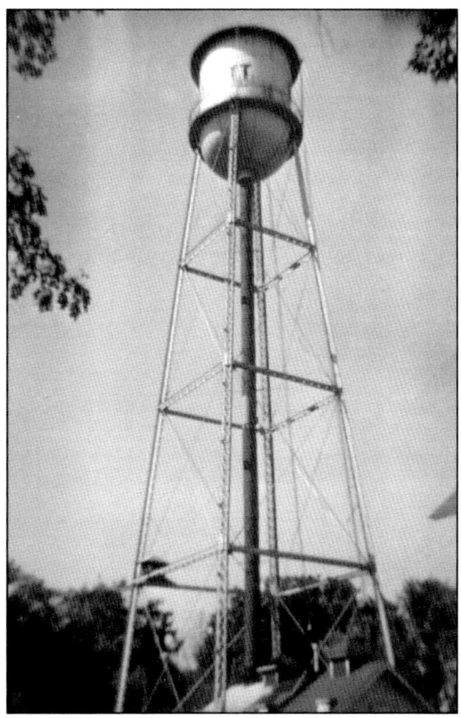

When it came time to dispose of the water tower that had loomed over the original Village Hall and served the needs of residents since its erection in 1923, the Village couldn't give the tower away. It seems that there was a glut in the market for small, riveted water towers in 1966, and the trustees were finally forced to accept a bid for $6,440 to have it demolished and hauled from town.

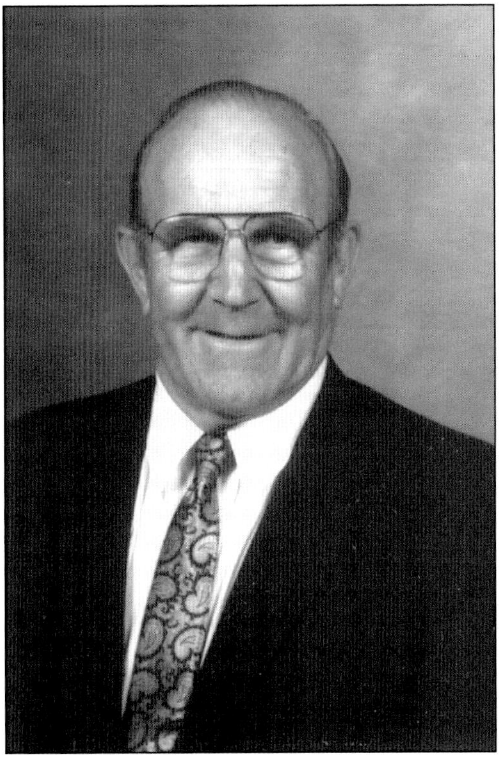

Upon his 1993 retirement, Orlo Benson wrote, "I have seen Bartlett grow, I have seen our wastewater treatment facility balloon into a major plant, our water system mushroom into miles of pipe and our streets stretch into three counties." Benson began as the Village's superintendent of Water and Sewer in 1958 and became the first Public Works Director in 1976. In 1998, the wastewater treatment plant was named in his honor.

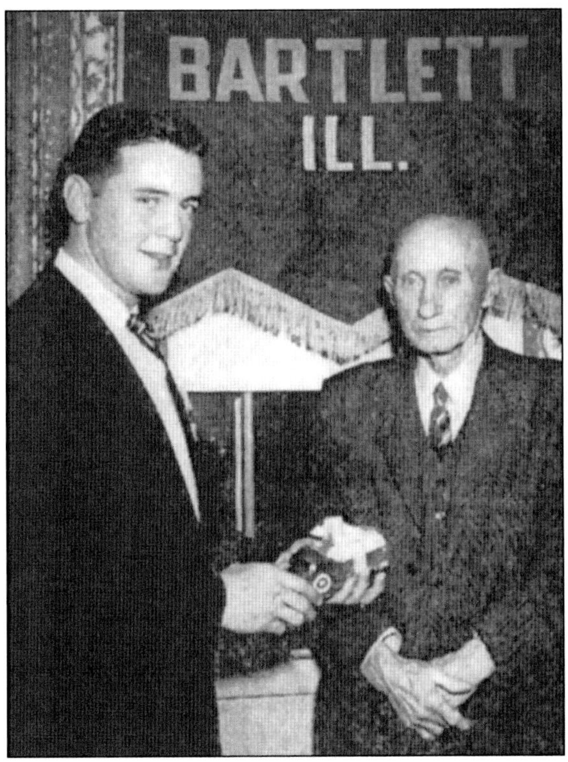

Born in Germany in 1879, Fred Hoth came to the U.S. when he was 2 years old. Fred was one of the earliest Village trustees and worked for the Village for 40 years. He was responsible for various public works activities and was also appointed police magistrate in 1920. The police department was established in 1891 and was essentially still a one-man force when Fred began serving as marshal. In 1957, Bartlett Lion John Alexander presented Hoth with 40 silver dollars, one for each of his years of service to Bartlett.

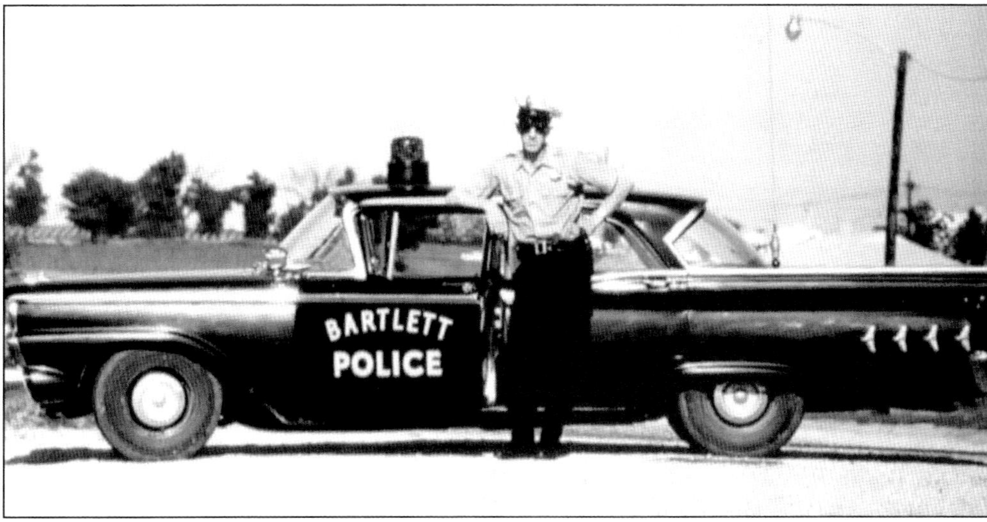

During the 30s, 40s, and 50s, the Bartlett Police Department routinely operated under the direction of one full-time officer, but special and auxiliary police were appointed during Village festivals, parades, and to fill in whenever duty called. Auxiliary Officer Ken Sorenson was dressed in uniform and ready to roll in this 1960s photo.

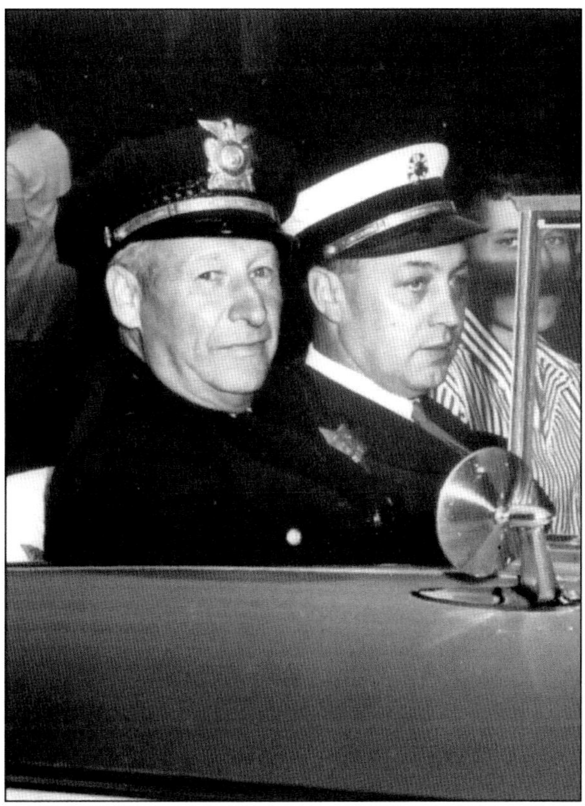

Ed Heinberg, far left, was appointed Police Chief in 1953. Heinberg's typical day would include answering police calls, acting as the school crossing guard, running radar on vehicles, keeping all police records, and maintaining his police car. He was also responsible for cleaning Village Hall for Village meetings. Lifelong area resident Harvey Rosenwinkel was with the Bartlett Volunteer Fire Department for more than 25 years, serving as Fire Chief from 1953 to 1960.

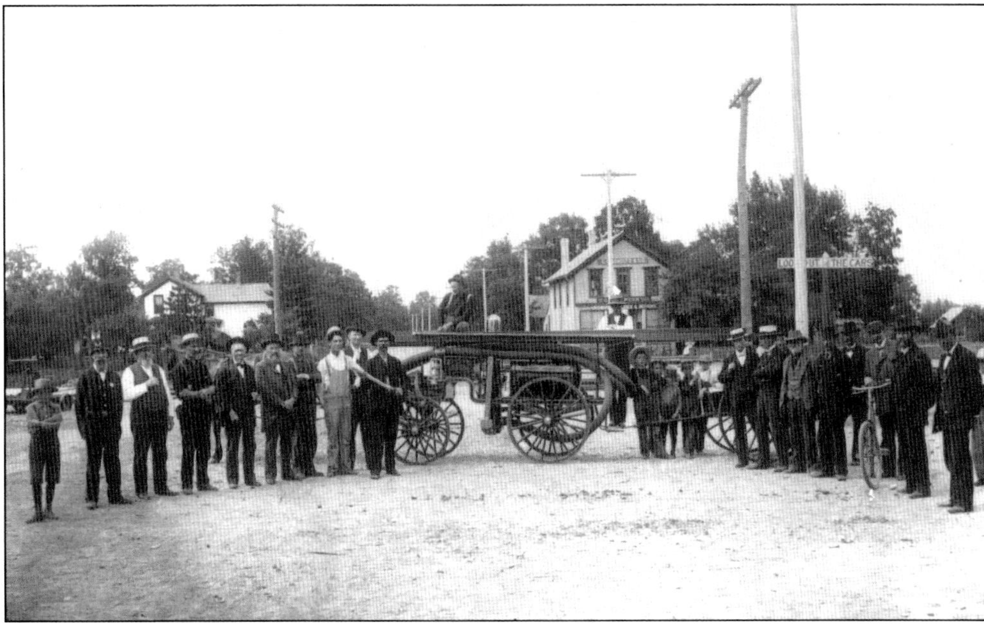

This c. 1897 photo was taken at Oak and Railroad Avenue looking north. The horse-drawn Howe Hand Pumper model #38 was delivered to Bartlett for $720, prior to the organization of the first Bartlett Volunteer Fire Company in December of that year. Today the restored pumper is on exhibit at Fire Station #1 in the Bartlett Fire Protection District Museum. Ernest Schwake, second from left, was Bartlett's police magistrate at the time.

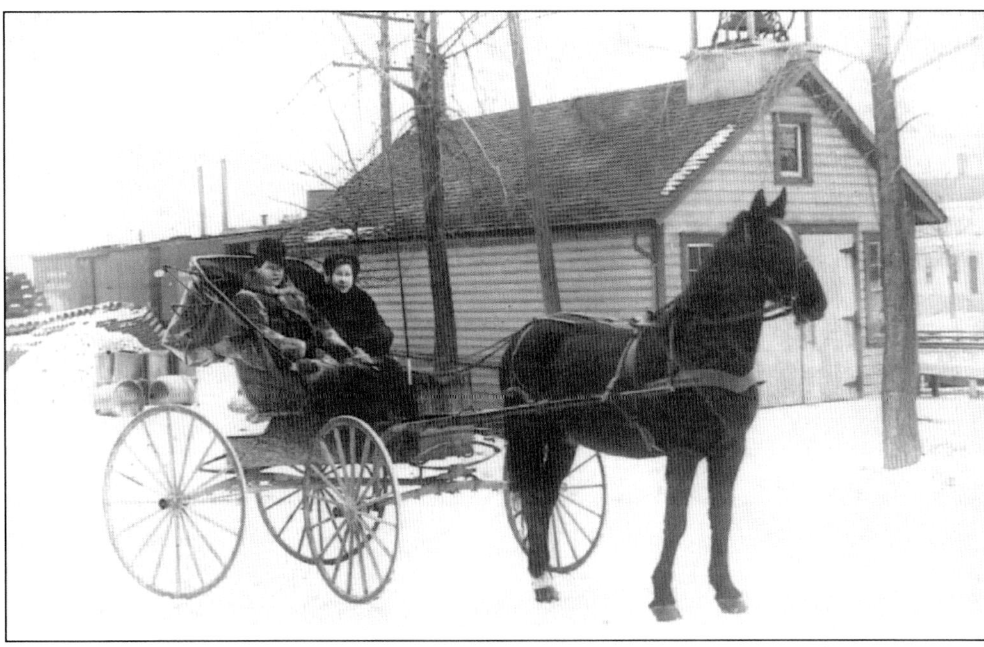

Christian and Katie Hoffman stop in front of Bartlett's first "Engine House" on Oak Avenue. A well was dug directly below the station as a ready source of water for the pumper. The rooftop bell was purchased in 1898 to summon volunteer firemen at the first report of fire. One such call came in on March 5, 1899, when a fire broke out on the roof of a house belonging to George Struckman.

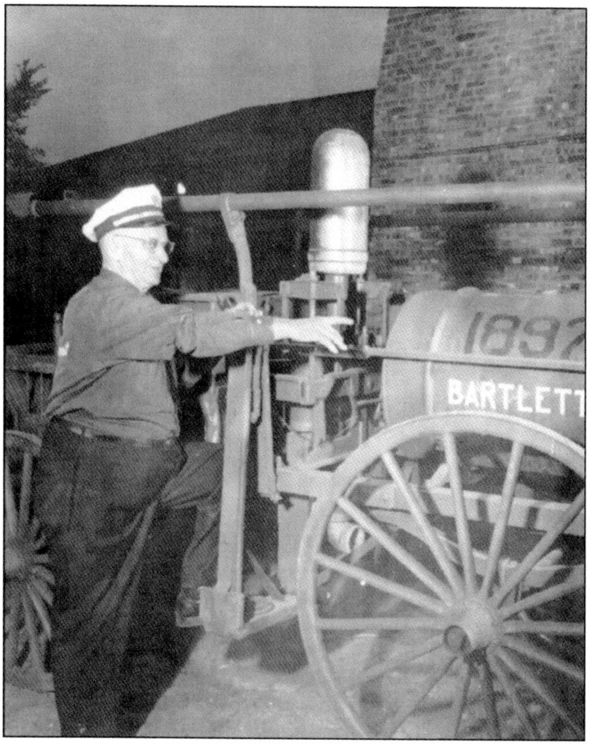

Fire Chief William (Billy) E. Bull stands beside Bartlett's first piece of fire equipment, a hand pumper purchased in 1897. Bull joined the department in the same year and spent the next 52 years in service to his town. He became the Fire Chief in 1931 and remained in that position until his unexpected death from a heart attack in 1949. This human sparkplug kept step with modern developments in firefighting equipment and under his direction, the Bartlett department became one of the most efficient in the area.

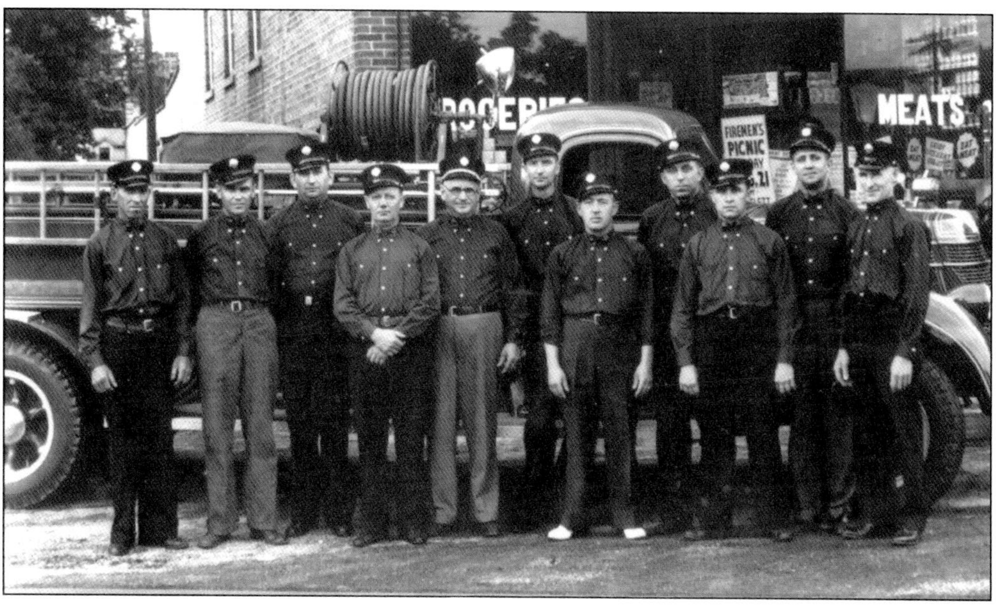

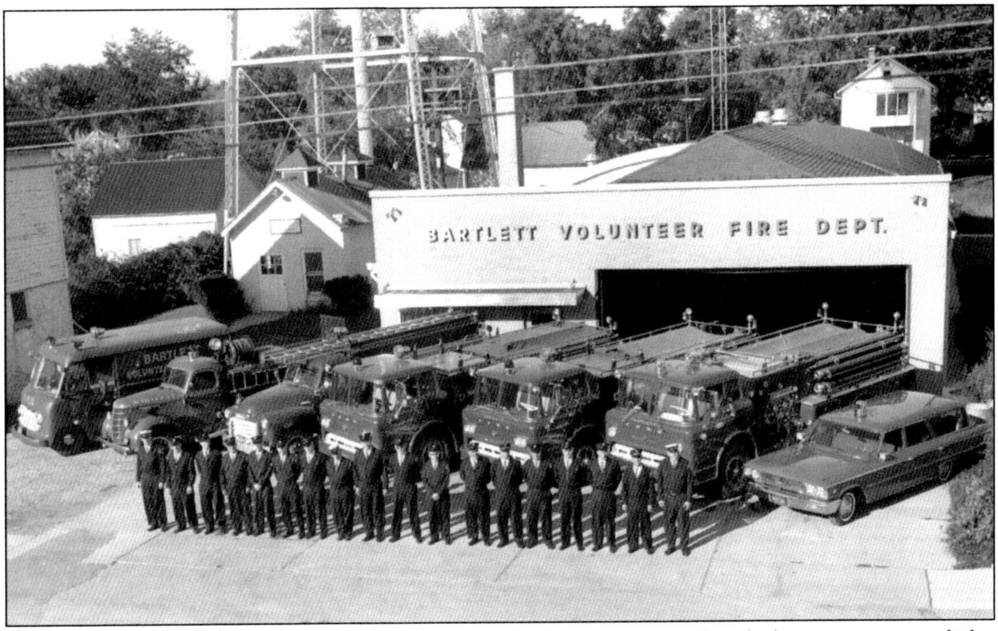

In January 1959, the Bartlett Volunteer Fire Department completed the expansion of the fire station at 220 Main Street. Most of the work on the building was done by the volunteers themselves. The building is owned by the volunteers to this day and is still used for many civic and community events. In 1989, due to the rapid growth in the Village, fire district trustees decided to go through the testing process and hire seven full-time firefighters.

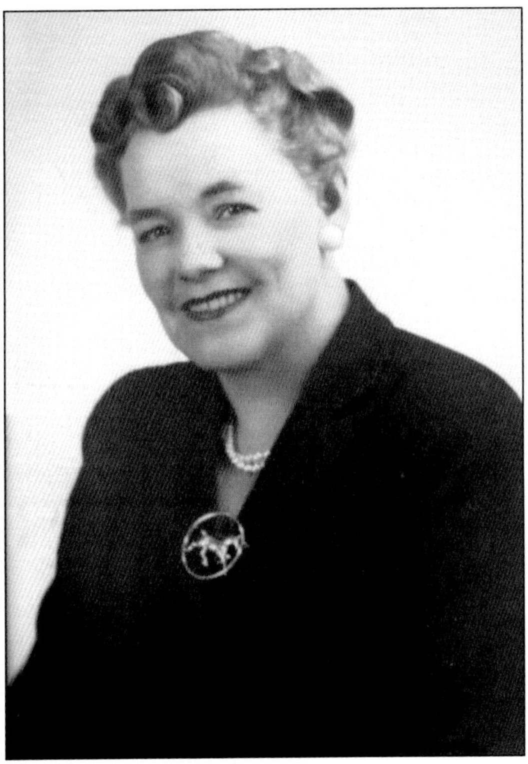

In 1951, Serena Jensen was awarded Honorary Fireman's Badge #13 for her dedication to the Bartlett Volunteer Fire Department. Serena owned and lived behind the Bartlett Tavern, and more importantly was willing to take on the late hours needed for sounding the fire alarm when night calls came in. After a call, the firemen always knew they could count on Serena to have coffee and sandwiches waiting at the tavern.

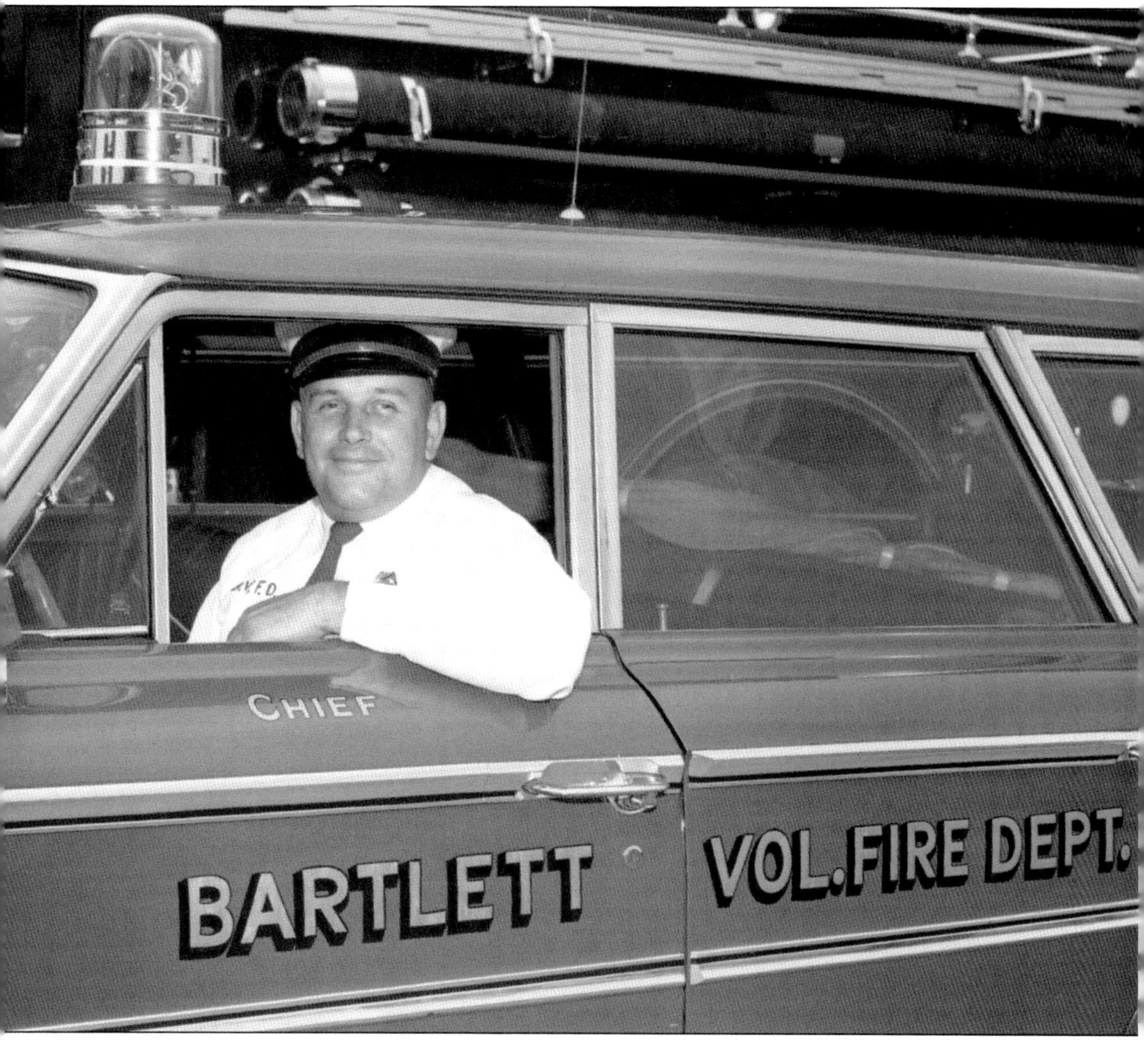

Elmer Hecht (b. 1926 – d. 2002) was raised on a prosperous farm in Hanover Township. Elmer's lifelong love of tractors grew from his boyhood, when he helped his father in the family threshing business. The Great Depression brought the loss of the family farm, prompting the Hecht family's move to Bartlett. He attended Bartlett School through his sophomore year, finishing at Elgin High. After returning from World War II, he married Mary Airhart, started a family and took his place in the community. Elmer joined the Bartlett Volunteer Fire Department in August 1952, became captain in 1956, and was elected chief in 1961, a position he held until his 1994 retirement. In 1968, fire district trustees recognized the need for full-time personnel and Hecht was the first full-time hire. During his 42 years of service, Elmer earned the respect and love of his department and his community. He was one of those rare bosses who didn't mind getting his hands dirty and was a firefighting innovator whose push for standardized hose thread helped assure mutual aid calls actually provided useful aid.

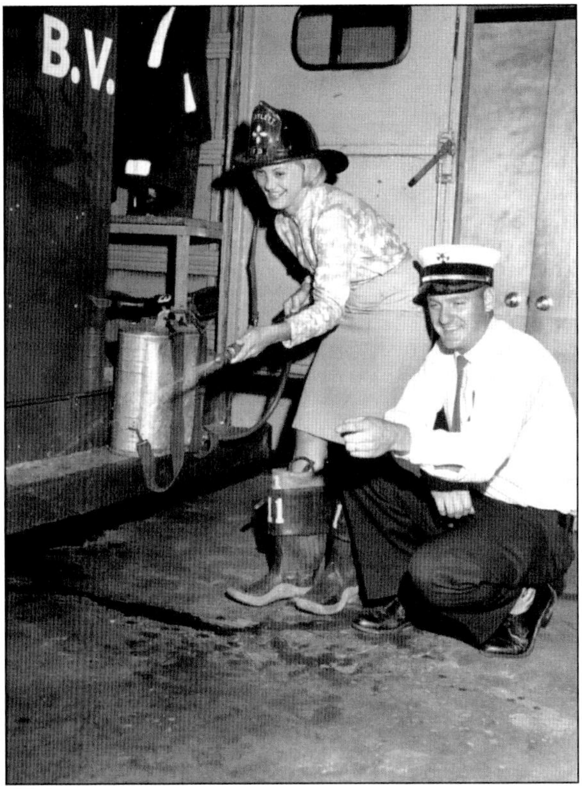

Fire Chief Robert Probst has fun instructing Miss Hanover Township Young Republican of 1964 in the proper technique for extinguishing a small fire with a handheld hose. Probst came to live in Bartlett with the Baxmann family in 1940. He was a volunteer fireman for 17 years and served briefly as fire chief.

For many decades, the Bartlett Volunteer Fire Department not only functioned as a fire-fighting unit, but as the center of social activity in the community. They held dances, picnics, turkey raffles, and the famous Firemen's Festivals, which began in 1938. Profits from the events were used for equipment, uniforms, training, facilities, and civic improvements. Volunteer and one-time Fire Chief Tony Whitmer, shown here second from right, holds court at a festival staple—the beer tent.

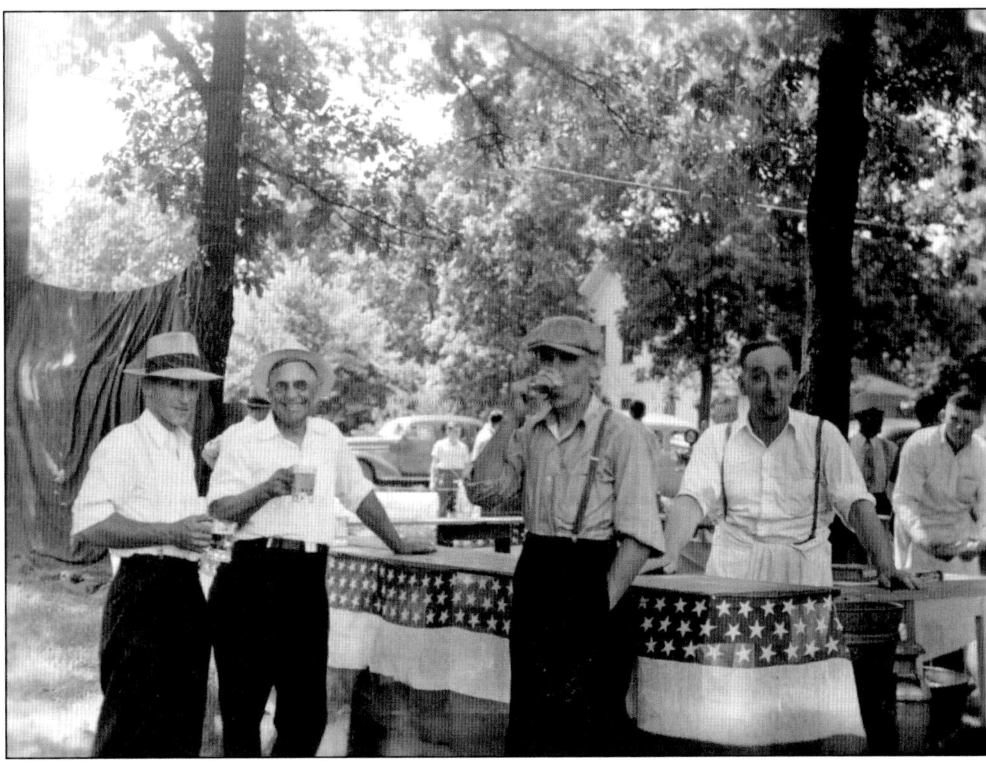

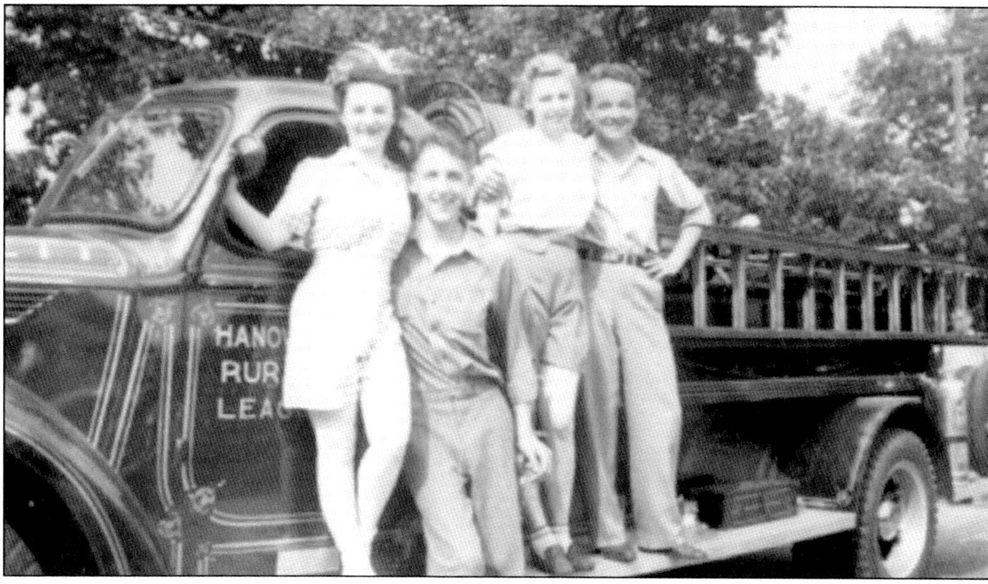

No one was too old to want to climb up onto the big red fire truck when it was August and Firemen's Festival days rolled around. By the early 1940s, when Elva Scholey, Gerald Faber, Elaine Jensen, and Allen Atchison, posed for a picture on the running board of this pumper, the greater Bartlett community was being served by what was now called the Hanover-Wayne Rural Fire League.

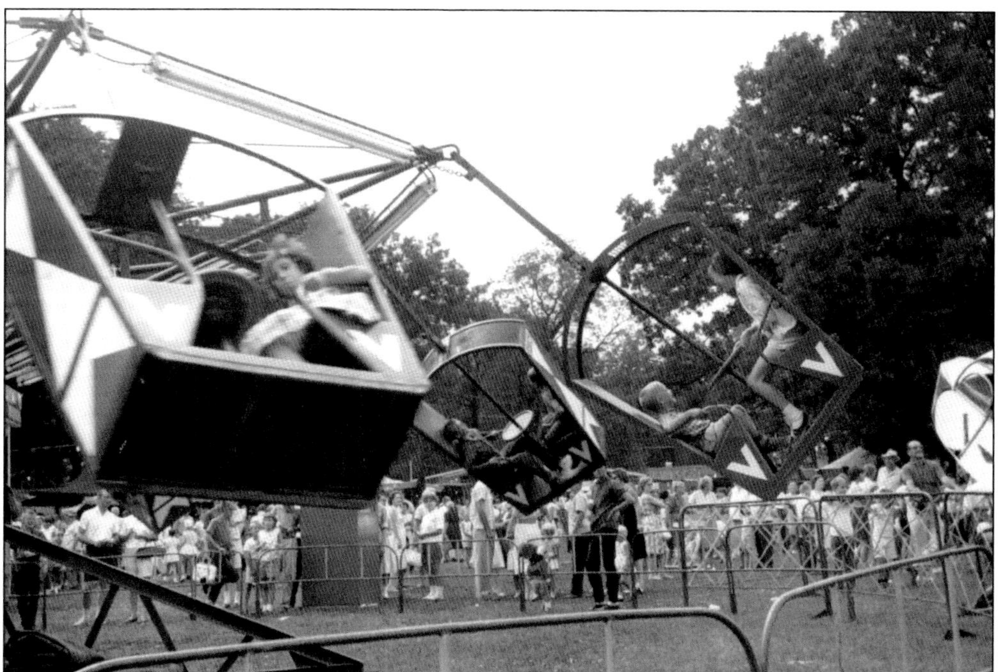

Children would save their money all year so they could play the games and ride the Tilt-a-Whirl, Ferris Wheel, and other rides offered by the Skinner Amusement Company. The carnival vendor would turn down two weeks of bookings to be available for the two-day Bartlett Firemen's Festival, kicked off annually by a parade through town and held at Bartlett Park.

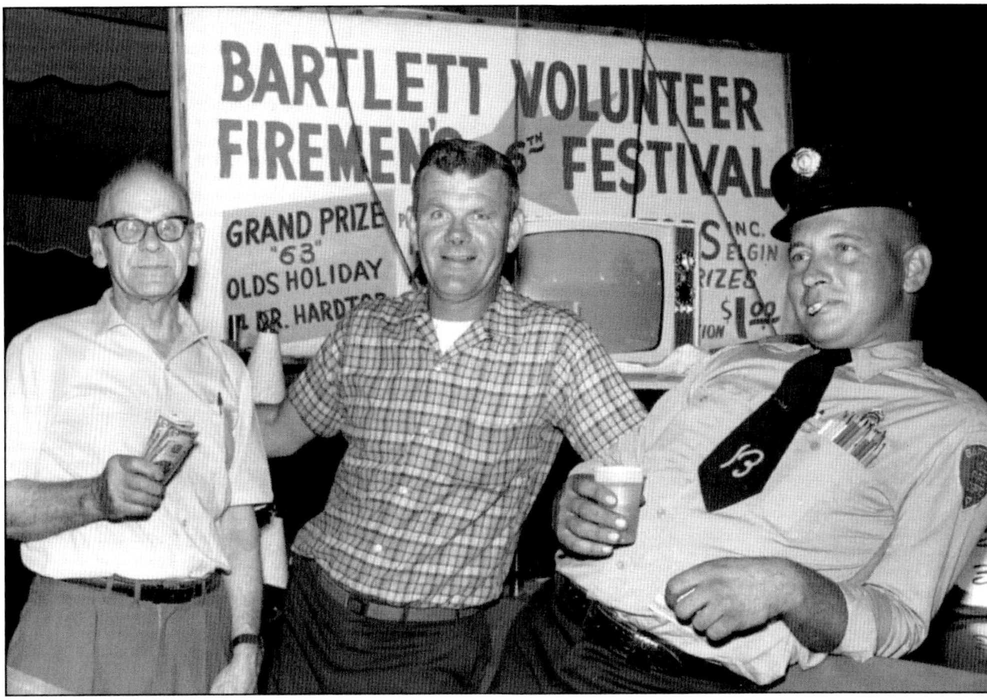

The festival was a non-stop party with something for everyone, including Bingo, gambling games such as Big 6, a car raffle, beer, food, a dancing band, and more. It took a week to set up and also a week to clean up after it was over. In this 1963 photo, Bill Schultz, Fire Trustee Pete Wehle, and Bob Van Alstine relax in the raffle tent. The last festival was held in 1969.

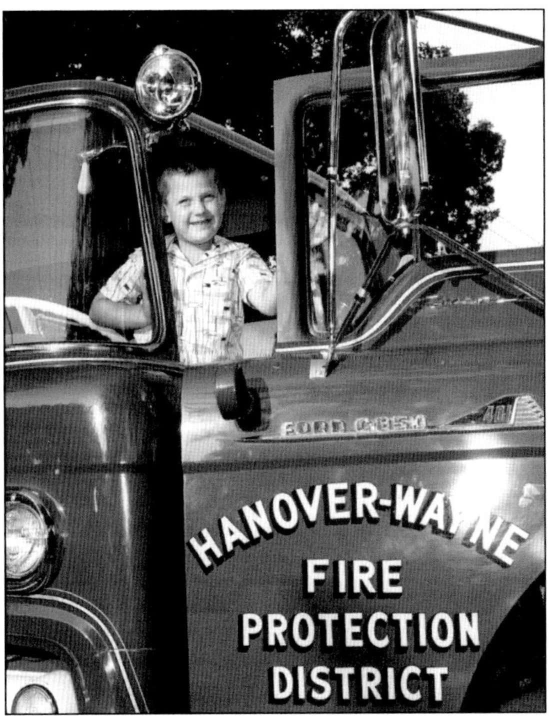

As a tyke, Paul Kuester, son of Clara and Fred, who was a volunteer fireman and an auxiliary policeman for Bartlett, didn't know that he too was destined to serve his childhood hometown one day. In 1974, Paul joined Bartlett's Public Works in the Streets Department and is today the Public Works Director for the Village.

Three

Growth and Commerce

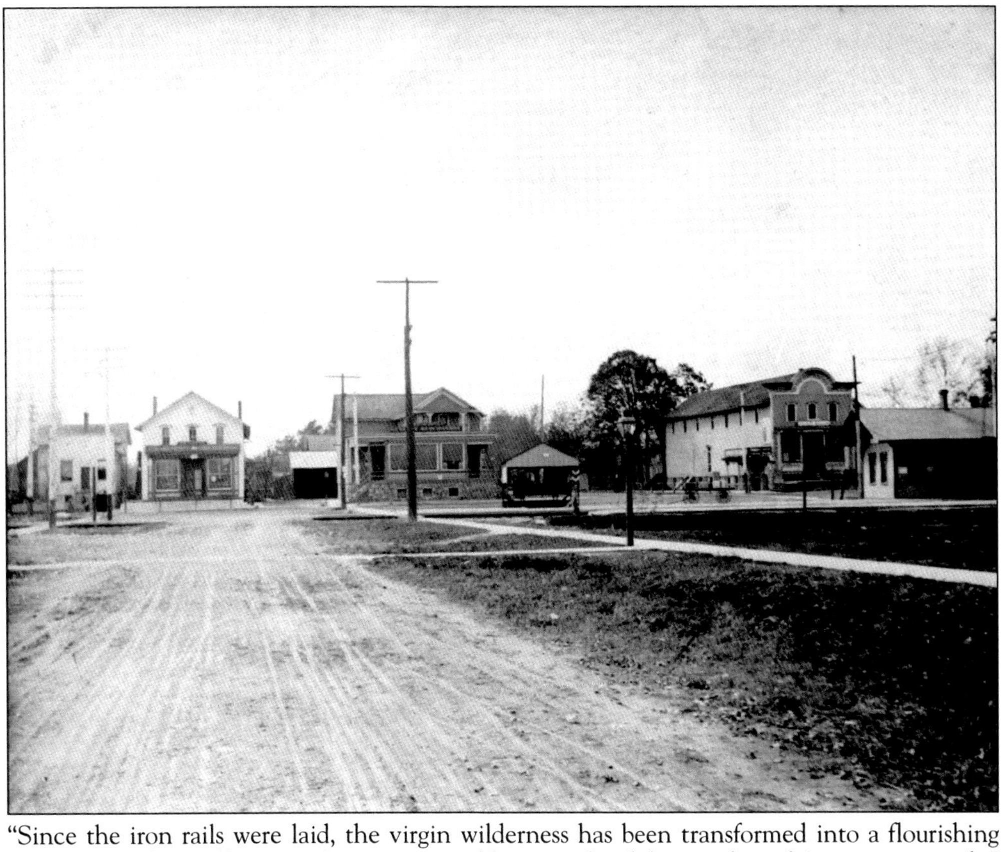

"Since the iron rails were laid, the virgin wilderness has been transformed into a flourishing little village that will in time become a notable example of the rapidity of American growth," so said the 1876 Elgin Advocate of Bartlett, "A Town of Three Years Existence and Still it Grows."

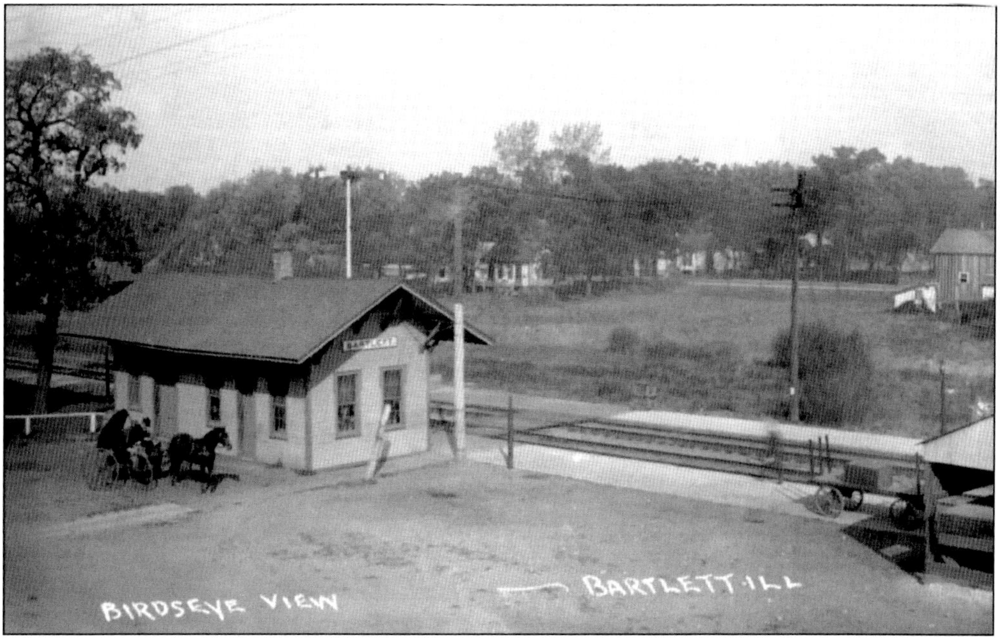

The centerpiece of downtown Bartlett, then and now, is the original Bartlett depot. Built in 1873, the train station was the hub around which the town itself and all its ensuing commerce were built. In addition to its traditional use as a passenger ticket office and baggage room, the clapboard structure also housed the town's first telegraph and post office.

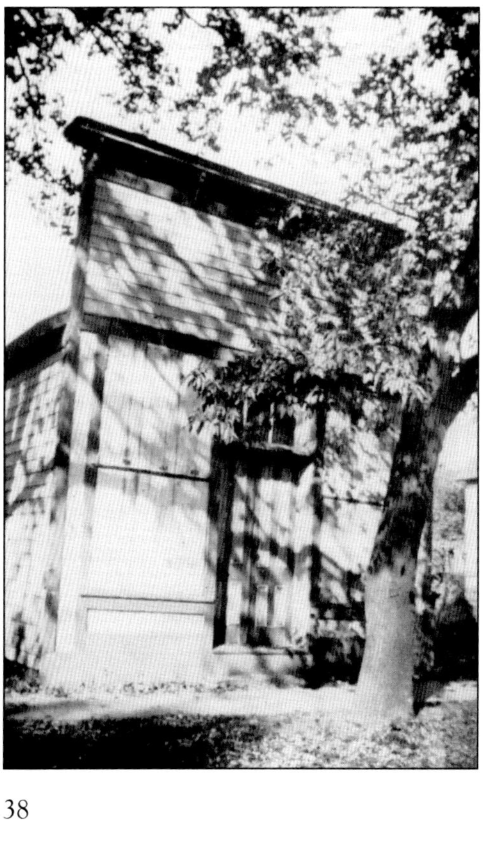

Pioneer businessman Carl Henry Krumfuss was a cobbler by trade and opened the first shoe repair and leather harness shop in town in the early 1870s. Most of Bartlett favored him with their orders for custom-made shoes and boots, allowing him to build a comfortable home at 120 S. Oak, next door to his shop, for his wife Dorothea and 11 children.

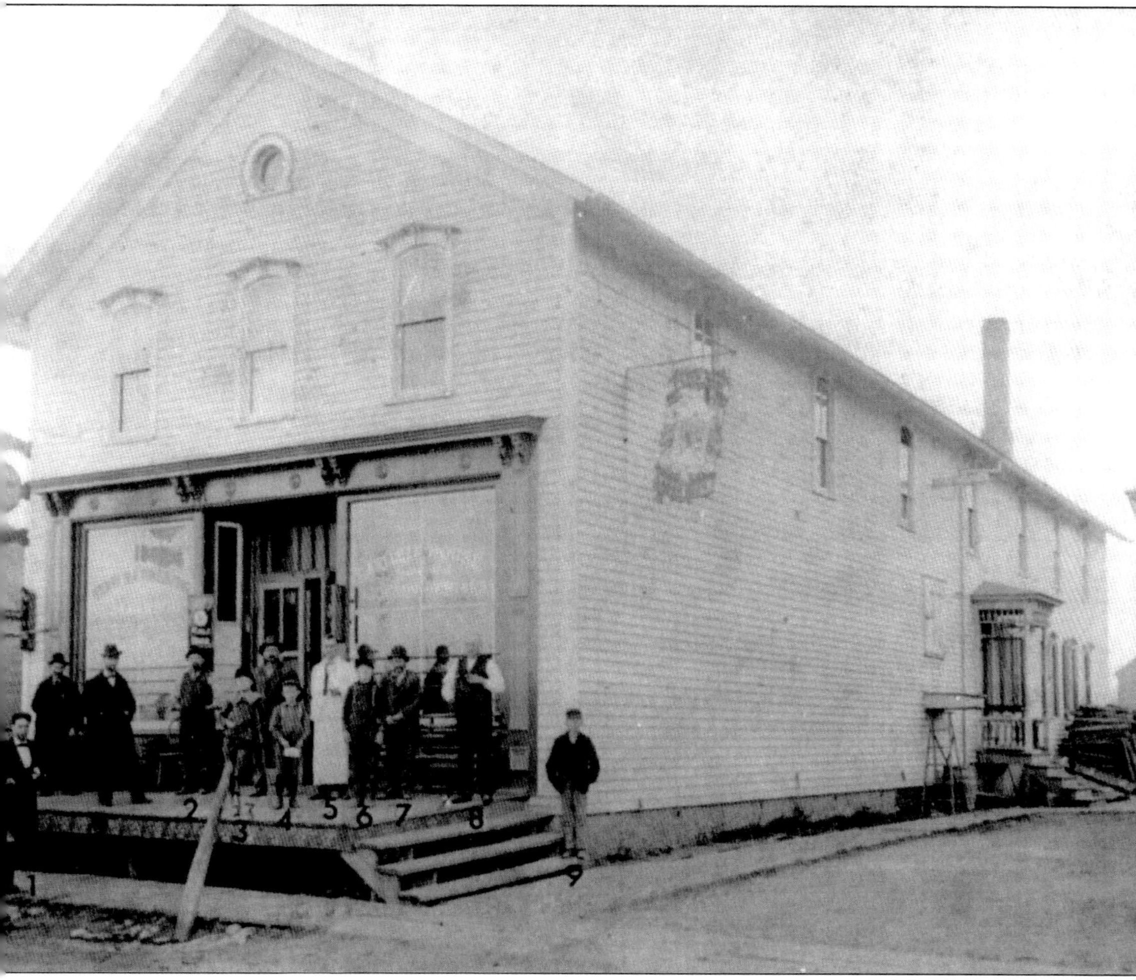

Who says there is no such thing as a free lunch? Just ask Caroline, wife of Bartlett House Saloon owner Henry Harmening Sr. (#8 in the photo), who cooked the tasty free lunch served daily at their establishment on Railroad Avenue. Rinderwurst (pot roast) was a special favorite of the saloon's patrons up until the time Harmening sold the business to his auctioneer partner, Herman Schnadt, in 1905. One of the first licensing ordinances in Bartlett was for saloons. To obtain a saloon license, the applicant had to be of good moral character, post $3,000 bond, pay $500 yearly, and abide by all licensing rules. One of the rules stated that a tavern owner "cannot sell to a minor without the parent's consent." The early records show it wasn't uncommon for the Village Board to brand someone as a "known drunkard." It would then be against the law for this person to patronize a local tavern. Any saloon keeper that sold "intoxicating beverages" to a town drunkard was subject to a fine.

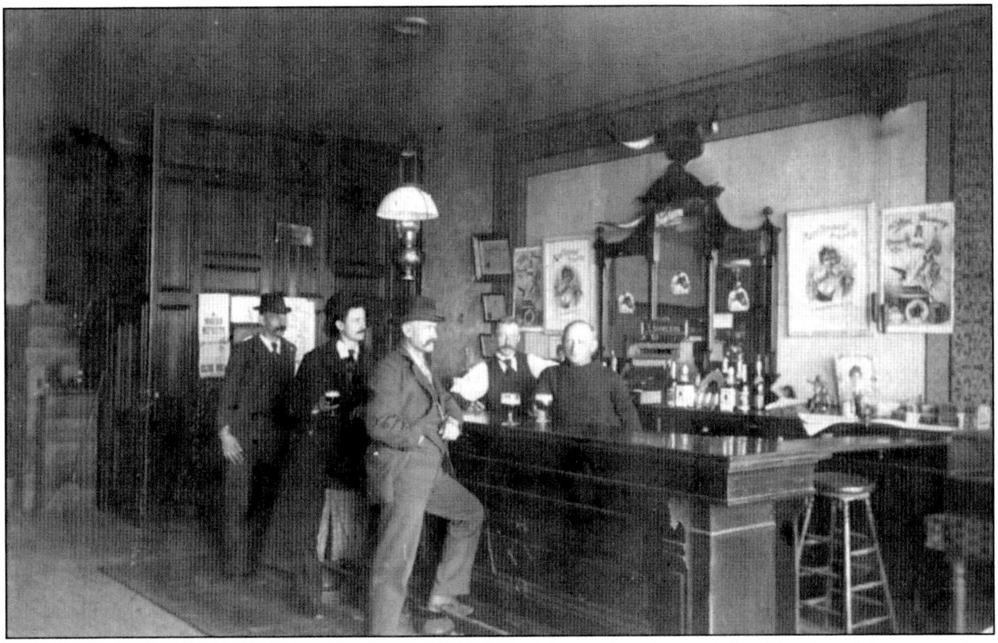

You didn't have to post a sign saying "For Men Only" on the door of the Bartlett Tavern in the early 1900s. Genteel women would never think to step foot into what was then an all-male bastion for whiskey, cigars, and pool. The mirrored back bar, which is still in service in the tavern today, was part of the 1893 Columbian Exposition and was then purchased by one-time tavern owner Henry Harmening.

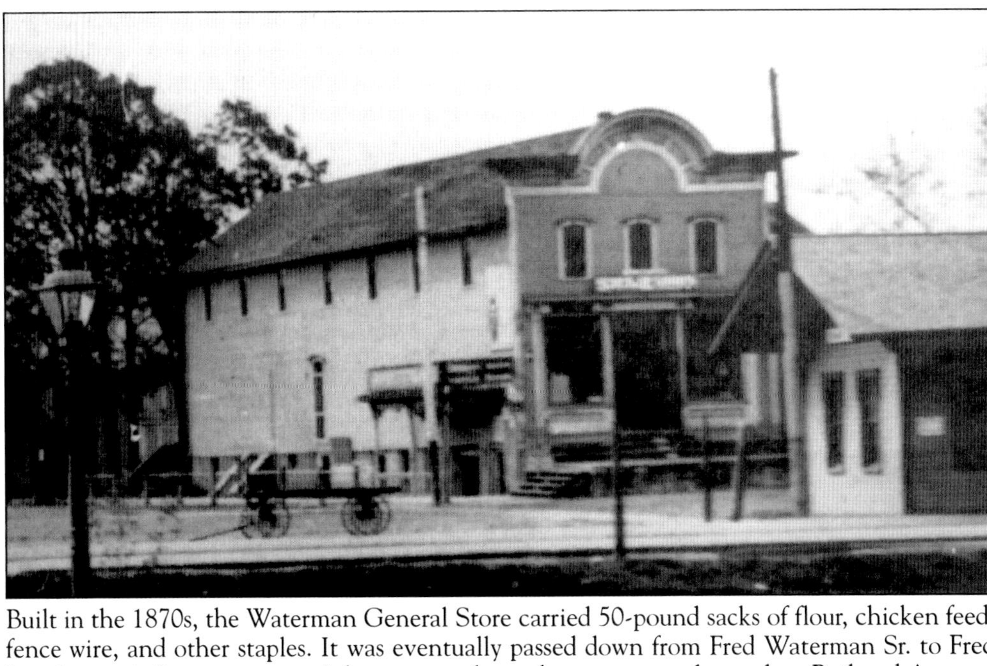

Built in the 1870s, the Waterman General Store carried 50-pound sacks of flour, chicken feed, fence wire, and other staples. It was eventually passed down from Fred Waterman Sr. to Fred Jr., who ran it for many years. A large room above the store, once located on Railroad Avenue, served as a dance hall where as many as 200 people would gather on a weekend evening to listen to German music.

Jacob Schmidt's wagon shop on Main Street in Bartlett was the all-inclusive, turn-of-the-century counterpart to today's big automakers and car repair shops. He provided the main mode of transportation for the day, wagons for commerce, carriages for leisure, and miscellaneous farm implements. The Bartlett Fire Barn now stands on the original site of his shop. Schmidt was also one of the first Village trustees, elected on March 24, 1891.

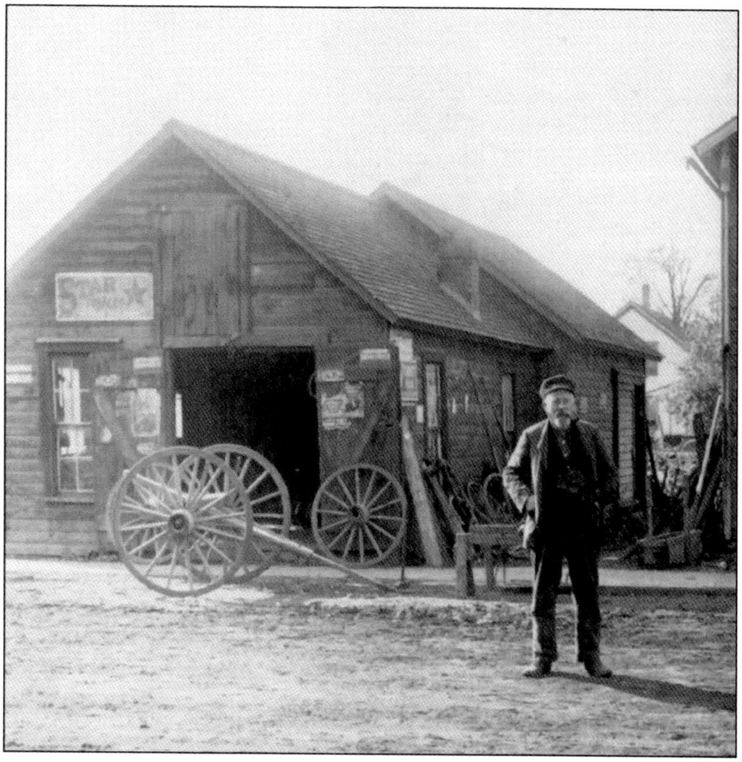

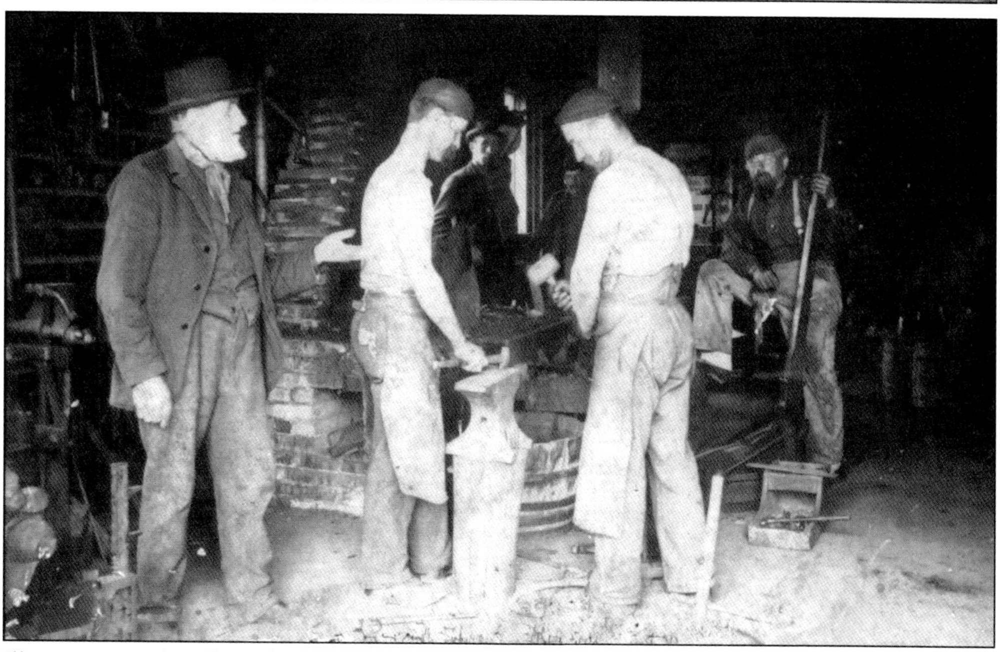

Illinois census data from the late 1800s listed the third most common occupation as blacksmith. Blacksmiths repaired everything from ditching plows to butter churns and baby buggies. Fixing a skillet or a part for a cook stove might be sandwiched between shoeing a horse and refurbishing a sleigh. "Routinely unroutine" is a phrase that reflects the breadth of the work the three Bartlett blacksmiths carried out for the farmer and town dweller alike.

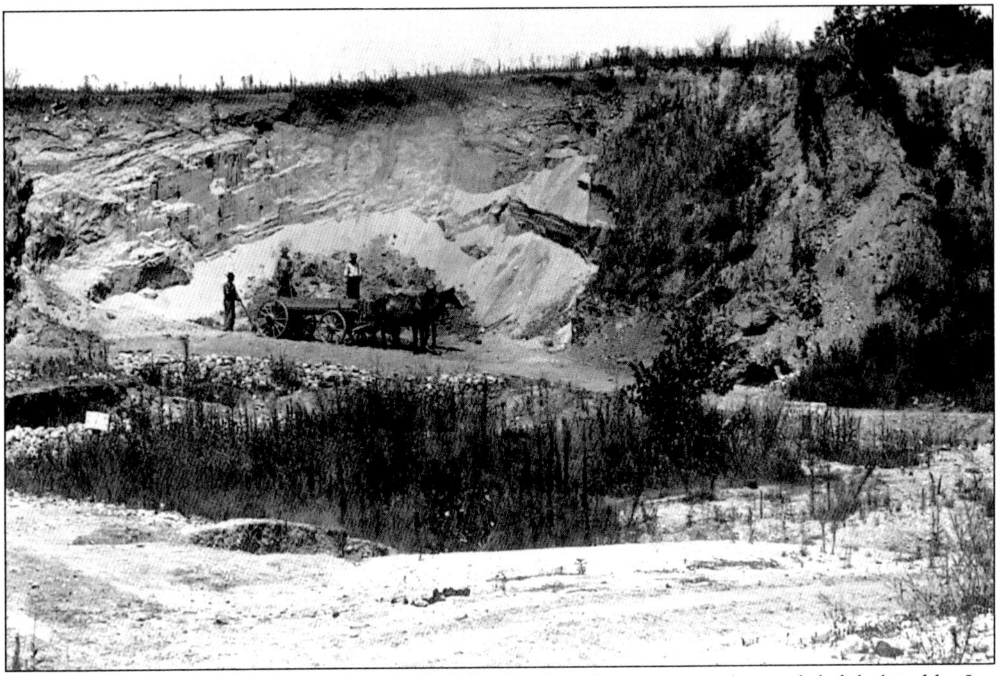

Scratch the surface of Bartlett and you'll find land rich in limestone and gravel, left behind by Ice Age glaciers and ready to be extracted from the earth by local mining companies for construction projects. Sand and gravel taken from pits, such as this one once located in the heart of town, were used to make cement block for building homes in the first decades of the 20th century.

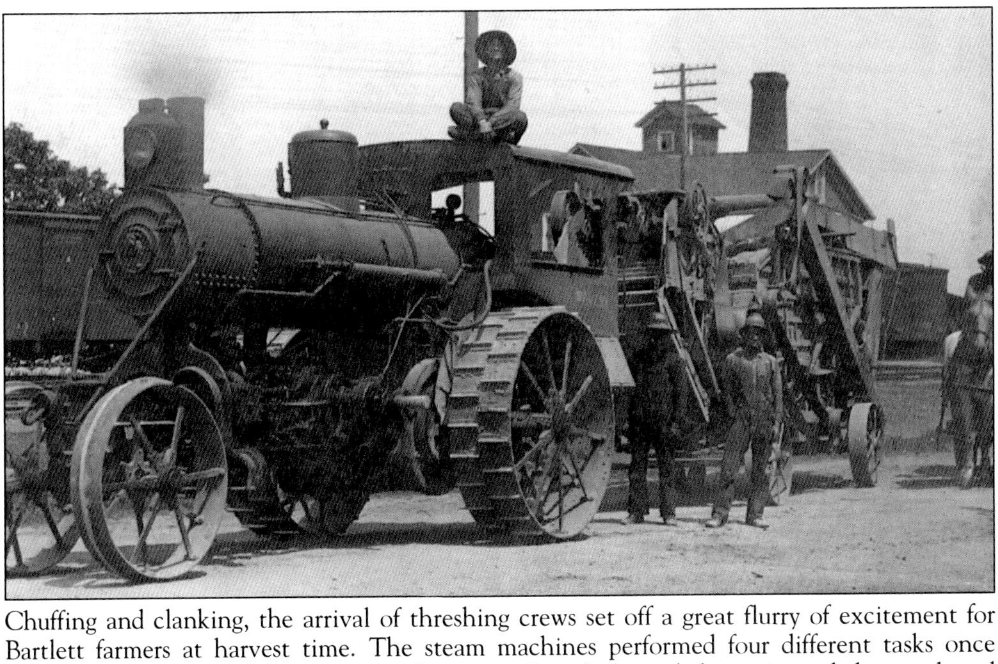

Chuffing and clanking, the arrival of threshing crews set off a great flurry of excitement for Bartlett farmers at harvest time. The steam machines performed four different tasks once done by hand or horse. They removed, separated, and cleaned the grain and then gathered or stacked it. Men and machines traveled from farm to farm in rural America because this equipment was too large and expensive for small farmers to purchase individually.

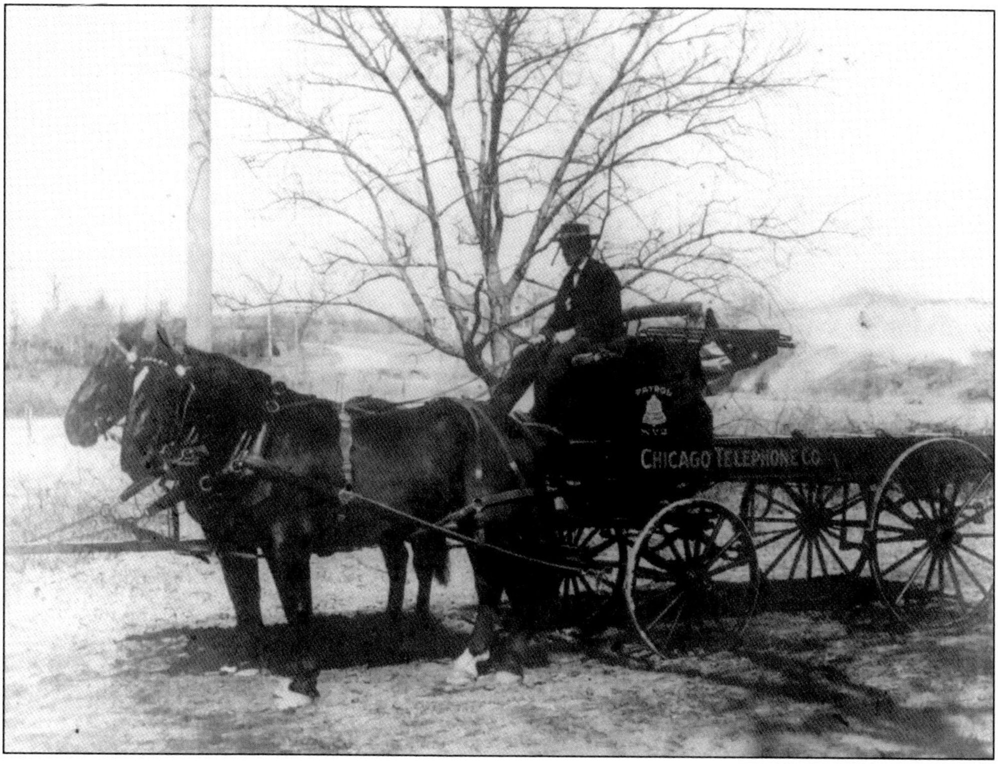

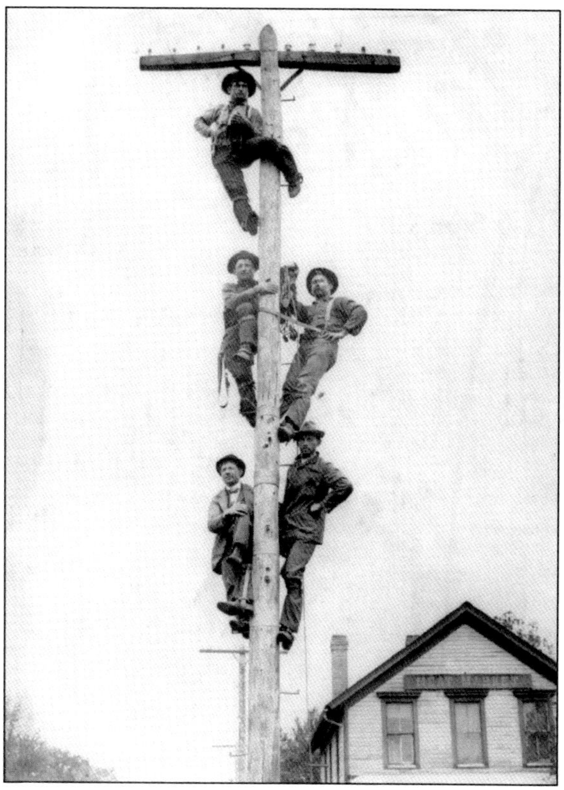

In 1901, the Village Board approved a franchise for two telephone companies, which eventually merged and became Illinois Bell Telephone Company. Gustav "Gus" Krumfuss was one of the first telephone linemen with Illinois Bell. Using a horse-drawn line-cart in the summer and snowshoes in the winter, he helped to string telephone wires over Bartlett and much of the northwest Chicago suburban area.

Gus retired in 1947 because the phone company felt that at the age of 61 he was too old to still be shimmying up phone poles (Krumfuss is at the very top in this photo). The first telephone switchboard installed in a rural area by Chicago Telephone was in Lena Kelley's home at 111 Railroad Avenue in 1901. Kelley's service was replaced by an automatic dial system in 1938, when the phone company pulled a switch and instantaneously put the more modern equipment into service.

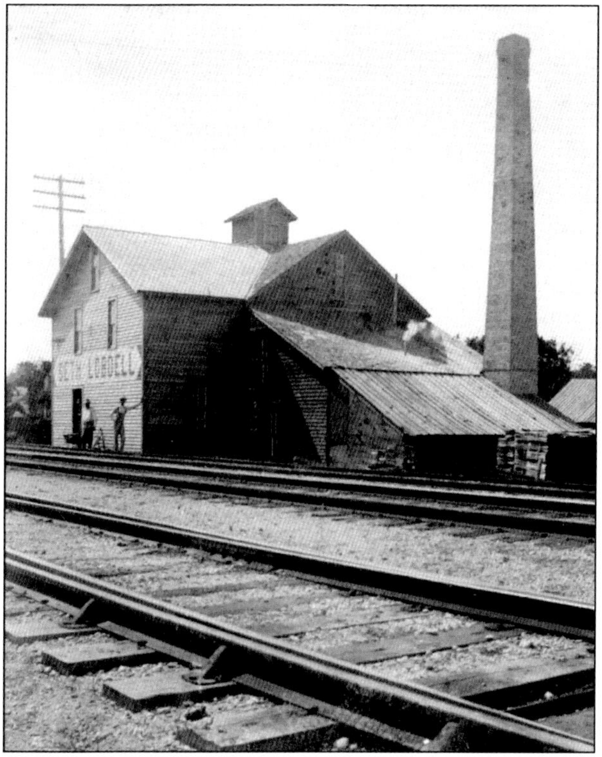

The Seth Lobdell Grainery, originally Carr & Lobdell, allowed Bartlett farmers to have their feed milled locally rather than traveling to Clintonville or Elgin. The main building of the steam-powered mill had "two run of stone" and a capacity of 4,000 bushels a day. Proprietors John Carr and Seth Lobdell were known to be genial fellows and their flour was said to be the best in the area.

The Huntley Dairy Company began construction on its new creamery and bottling plant in Bartlett in July 1907. The two-story brick building cost approximately $12,000 and the railroad company put in new sidetrack to help speed pickups and deliveries to the factory. The company hoped to have the work completed quickly so it could begin taking in milk on November 1.

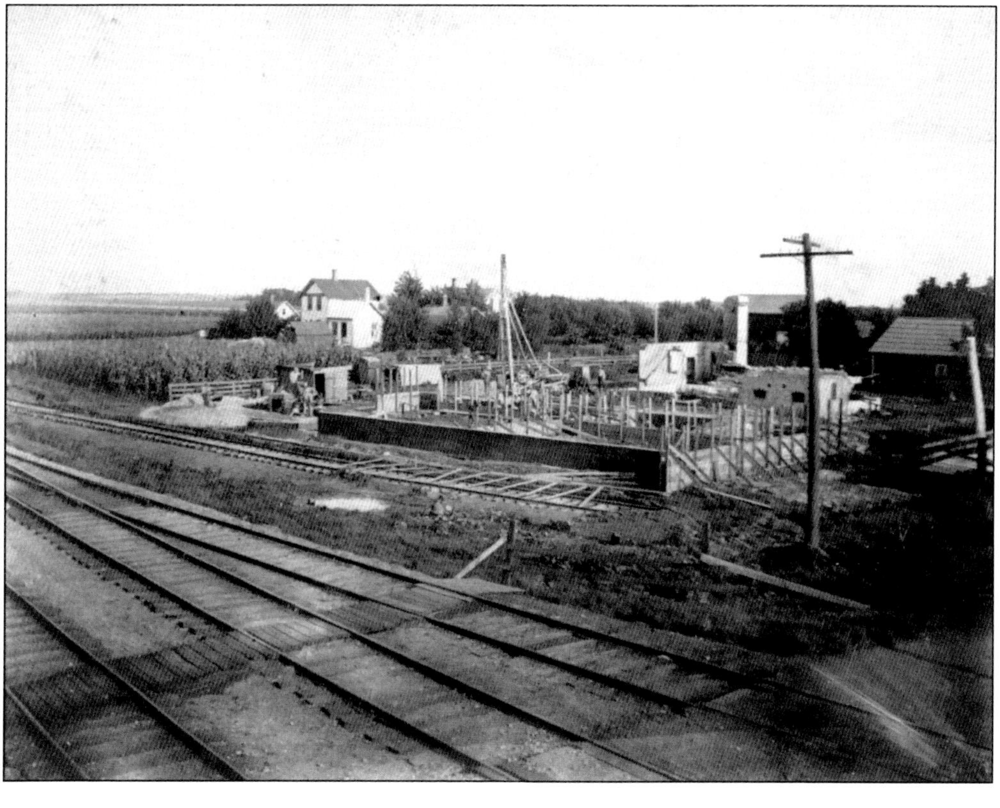

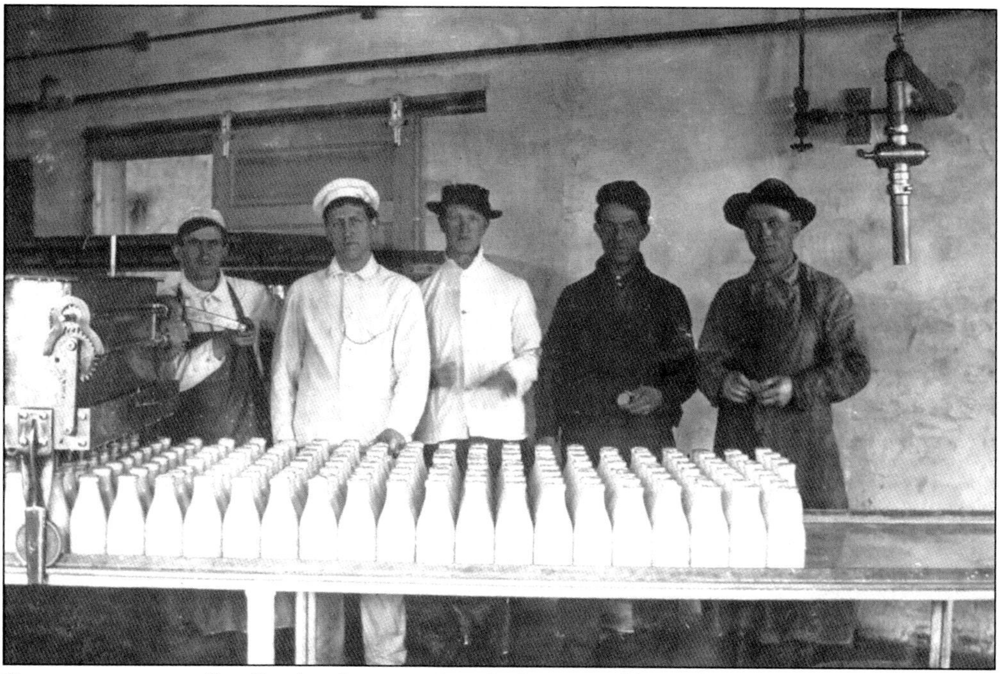

"Let anyone stop off at Bartlett between 8 and 10 a.m. and he will be astonished at the hustle and hurry in a village of this size," reported the *Cook County Herald* in 1909. At the height of operations, 60 to 80 farmers would line up their milk wagons as far back as Lake Street, waiting to deliver as much as 30,000 pounds of milk daily for pasteurization and delivery to Chicago.

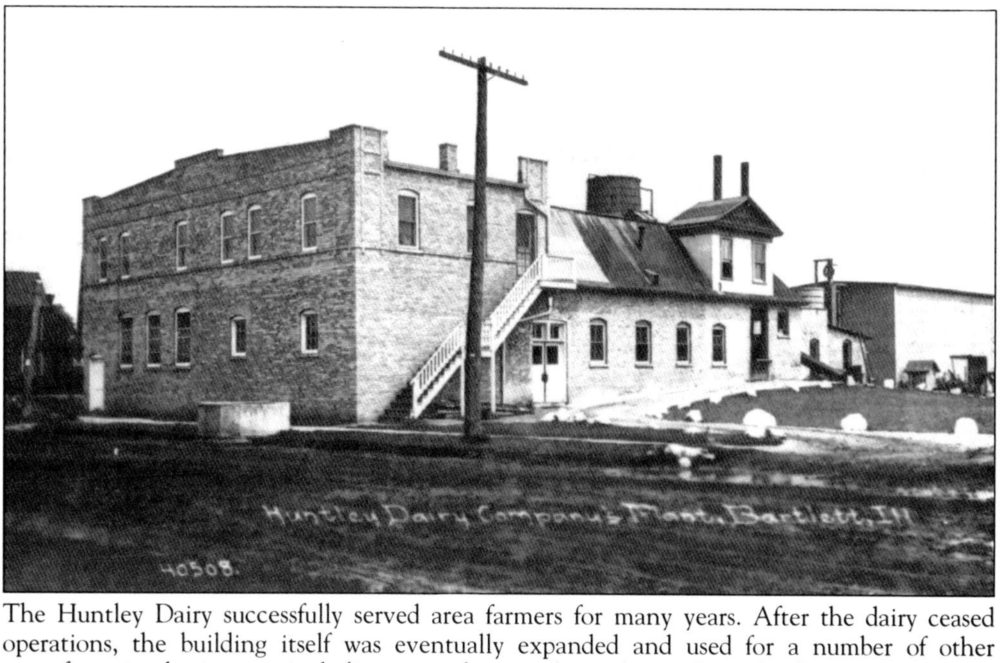

The Huntley Dairy successfully served area farmers for many years. After the dairy ceased operations, the building itself was eventually expanded and used for a number of other manufacturing businesses, including a toy factory, the making of wood cabinetry and finally Setko Fasteners, a manufacturer of set screws. The structure at Railroad Avenue and Main Street was torn down in 2001 to make room for downtown redevelopment.

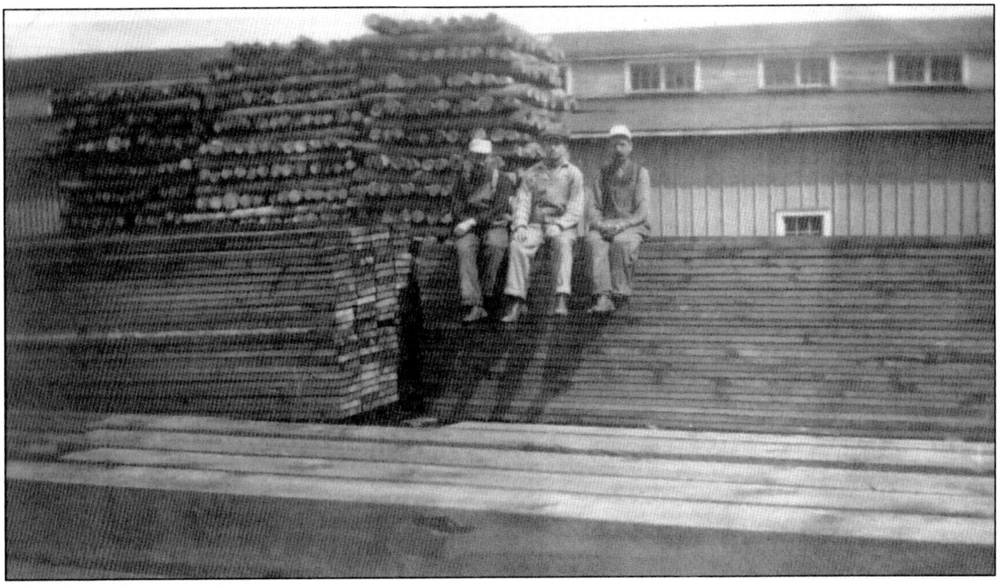

The demand for construction grade wood for farmsteads, homes, and businesses made lumber a profitable endeavor in Bartlett. In the early 1900s, John Fenz owned Bartlett Feed & Lumber at the east end of Bartlett Avenue. Local builders John Wendler (above left) and Herman Wendler (right) relied on Fenz for their materials. By the 1930s, O.H. Wright acquired the property and opened Wright's at Bartlett. "A dependable place to trade," Wright's carried lumber, millwork, fuel, and feed. Two of the frame buildings were accessible to the railroad siding where coal and other goods were unloaded. Three more buildings were across the roadway to the north. An in-street scale allowed customers to have their trucks weighed to determine the total price of their per pound purchases. One of the original buildings at 108 Bartlett Avenue is still used for commercial purposes today. The rest were razed for parking.

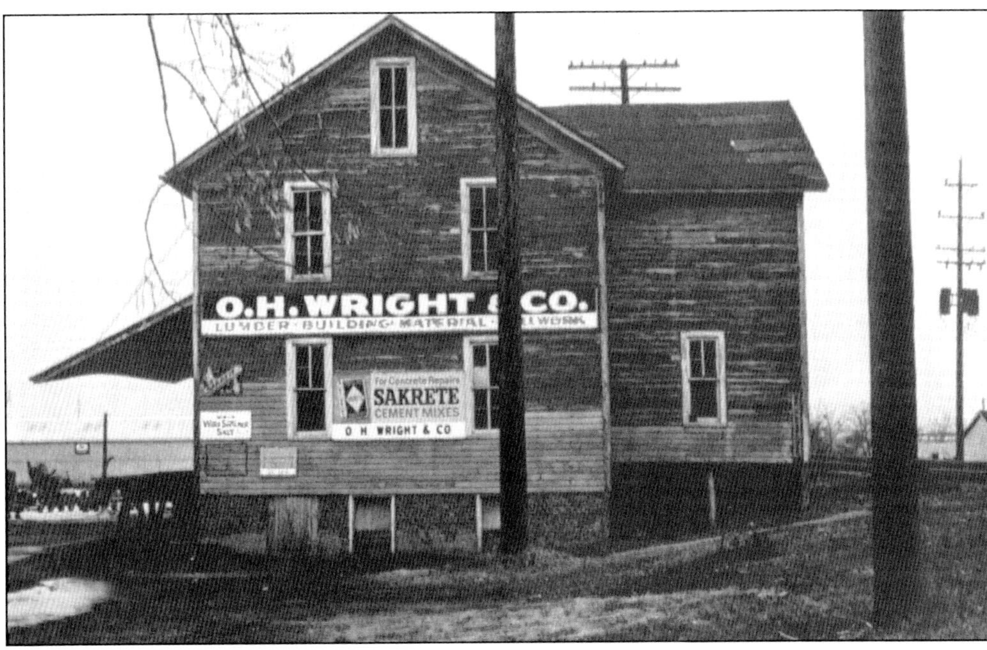

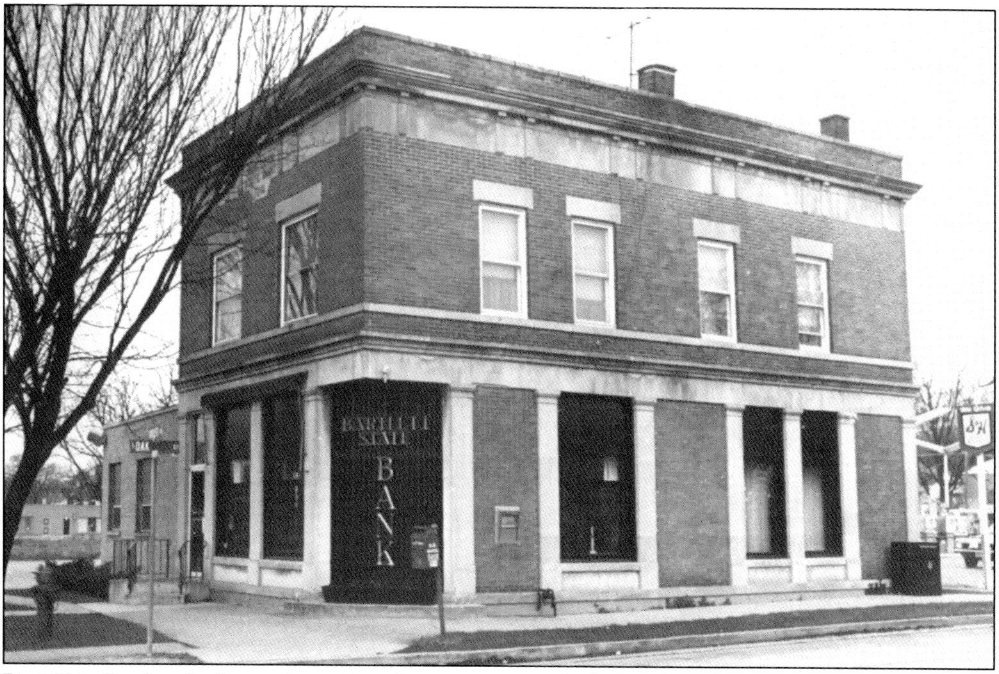

By 1910, Bartlett had experienced an "energetic period of growth and it was obvious a bank was needed." On December 17, 1910, Bartlett State Bank opened for business at 200 Bartlett Avenue. The bank grew and prospered through a number of wars and withstood the Depression and Black Monday. In 1973, the bank moved to its new facility at 335 S. Main Street and is now Harris Bank.

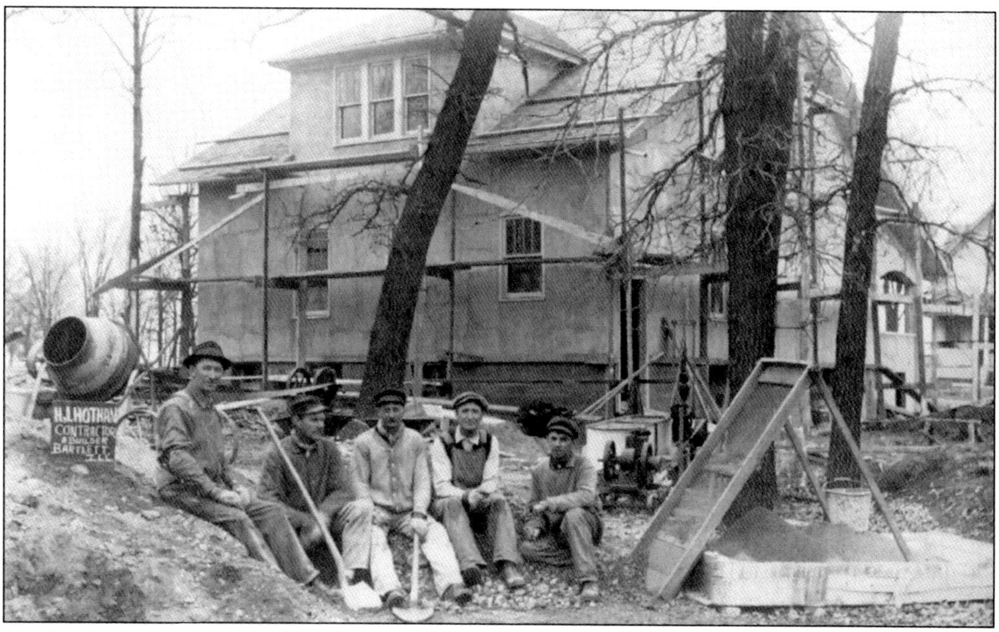

Bartlett contractor and builder Henry Hothan (first on the left) and his crew take a break from work on the stucco home at 148 N. Oak. Constructed in the 1920s, the house still stands today at its original site. In addition to building homes, Henry also contracted with the Village in 1918 to install cement sidewalks in town at a cost of 9¢ per square foot.

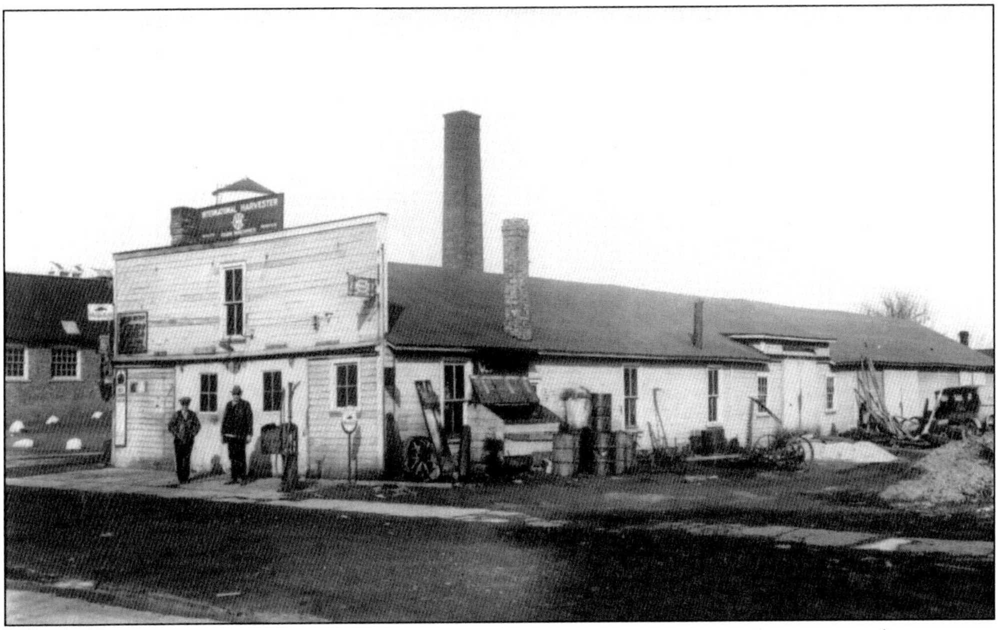

Edward D. Thurnau and Edmund G. Krumfuss, shown here in front of their original garage on Main Street, started out selling and repairing John Deere farm machinery and later added an automobile dealership. The growth and expansion of the business prompted the two men to build a new garage complete with a gas pump in 1925. In 1941, after 30 years of partnership, Thurnau & Krumfuss was dissolved.

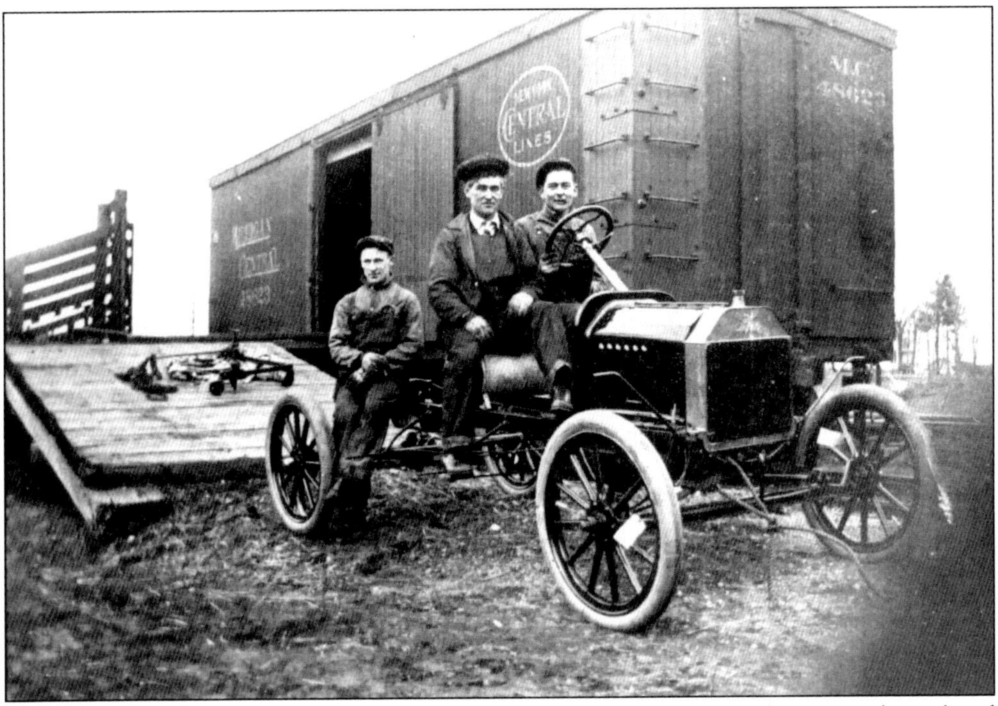

New shipments of automobiles and farm implements meant a short walk over to the railroad siding to accept delivery of the stock for the Thurnau & Krumfuss partners and their help.

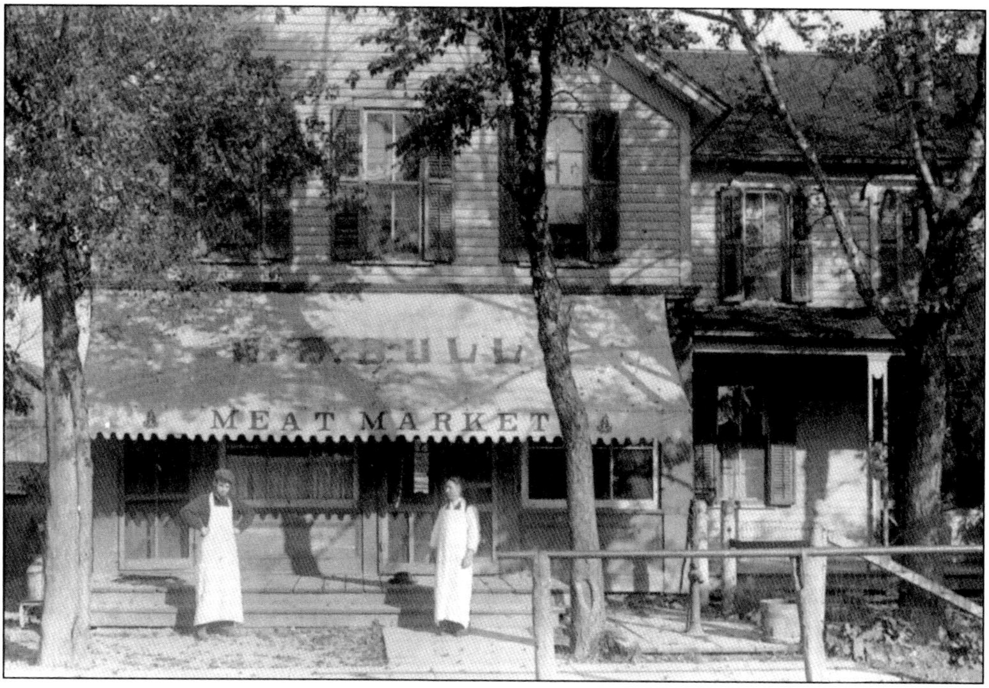

Bartlett housefraus often made Bull's Meat Market a daily stop for fresher than fresh chops, roasts, and sausages. First located on Main Street, butcher/owner William Bull shared the building with the Baxmann family who resided there. Bull's young butchers and apprentices, Raymond O'Brien, Conrad Baxmann, Fred Baxmann, Fred Wendler, and George Grey in this c. 1935 photo, were easily recognizable by their crisp white coats and aprons and the hair caps that signaled to patrons the strict sanitary conditions adhered to in the shop.

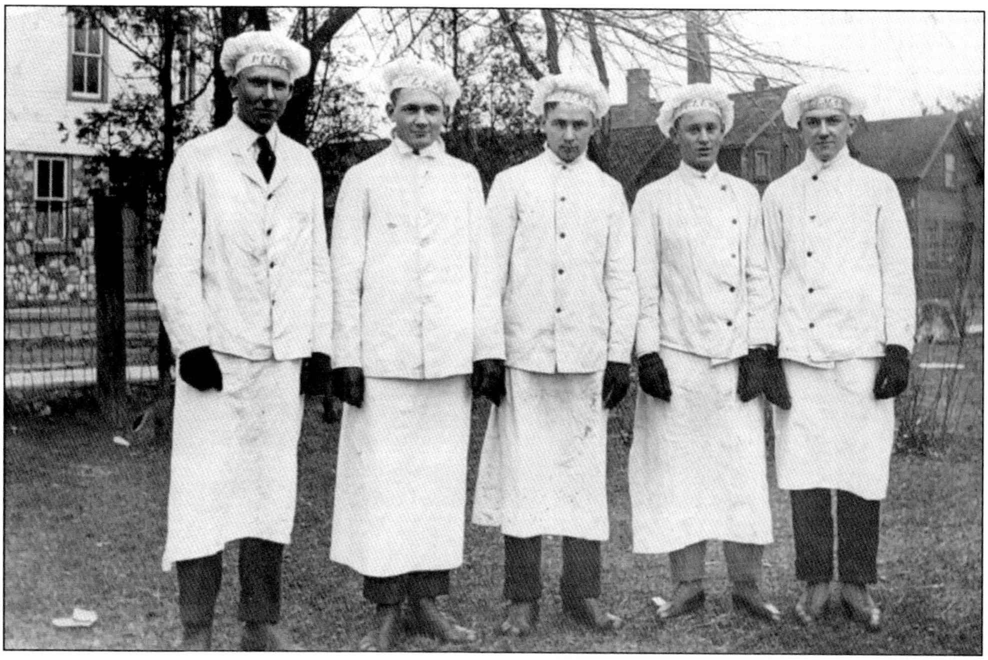

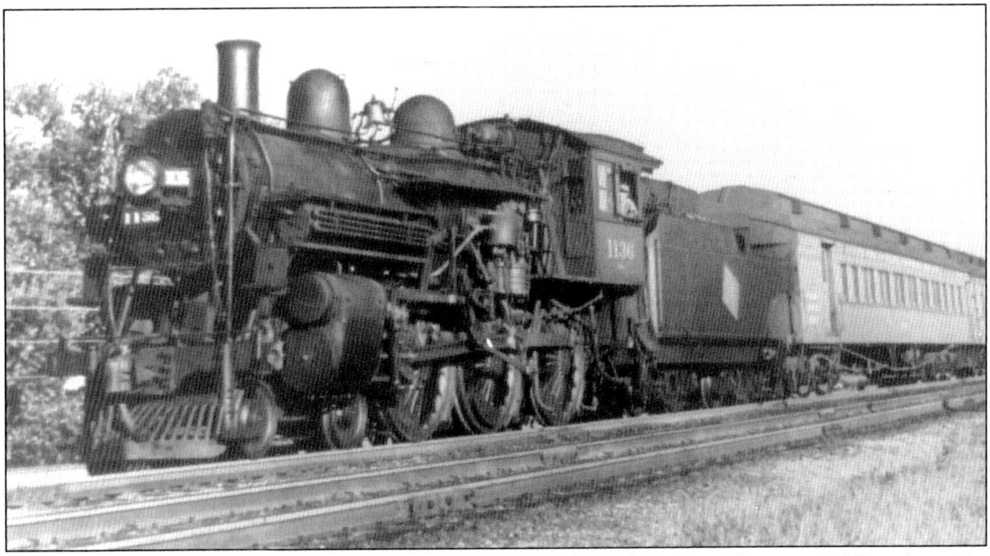

The Chicago & Pacific Railroad gave birth to Bartlett, but the Chicago, Milwaukee, St. Paul and Pacific Railroad Company, known as the Milwaukee Road, was a town builder. Before METRA, the Milwaukee Road's steam-powered trains offered reliable service to area commuters, transforming Bartlett into a burgeoning bedroom community. The company's beautiful streamliners provided the greater Bartlett area with a gateway to San Francisco, Los Angeles, Portland, and other cities.

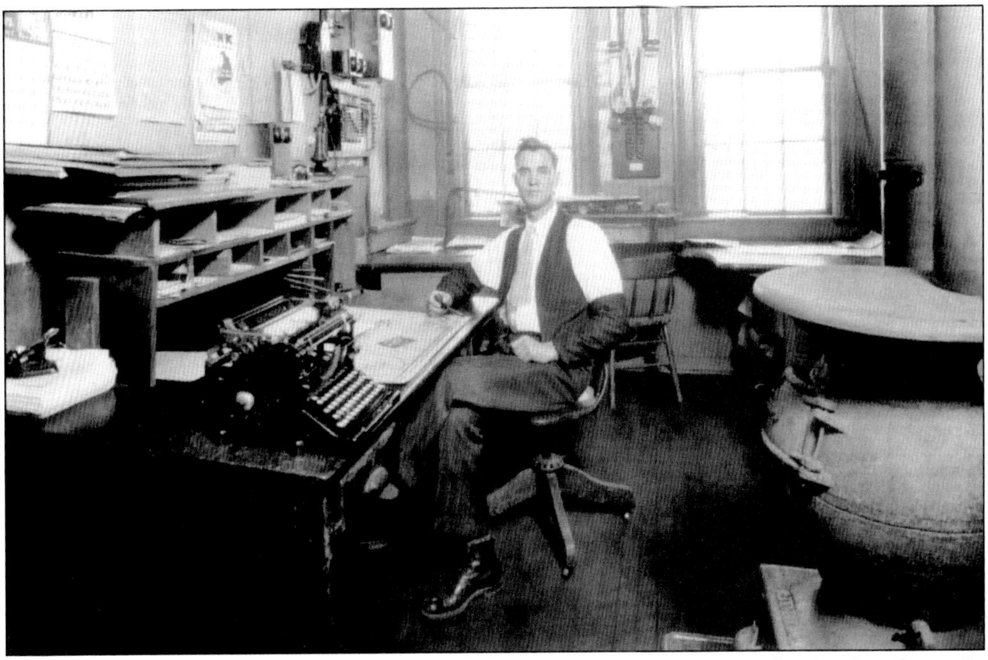

Joseph Charneskey, shown here in 1930, was a long-time stationmaster at the Bartlett depot. In addition to selling commuter and long-distance passenger tickets, early Bartlett station agents were responsible for shipping and receiving all freight traveling through the community, including autos, farm implements, livestock, and even the Fourth of July fireworks, eagerly awaited by mischievous boys. The depot was also the central location for postal services and telegraph communications.

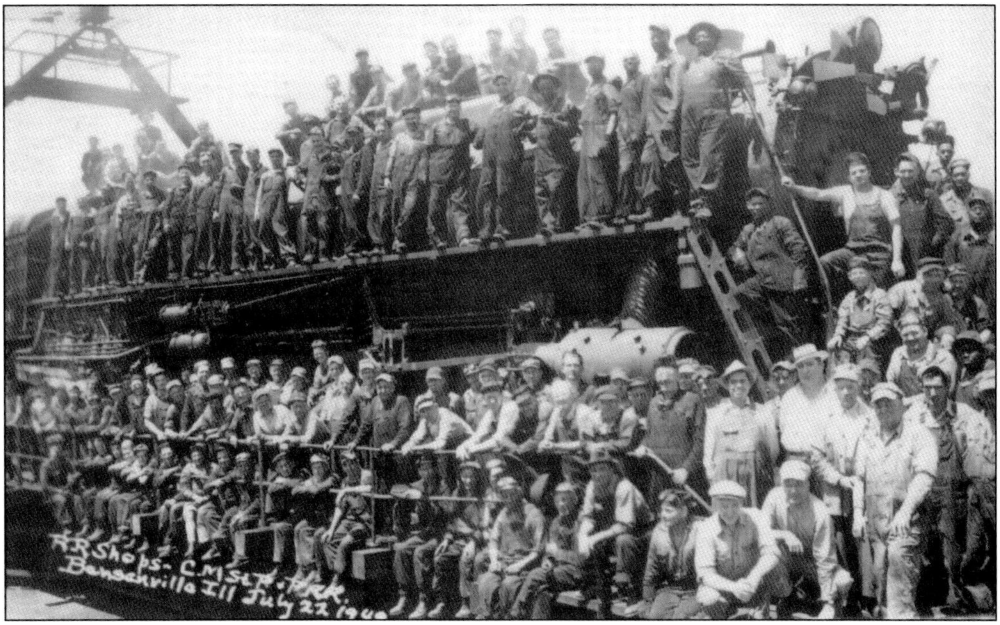

The Milwaukee Road provided a job and a free ride to the workplace for many a Bartlett resident. Roy Hinz, row three, second from right, would hop the train each morning to catch a ride to his machinist job in the Bensenville yards and later as a foreman at Galewood. He retired in 1970 after 47 years of service.

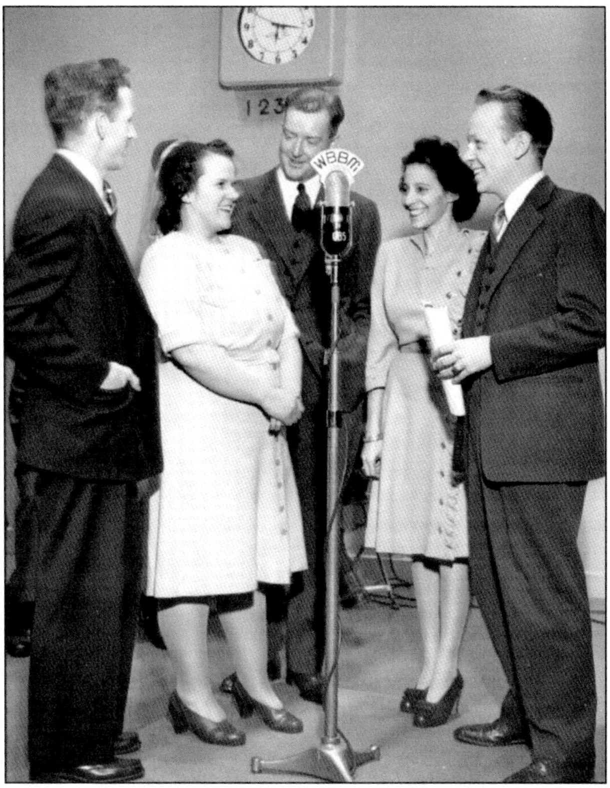

Long-time Bartlett resident Dorothy Heinberg (second from left) didn't need a lifeline when she helped her team from the Chicago, Milwaukee and St. Paul Railway win against the New York Central team on WBBM Radio's Monday evening "Brain Battle." In addition to being a 37-year railroad employee, she also was a driving force behind the organization of the Bartlett Historical Society in the early 1970s.

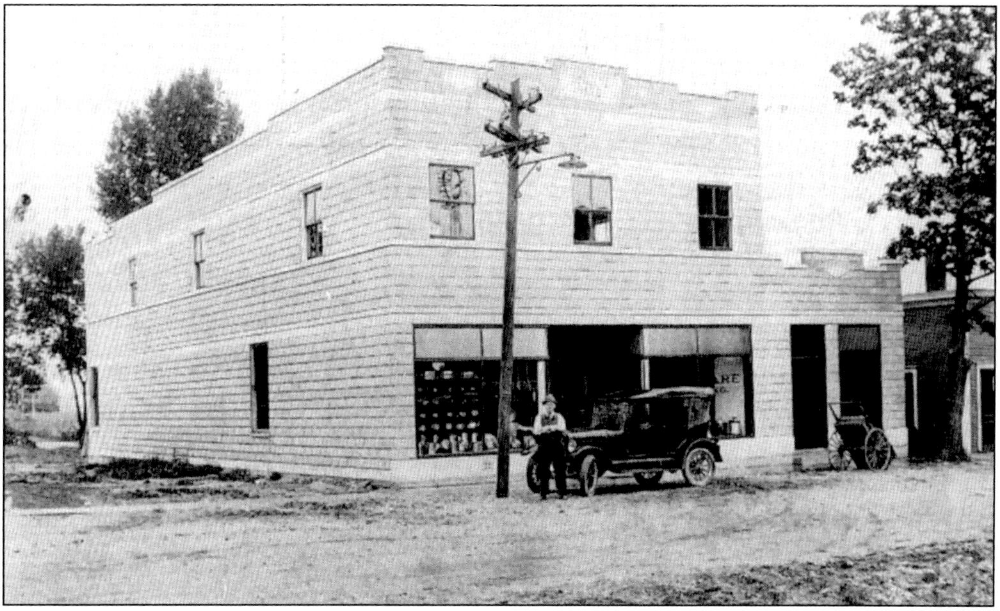

In 1926, Herman Henry Schultz constructed a new building at 110 Bartlett Avenue to house his growing hardware business. A rolling ladder put the boxes of nails and screws on the floor to ceiling shelves within easy reach. Upon the death of Herman, son Bill and his wife Ruby operated the business until his retirement in 1964. It continued as a hardware store until 1999, when it was renovated for other uses.

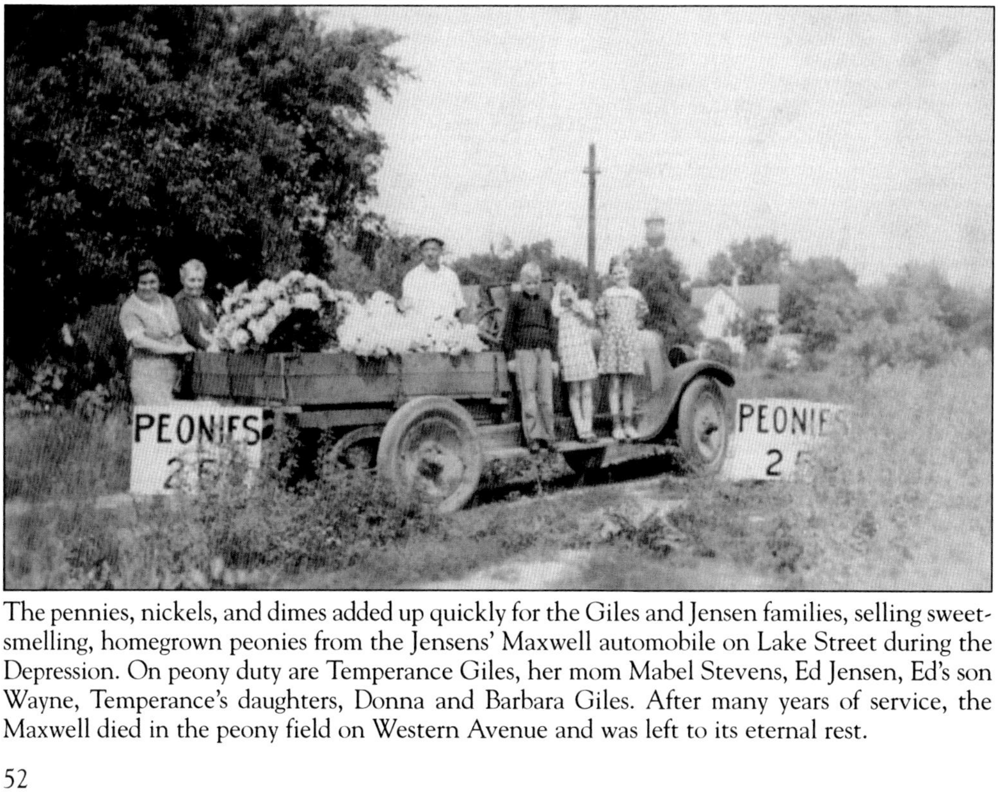

The pennies, nickels, and dimes added up quickly for the Giles and Jensen families, selling sweet-smelling, homegrown peonies from the Jensens' Maxwell automobile on Lake Street during the Depression. On peony duty are Temperance Giles, her mom Mabel Stevens, Ed Jensen, Ed's son Wayne, Temperance's daughters, Donna and Barbara Giles. After many years of service, the Maxwell died in the peony field on Western Avenue and was left to its eternal rest.

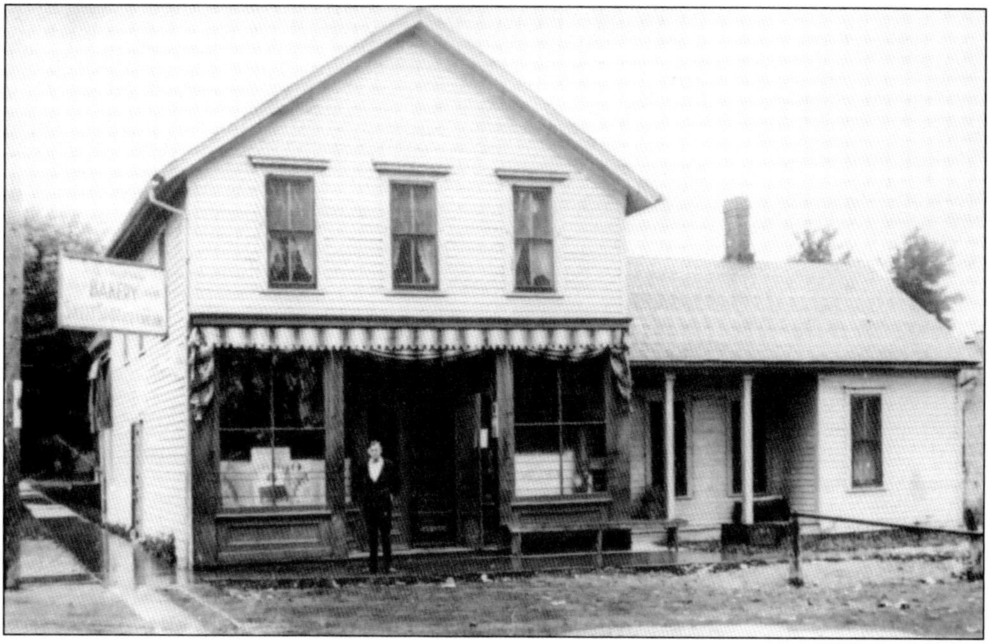

Henry C. Thurnau, born in Bartlett in 1888, stands in front of his bakery, confectionery, and ice cream shop at the corner of Oak and Bartlett Avenues. Thurnau was also a cattle dealer, the sixth Village president, a Hanover Township clerk for 30 years, a school trustee, and senior partner in Thurnau and Benicke Implement Co. In 1913, he married his "sweet shop partner" Melinda Kaiser.

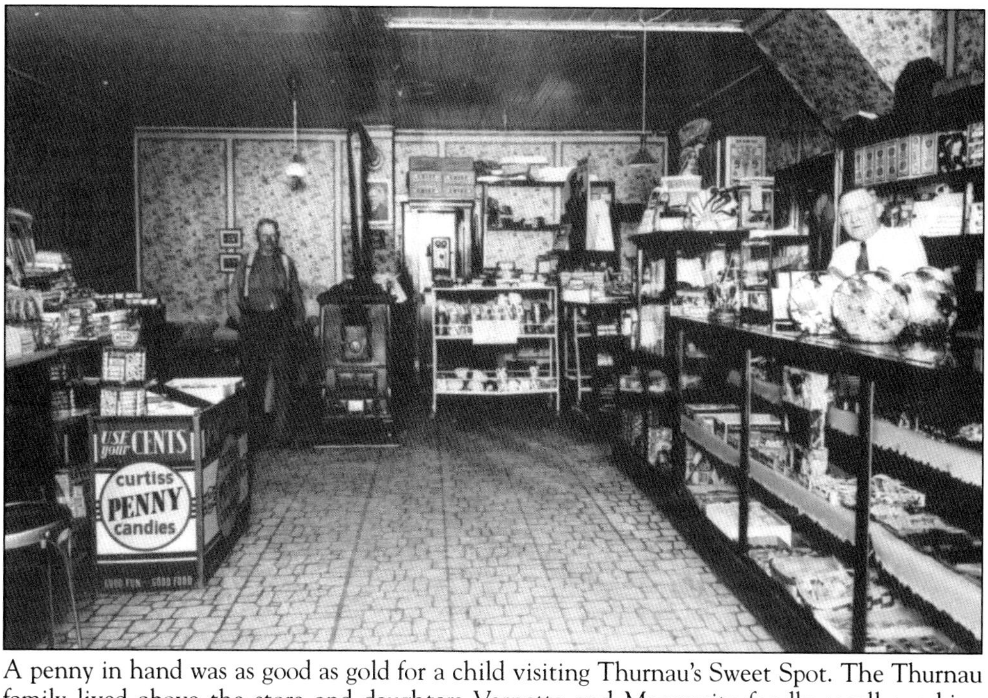

A penny in hand was as good as gold for a child visiting Thurnau's Sweet Spot. The Thurnau family lived above the store and daughters Vernetta and Marguerite fondly recall sneaking downstairs after hours and savoring ice cream delights and Curtiss Penny Candies during the Depression.

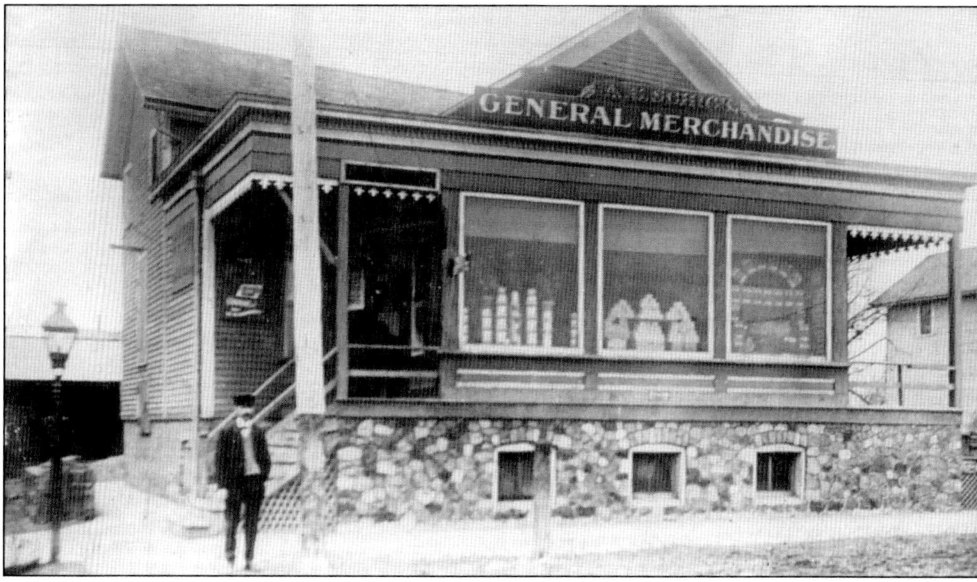

The clapboard building at the corner of Railroad and Oak, shown here in the early 1900s, has housed many a Bartlett business, including both A.C. Schick's and L.F. Stumpf's general stores. Later it became a restaurant and tavern, operating under various names, including Hugo's, The Eck (German for the corner), and now Lucky Jack's. The lower level, which is currently home to Sunshine's Victorian Gifts, was once Henry Hoth's butcher shop and O'Brien's and Baxmann's general stores.

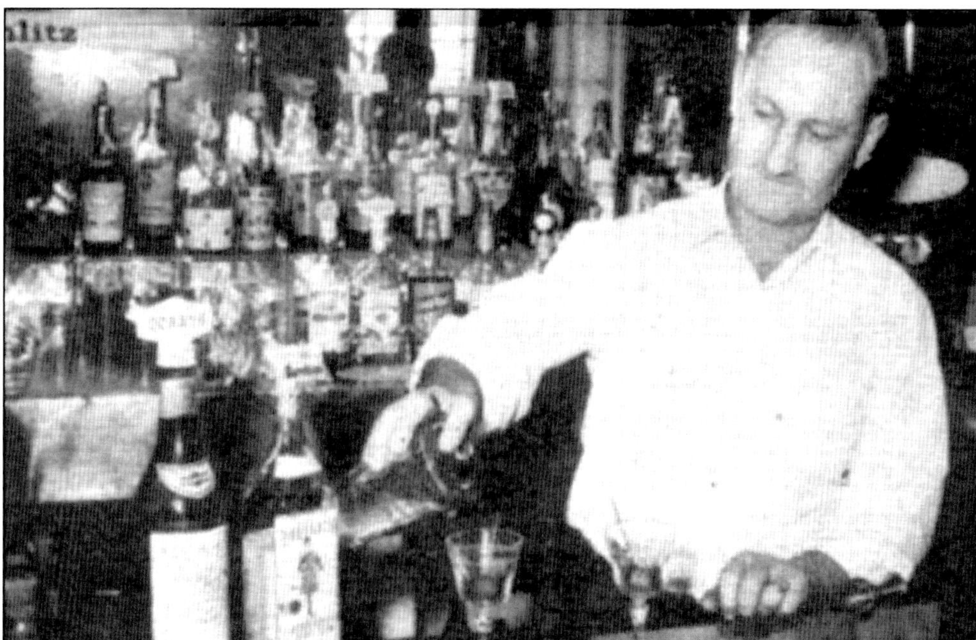

"What'll it be?" Basil "Doc" Ping, owner of the Eck from 1955 to 1968 and "mixologist" of fine libations, took pride in stocking just about every favorite brand a customer could ask for. Martini or Manhattan, you could count on Doc to shake or stir a liquid refreshment bordering on perfection every single time.

Newly widowed by a tragic train accident that claimed her husband Royal and young daughter Virginia Mae, Emma Krumfuss O'Brien set up shop across from the train depot in the early 1930s, in what was formerly Waterman's General Store. "Emy" always had warm gloves and caps for the school kids standing patrol.

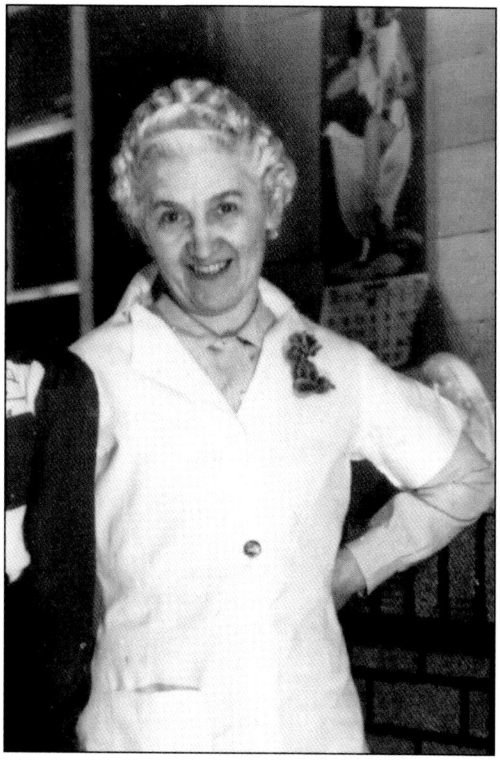

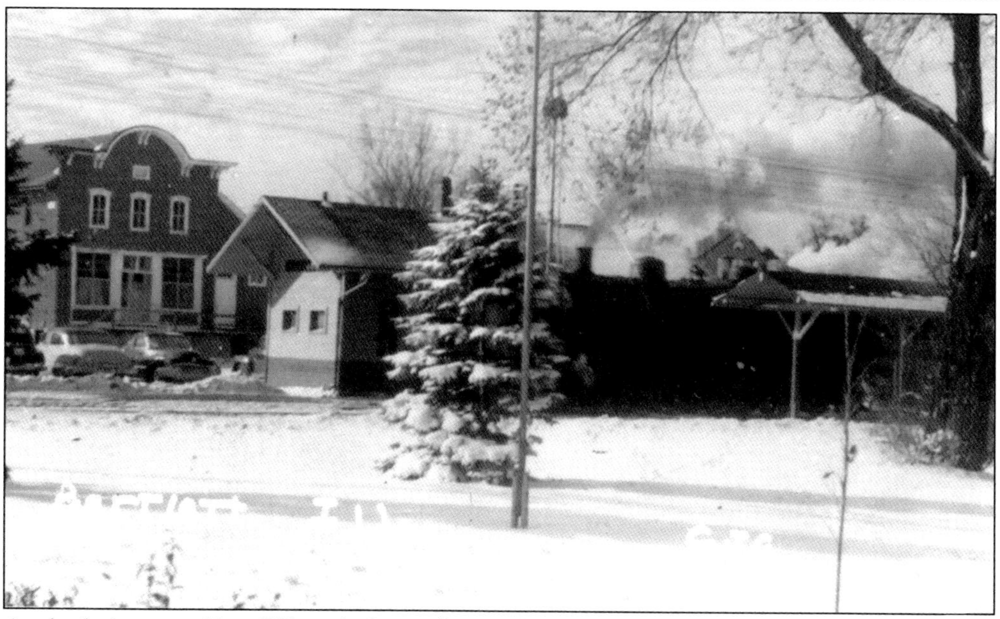

As the kids grew older, O'Brien's General Store became a comfortable hangout for the teens, including Emma's own sons, Roland and Paul. During World War II, Emy further endeared herself to the Bartlett servicemen with letters and care packages, making it natural for them to head to O'Brien's upon their return to town. In 1953, Emma's landlord Worthington Dawkins Genck converted the building into apartments and O'Brien's found a new home across the street below the Eck Tavern. The store was sold shortly before her death in 1962.

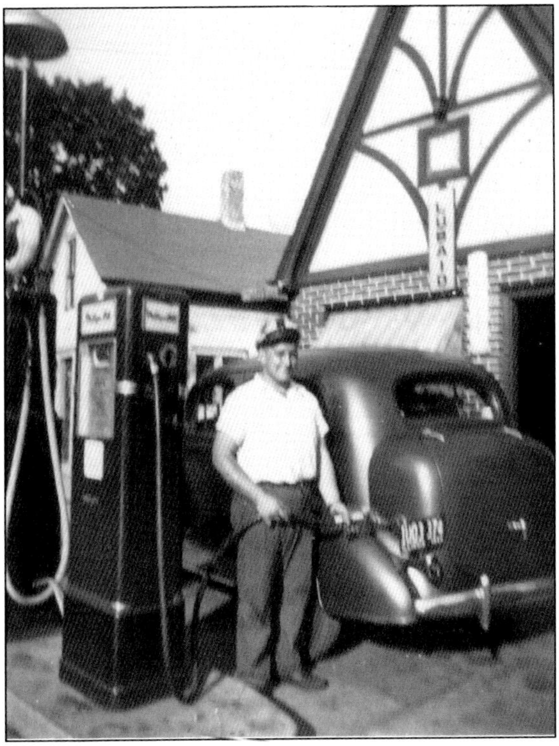

In days gone by, the customer said "fill 'er up" from the upholstered comfort of the driver's seat and pump jockeys, such as Paul Heinberg, would provide full service with a smile. The filling station was built at 151 S. Oak in 1932 and was originally operated by Harvey Schnadt. Bob Van Alstine ran the station as Van's 66 until 1975, when Jim Jensen purchased the business and operated it until his death in 1997.

After returning from World War II, Earl Humbracht took over the business that once was Thurnau's Sweet Spot. More than a candy store, Humbracht's Confectionery (second from left) sold newspapers, magazines, sundries, and coffee. Early on, the farmers would pick up their mail at the post office next door and stop for a cup and a chat, but soon Earl was pouring "Joe" for the commuters hurrying to catch the morning train.

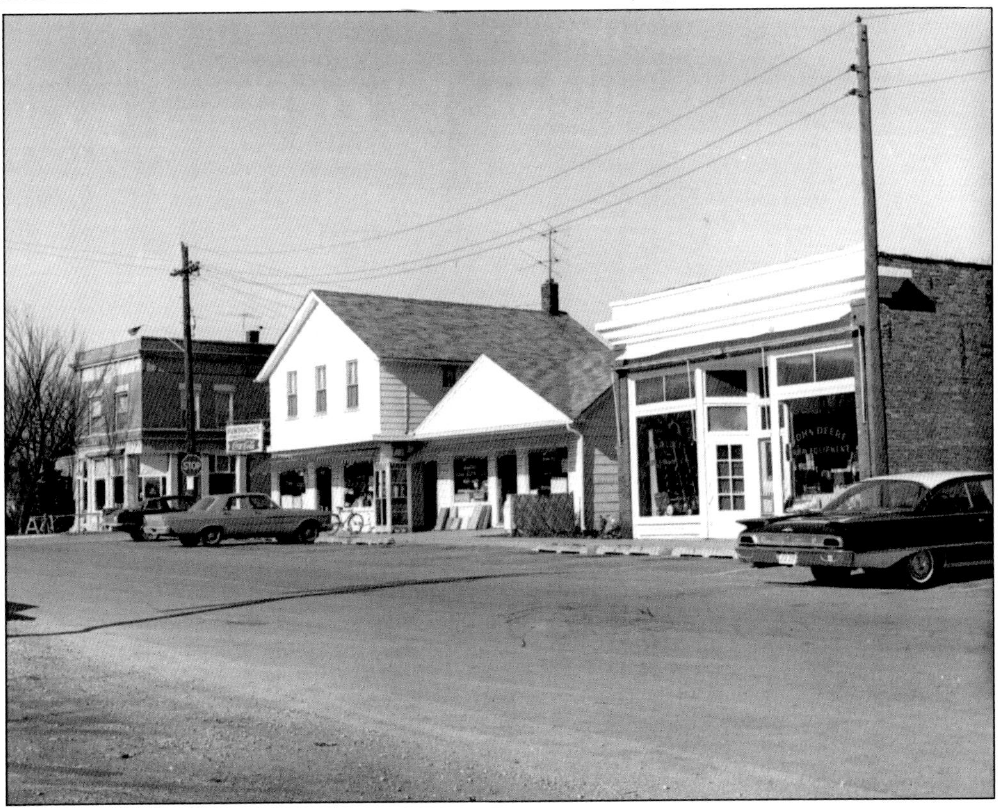

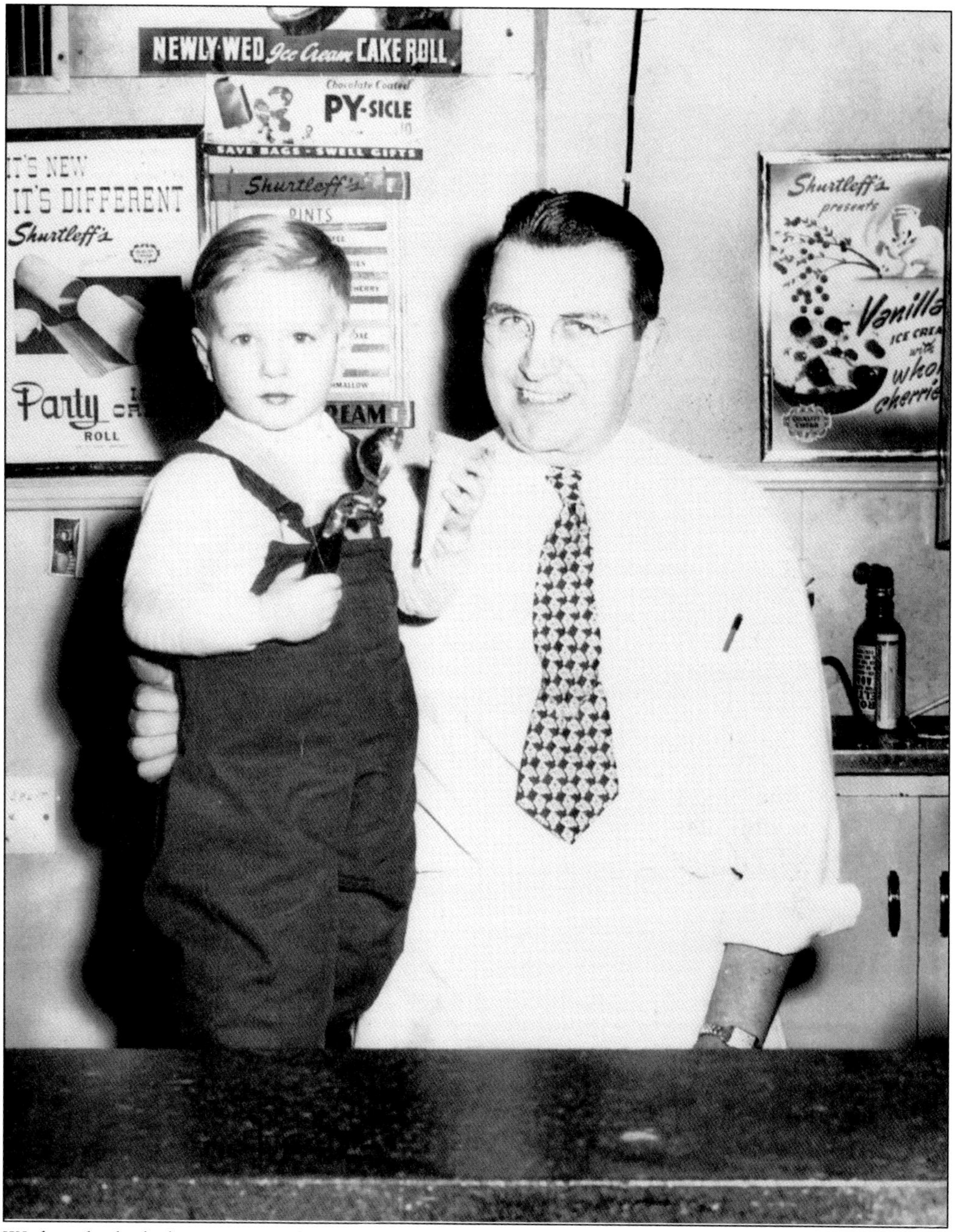

With a little help scooping from young son Greg, Earl also fixed a variety of soda fountain creations for anyone with a sweet tooth. In 1980, Humbracht's was dubbed "King of the Malts" by the *Daily Courier News*. The malts were made with double rich Wisconsin ice cream, but a long-time Humbracht employee, said "love and care" were the extra ingredients that made the malts the best in the Fox Valley. Earl sold the business and retired his "crown" in the mid-1980s.

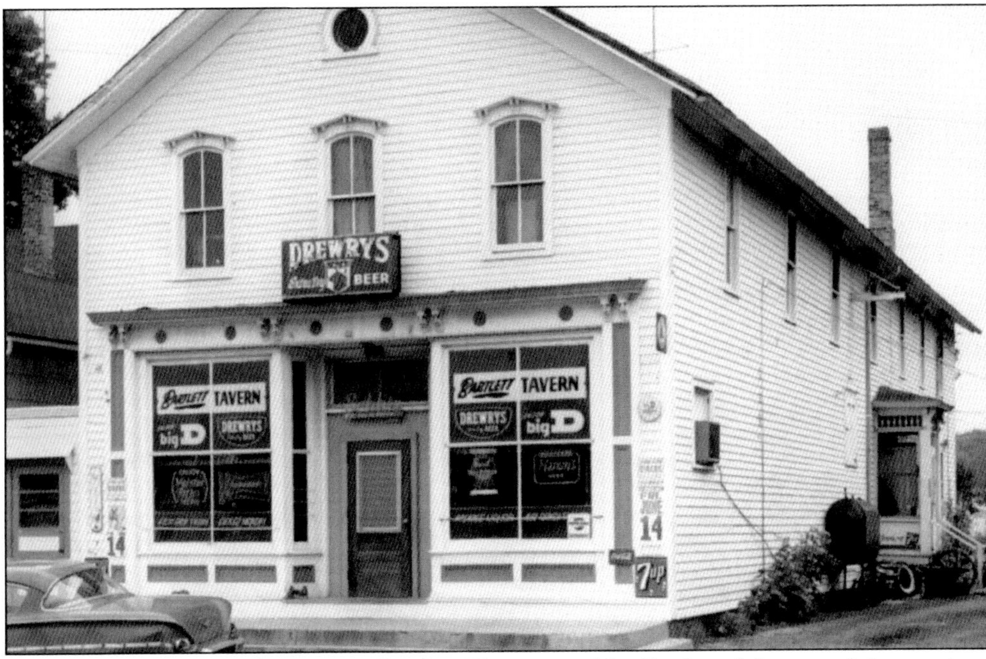

If old walls could talk, the ones at Bartlett Tavern would tell tales of dances, civic meetings, Friday night Fish Fries, and of course, the Niewisches, Harmenings, Schnadts, Jensens, and now the Lomeos—five of the families who owned the tavern and called it home. Built in the late 1880s, the Bartlett Tavern is the oldest continuing business in the Village and was the site of the election for Bartlett's incorporation.

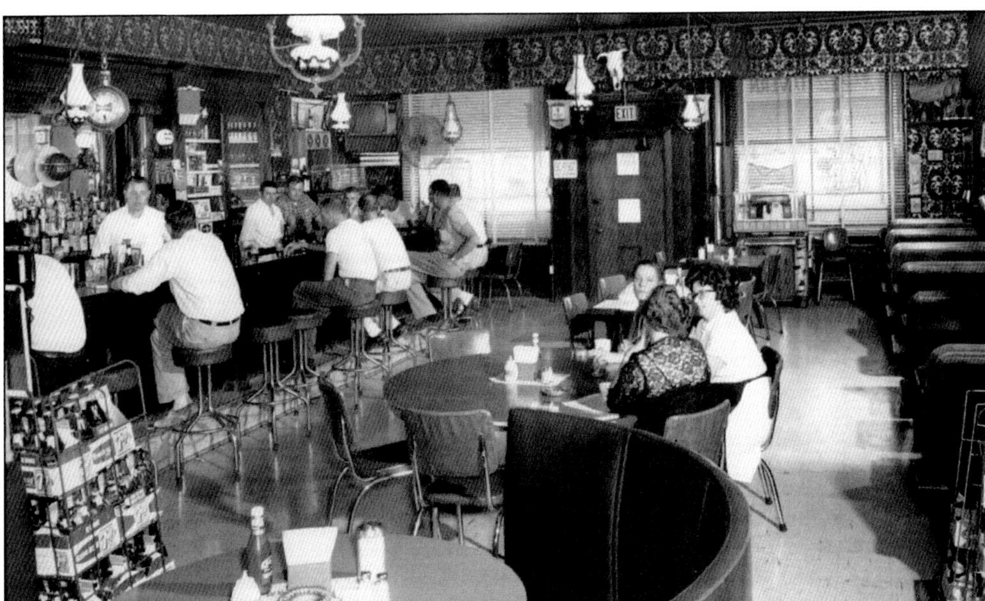

The Jensens purchased the Tavern in the early 1940s and made the business a family endeavor. Under the watch of Ed, and that of his wife Serena after his death in 1952, the pool table was removed, the walls were given a fresh coat of paint and attractively wallpapered, comfy booths were added and the menu was expanded, making the old tavern much more family friendly.

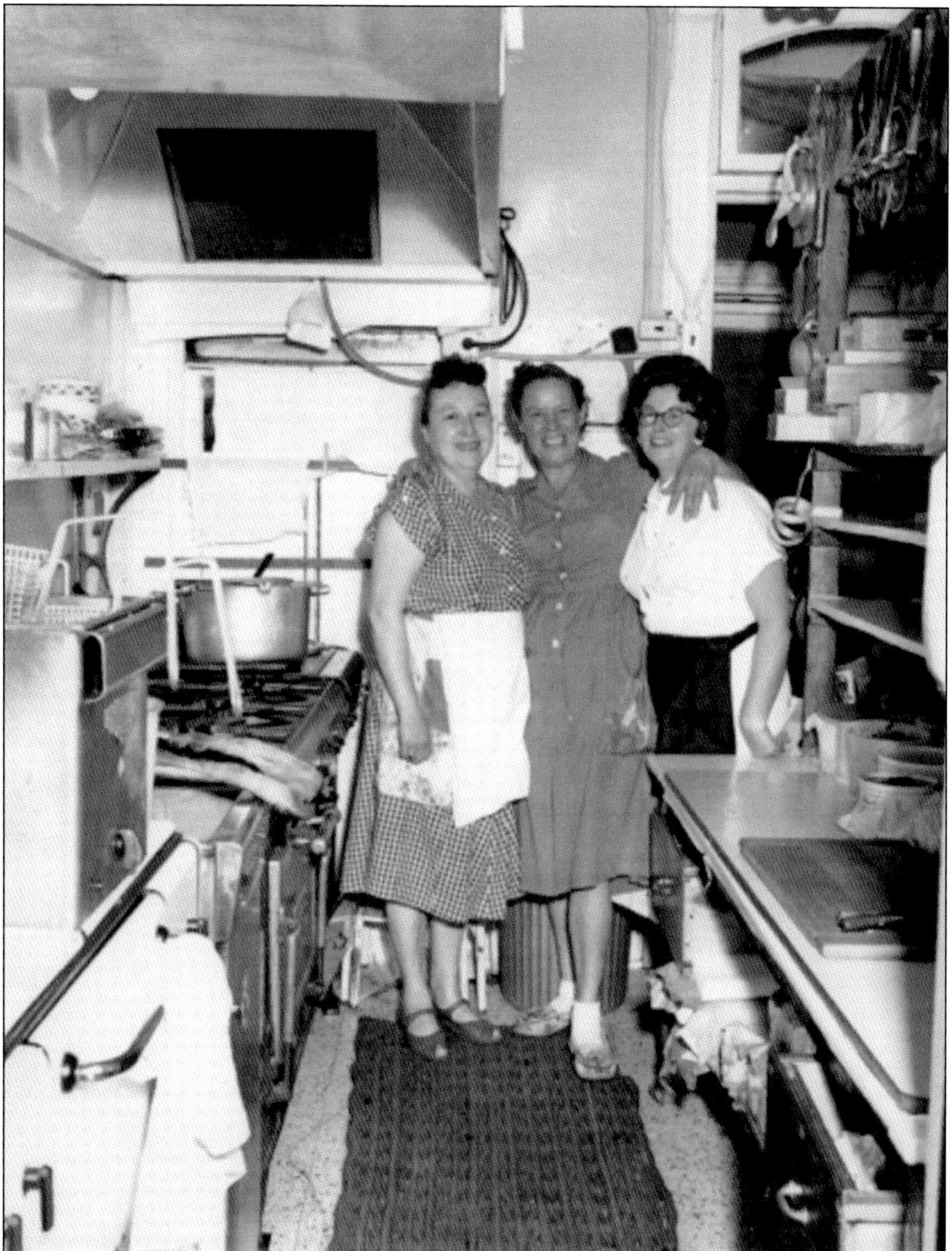

By the time Serena and Ed bought the Tavern, the Fish Fry had become a Friday night mainstay. The Jensens' chief cooks and bottle washers, Marge "Tootie" Klein Marxen, Margaret "Mike" Stark Boychou, and an another waitress, used the family bathtub in the rear to thaw the fish and prepared Serena's special coleslaw recipe, which is still served on the side with every fish dinner sold at the Tavern today.

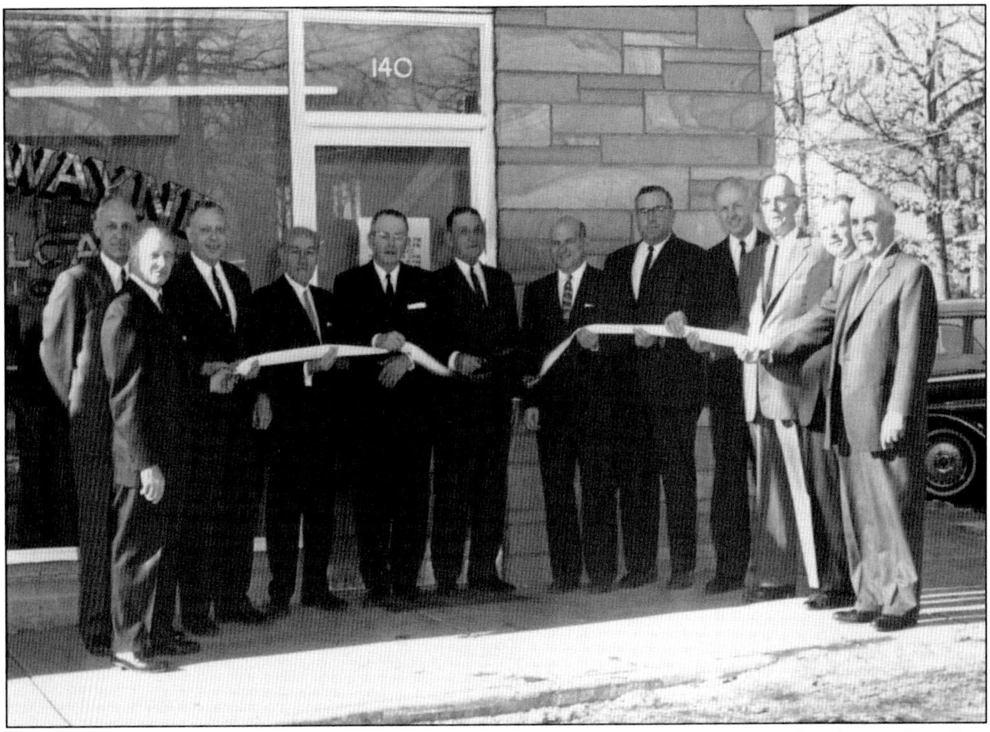

Bank president William Leiseberg (fifth from left) and on his right, Leo Blanchette, Bartlett Village President from 1963 to 1973, cut the ribbon at the grand opening of the Hanover Wayne Savings & Loan at 140 S. Hickory. "A beautiful Danish Modern ice cream scoop" was the bank's incentive gift to lure new account holders in July of 1964.

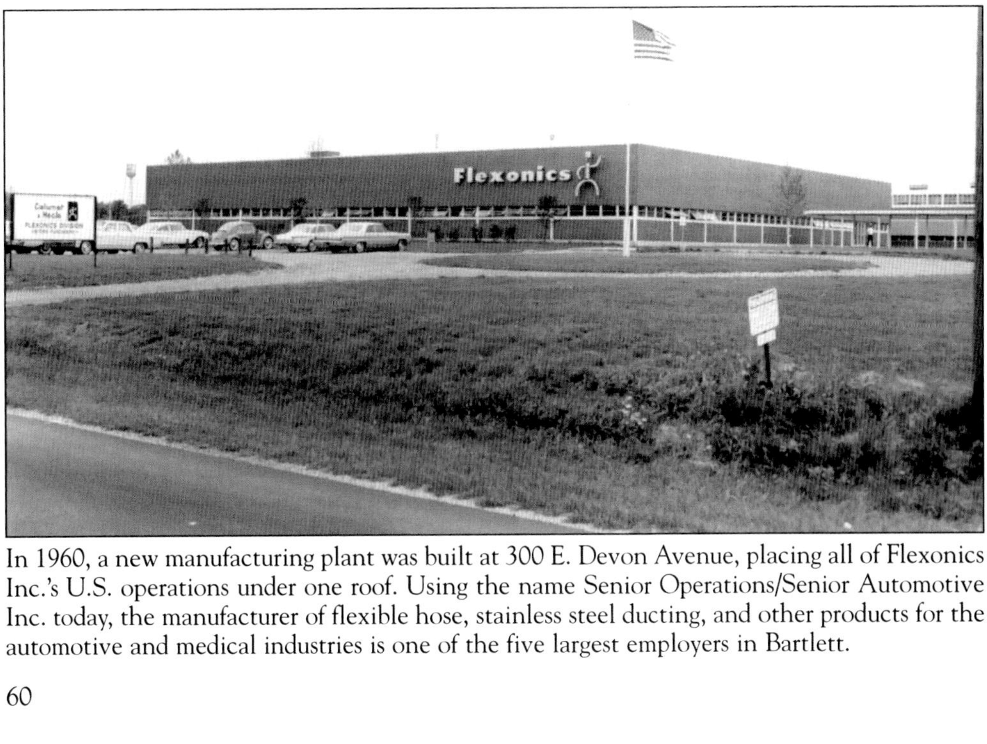

In 1960, a new manufacturing plant was built at 300 E. Devon Avenue, placing all of Flexonics Inc.'s U.S. operations under one roof. Using the name Senior Operations/Senior Automotive Inc. today, the manufacturer of flexible hose, stainless steel ducting, and other products for the automotive and medical industries is one of the five largest employers in Bartlett.

Four

Civic Groups and Social Clubs

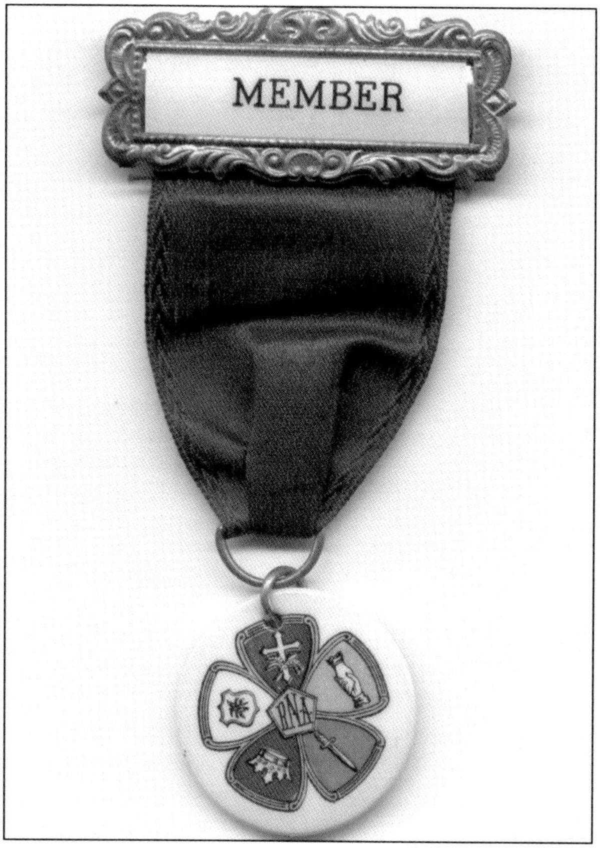

From its beginning, Bartlett was a town of joiners and organizers. Among the original civic groups formed in the early 1900s were the Modern Woodmen of America, a fraternal benefit society and its female auxiliary, the Royal Neighbors of America. The Bartlett "camp" had as many as 45 members who held social events and carried out benevolent work. The Royal Neighbors emblem, shown here, symbolizes the five principles of the Society: Faith, Unselfishness, Courage, Endurance, and Modesty.

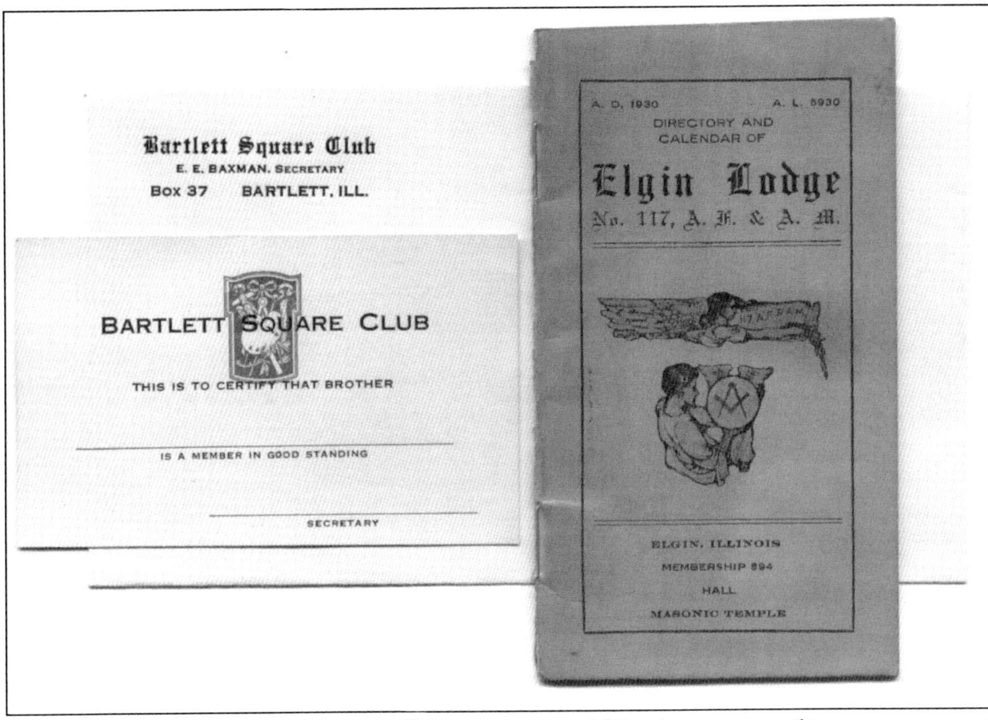

In January 1931, the Bartlett Square Club was organized "for the purpose of improvement and instruction in Masonry and for the furtherance of Masonic good fellowship." They were an adjunct to Elgin Lodge No. 117. Members met twice each month in Waterman's Hall, hosting "distinguished" guest speakers and a variety of social events. Dues were $3 per annum.

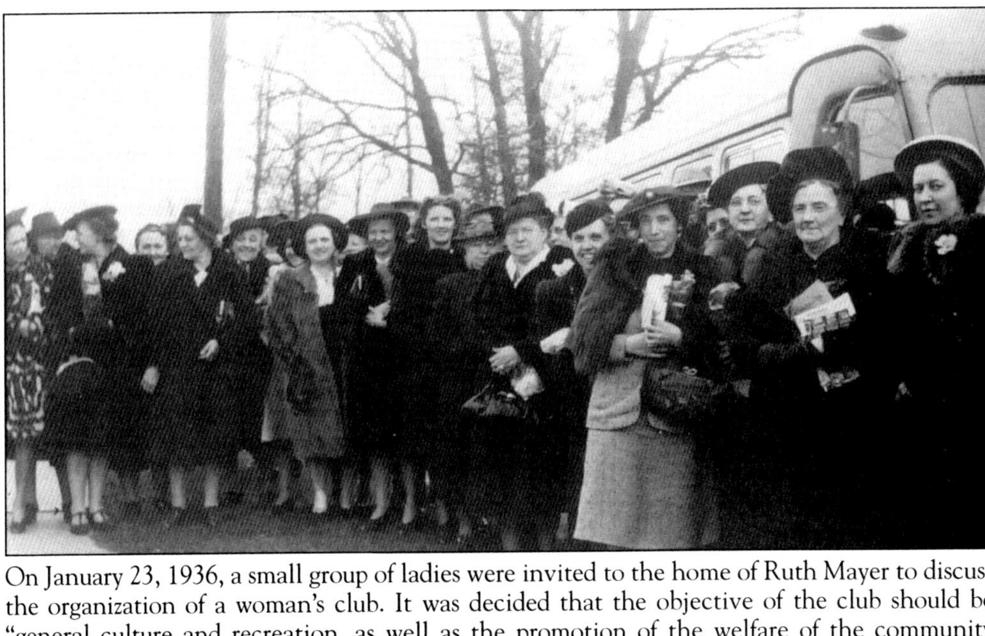

On January 23, 1936, a small group of ladies were invited to the home of Ruth Mayer to discuss the organization of a woman's club. It was decided that the objective of the club should be "general culture and recreation, as well as the promotion of the welfare of the community whenever possible." This was the start of the Bartlett's Woman's Club, the oldest service organization still in existence in the community today.

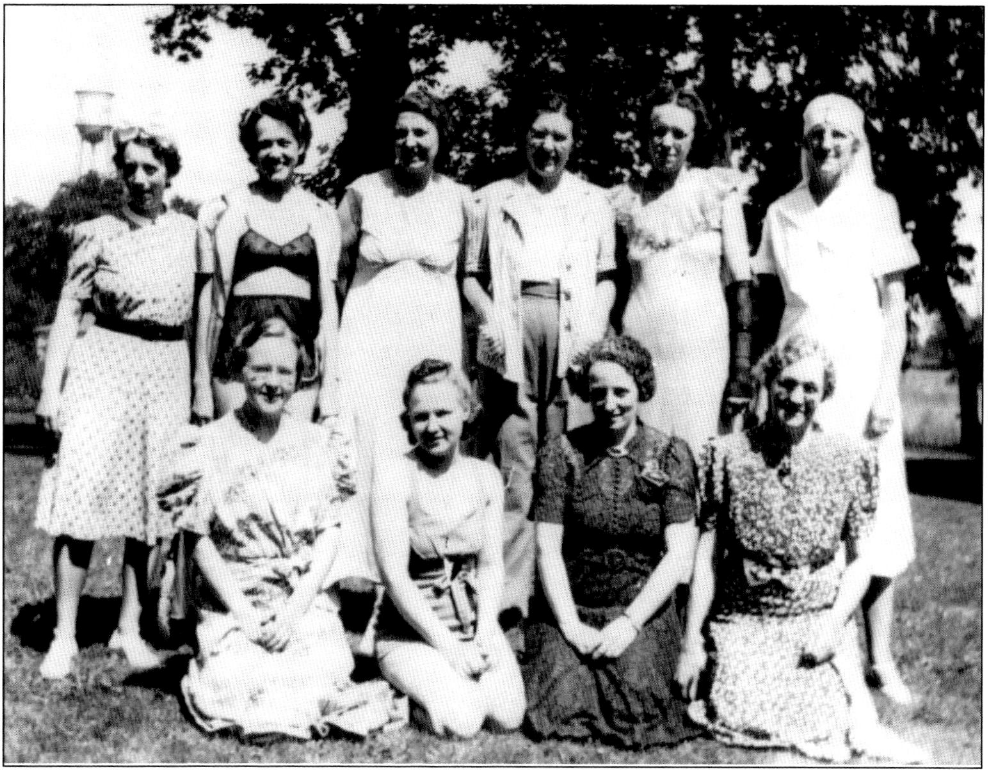

In 1940, the Bartlett Woman's Club held a fashion show to celebrate 50 years since "The General Federation of Women's Clubs" was organized. The show featured fashions of 1890 and their 1940 counterparts, which were heralded in a poem written for the occasion by Bartlett's own published poet Mrs. Edmund Krumfuss. Under her pen name Esskay, Stella wrote, "50 years of labor by women of every creed, 50 years since women took the lead."

On November 15, 1939, 28 Bartlett men assembled to celebrate the charter for a new chapter of Lions International. So began the Bartlett Lions Club's generous and extensive record of service to the world and community. In addition to fundraising for the deaf and blind, the Club extended helping hands to local scout troops, Bartlett School, the Park District, Little League, and children's activities such as Operation Santa, the Easter Egg Hunt, and the Halloween Parade.

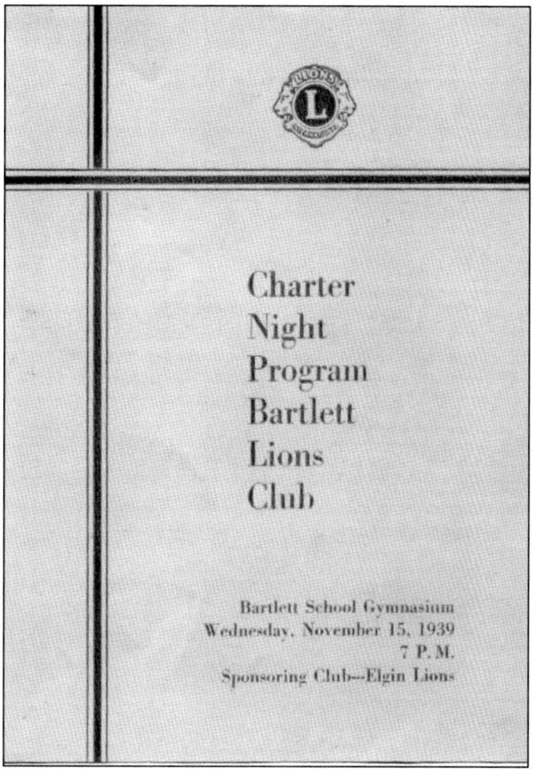

Charter
Night
Program
Bartlett
Lions
Club

Bartlett School Gymnasium
Wednesday, November 15, 1939
7 P. M.
Sponsoring Club—Elgin Lions

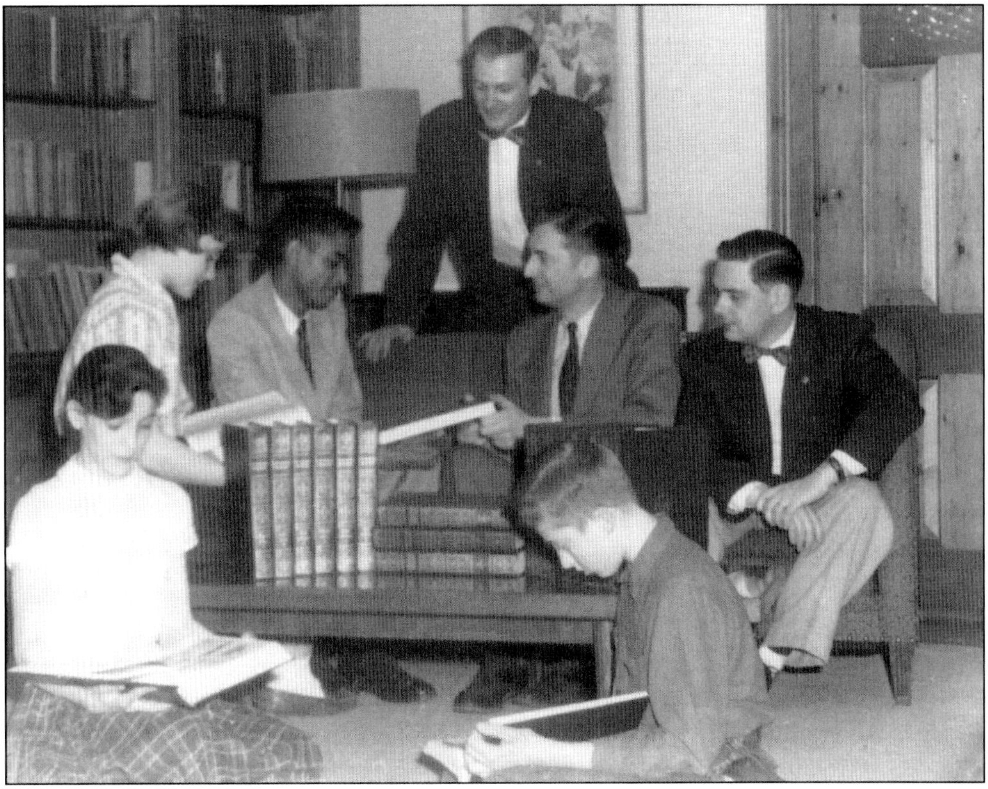

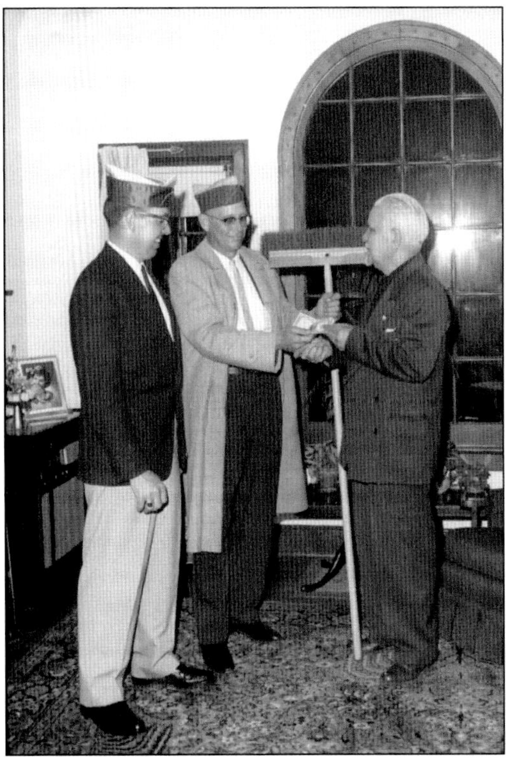

In 1955, the Bartlett Lions Club presented a gift of encyclopedias to the young people at Bartlett's Herrick House, a convalescent home for children recovering from rheumatic fever. A frequent beneficiary of the Club's charitable efforts, Herrick House was also given funds for its building program and to send children to the circus. Tom Giles, sitting center, and Ollie Hardt, over Tom's shoulder, were still serving as Lions, almost 50 years later.

Old time residents will recall buying a variety of brooms from Lions Club members starting in the 1940s. These useful household items were made by handicapped individuals and the sales were just one of the popular fundraising activities sponsored by the Lions. Other eagerly anticipated fundraisers included the annual pancake breakfasts and beer sales at Bartlett's Volunteer Fire Department Festival. Pictured here is Village President John Buelting buying a push broom.

Village President Henry Thurnau accepts the deed to Bartlett Park property from Fire Chief William Bull. Chief Bull, the Bartlett Volunteer Fire Department, and other civic groups were largely responsible for the creation of this first Village park and community field house; they raised money to purchase the six lots that completed the acreage of the park, turned it over to the Village in 1948, and planned the construction of the Log Cabin.

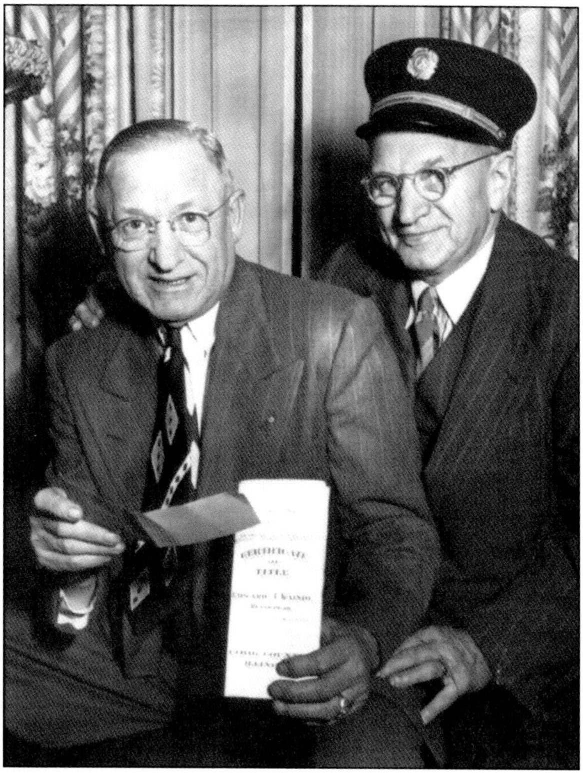

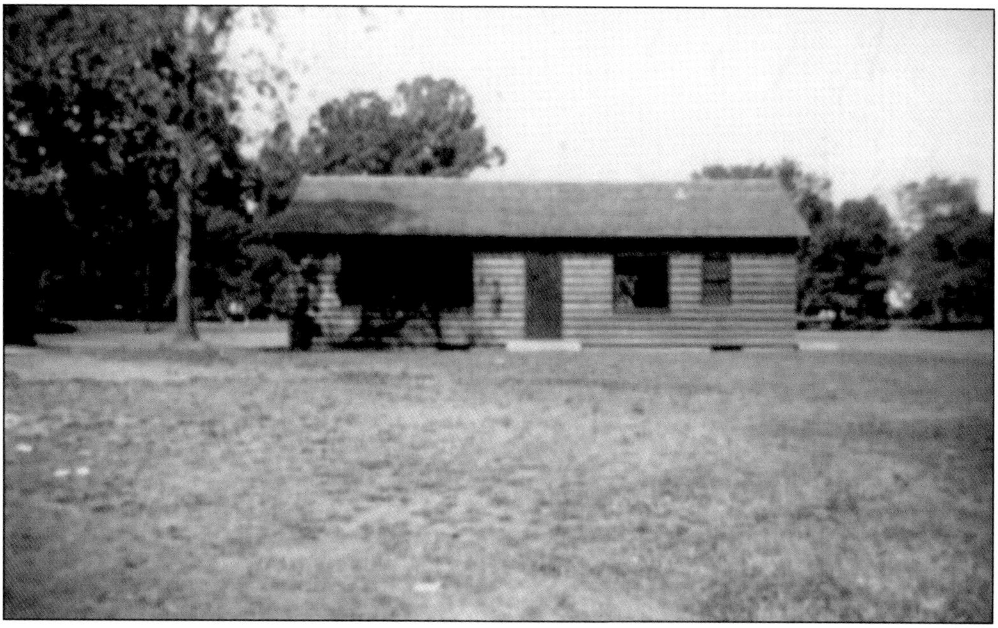

Much time, work, money, and community effort went into building the Bartlett Park Log Cabin, the very first community center in the Village. The Volunteer Fire Department built the structure, the Lions Club donated money to furnish the facility, and the Woman's Club made the curtains and equipped the kitchen. The residents and civic groups enjoyed and maintained the Log Cabin until the establishment of the Bartlett Park District on January 18, 1964.

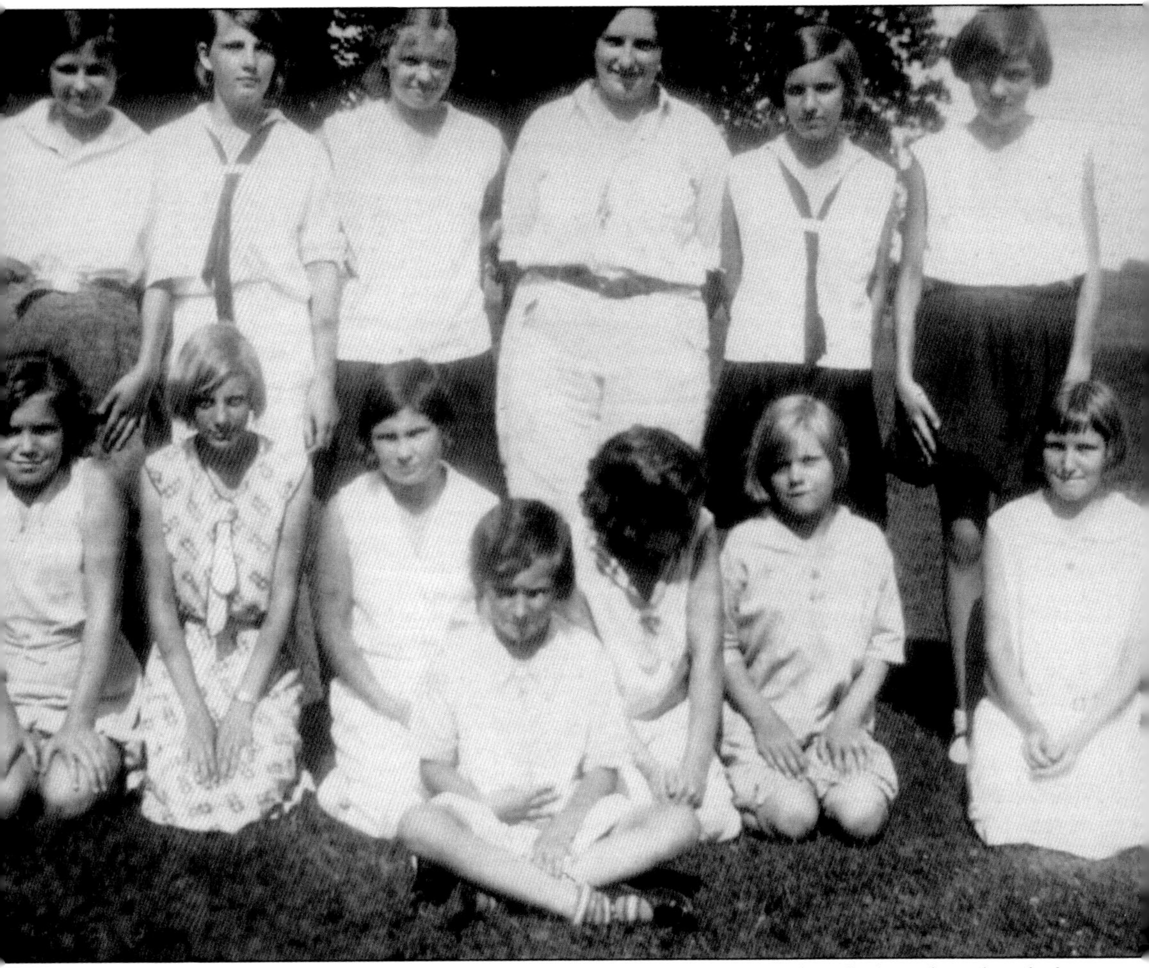

Girl Scouting in the Village of Bartlett began in 1929. Estelle Schnadt (standing fourth from left) started this "lone" troop, unaffiliated with other councils, and continued as the leader until 1942. The girls met in the old Krumfuss Shoe Shop on Oak Avenue between Oneida and North. They paid rent of $3 per month. The girls accumulated the necessary furniture for the meetings and made curtains for the windows. Stella would start a fire in the old coal stove approximately three hours prior to their meeting, so it would be warm when the girls arrived. Meetings were also held in the Bartlett Grade School gymnasium at the corner of Eastern and North Avenues. Original members of this troop included Ruth Harmening Giles, Ruth Krumfuss Regenburg, Evelyn Rieckhoff O'Brien, Lucille Hothan Drew, Genevieve Bowman Schick, and Myrtle Haase Kunos.

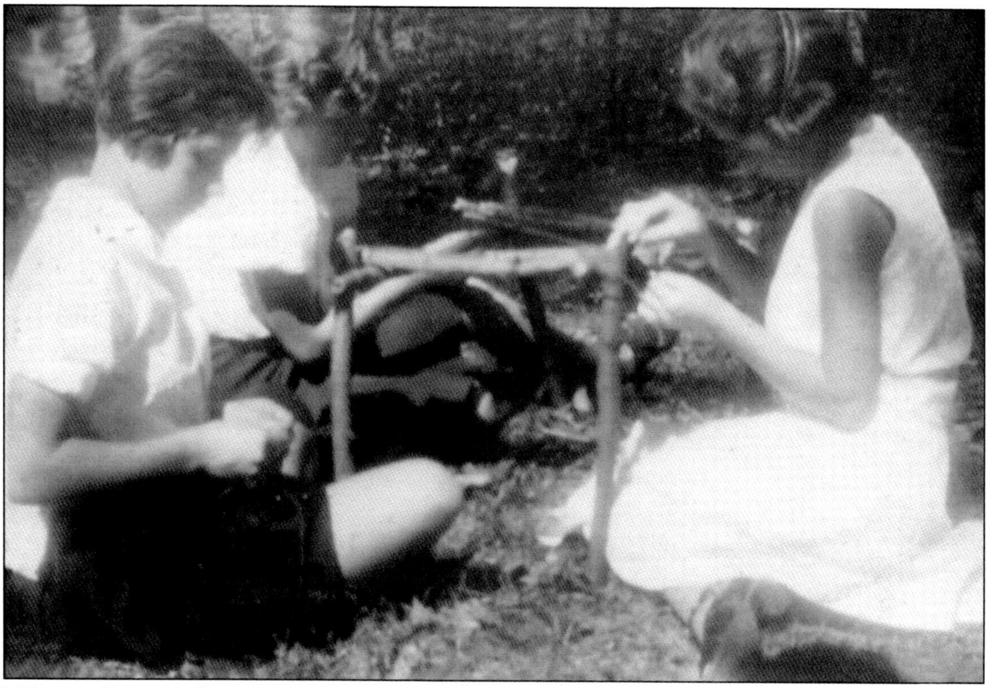

Hikes and overnight camping trips were frequent activities enjoyed by Bartlett Girl Scouts. During these outings, everyone was kept busy, setting up tents, cooking over an open fire, lashing together branches, and learning other scouting skills.

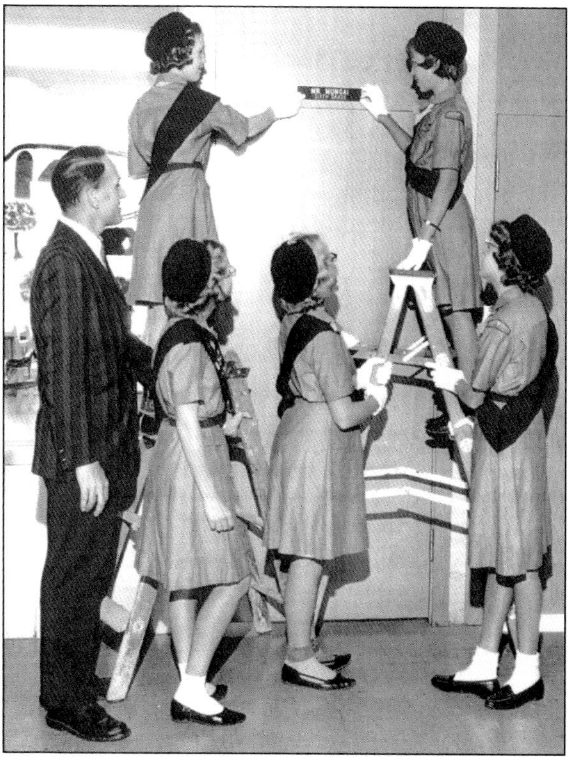

Mrs. Earl Shaw organized Girl Scout Troop 452 in the fall of 1962. It consisted of fifth and sixth graders from Bartlett Elementary. For one of their service projects, the girls used $40 from cookie sales to purchase nameplates for each room at their school.

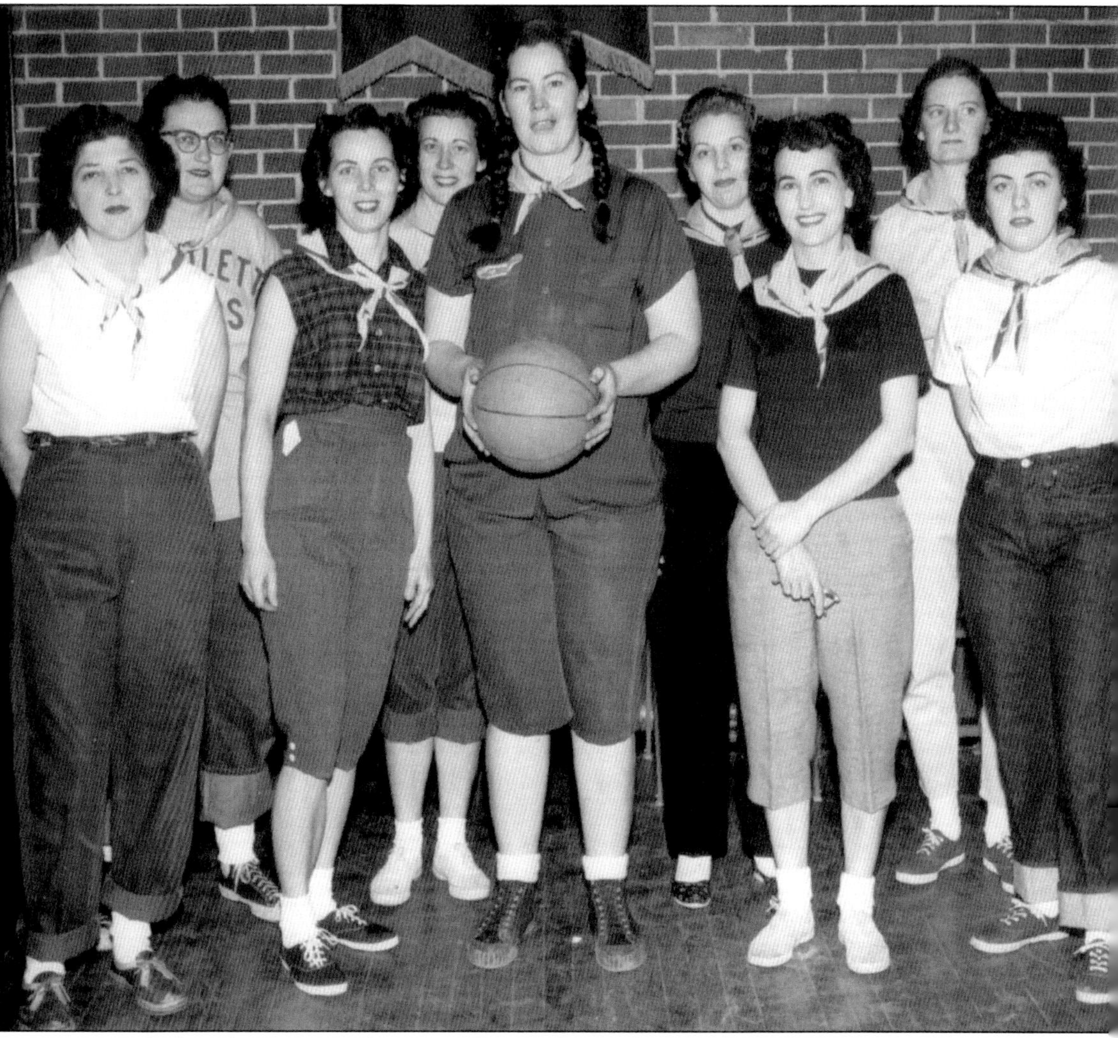

Long before the WNBA, there was the Bartlett Cub Scout basketball moms. These "driving athletes," sporting their sons scout neckerchiefs, challenged the Girl Scout mothers in an annual charity game at Bartlett Elementary School gymnasium. Pictured in this March 20, 1959 photo are, from left to right: (front row) unidentified, Dorothy Peterson, Ruby Roth, Tina Faber, and Charlotte Tiknis; (back row) Mick Jervey, unidentified, Jo Reif, and Carol DuBois.

The Bartlett Cub Scouts came into being in May 1951, under the sponsorship of the Bartlett Elementary School PTA. Robert Vogt was the first Cub Master. Cub Scout Bill Peterson of Pack 23 was a fine representative of Cub Scouting in 1957 Bartlett.

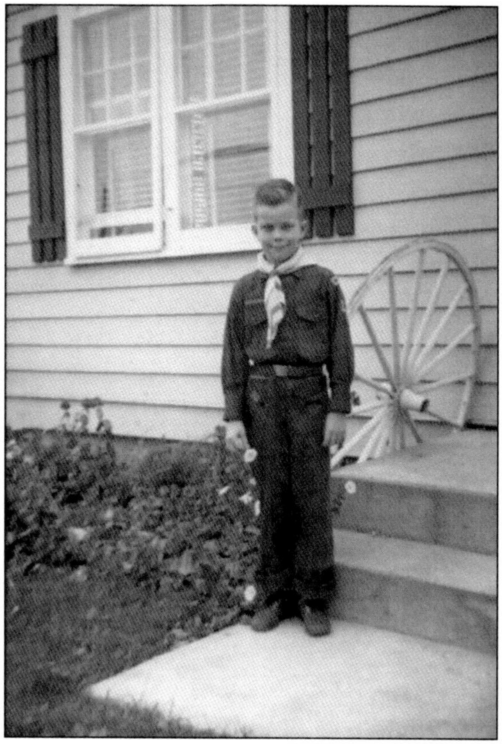

Boy Scout Troop 23 wishes departing Scoutmaster Bill Jervey a fond farewell on November 24, 1963. Jervey Lane, a local street, was named in Bill's honor because of the many years he spent guiding Bartlett boys through the scouting ranks.

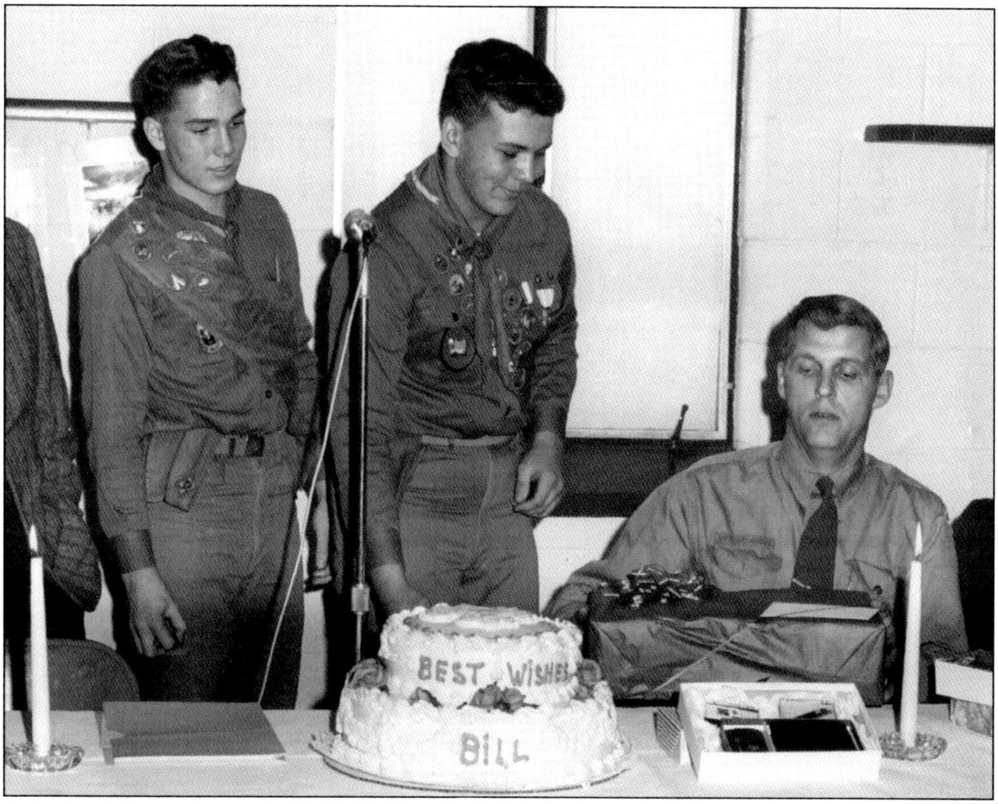

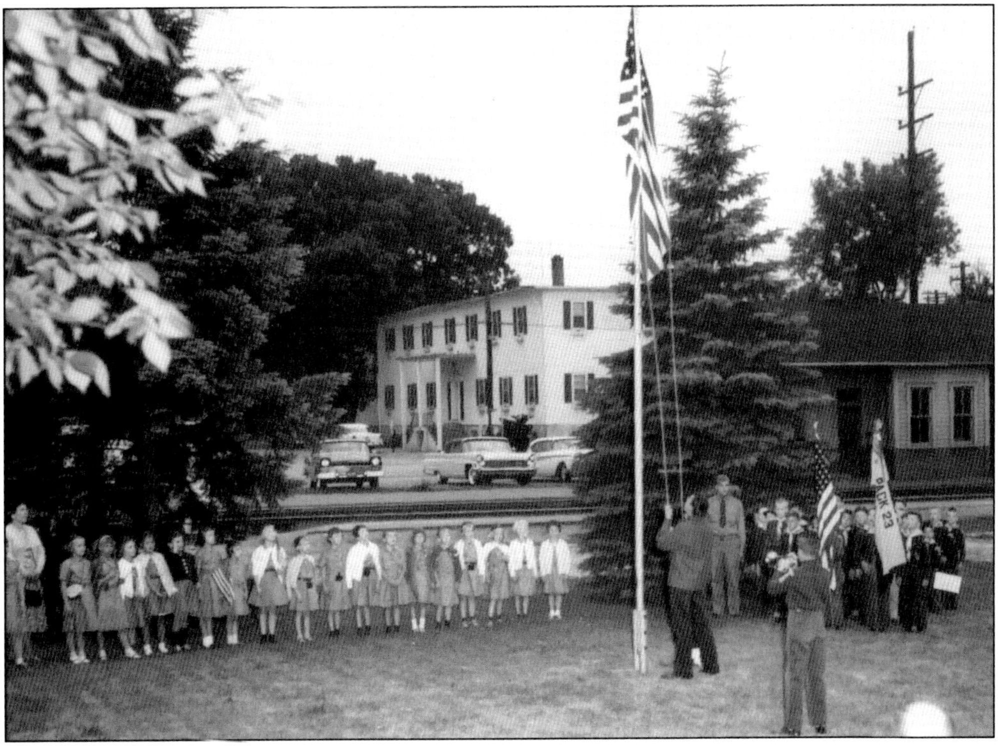

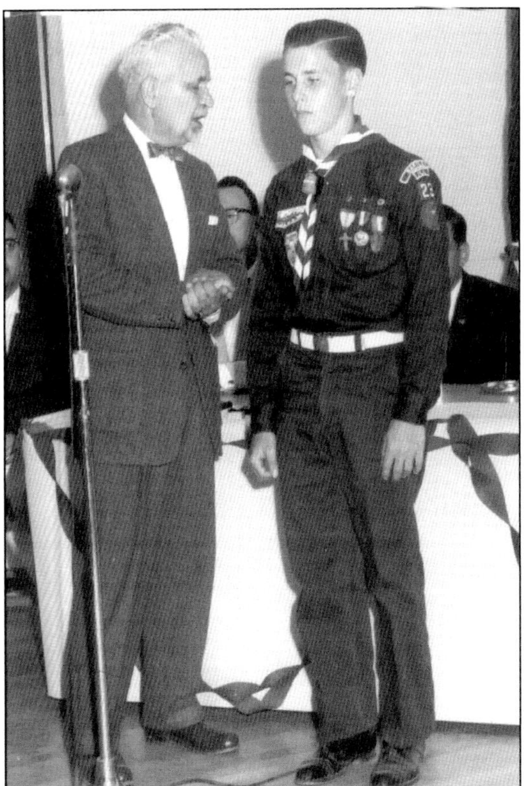

John Hilliard was the first young Bartlett resident to be awarded the rank of Eagle Scout on June 14, 1959. This lofty achievement drew the attention of the entire town. A parade in John's honor began at Bartlett Park and paused at the flagpole outside Bartlett State Bank for posting of the colors. Then all of Bartlett continued to the newly completed Fire Barn on Main Street for the Eagle Court of Honor followed by a celebratory reception. Village President John Buelting offers his congratulations to the Village's new Eagle Scout.

In their version of the modern day quilting bee, from left to right, Ethel Hinz, Violet Haase, Mary Reed, and Elaine Atchison stitch up a bit of holiday finery for Christmas 1951. The gals met regularly for Sewing Club meetings and fun chitchat.

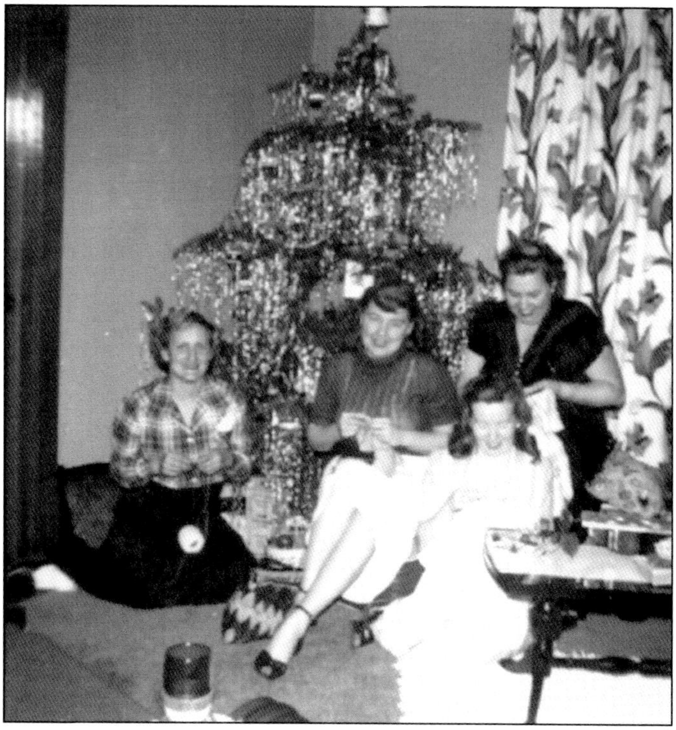

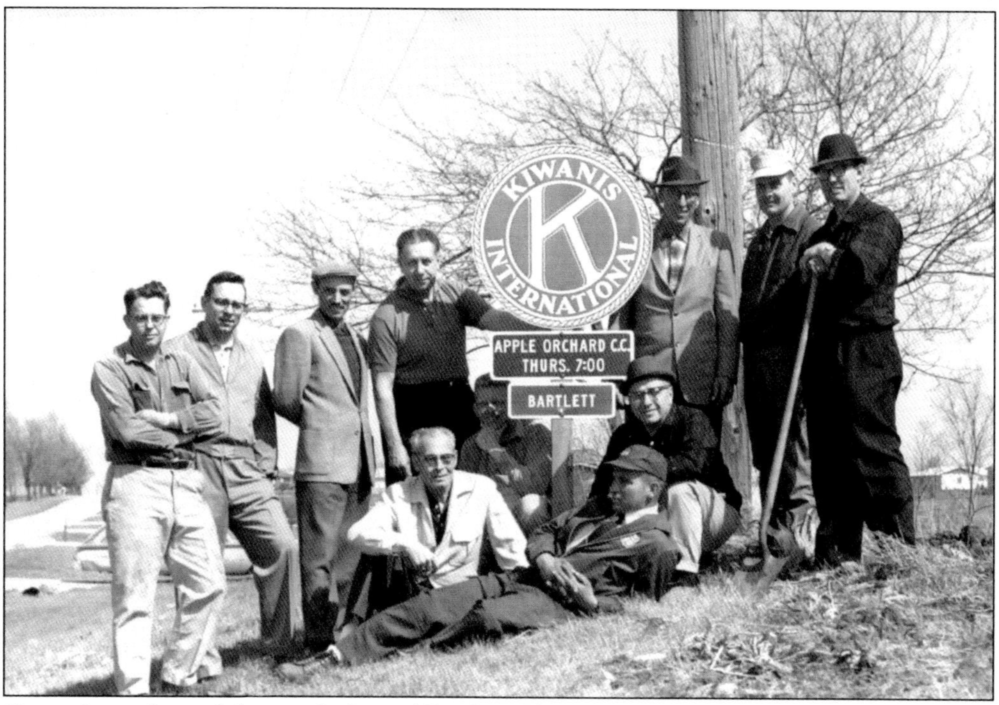

Original members of the newly formed Bartlett Chapter of Kiwanis International post a sign at the town's border in 1962, announcing their Thursday evening meetings at Apple Orchard Country Club. Kiwanis is an organization of service and community minded individuals who support children and young adults around the world.

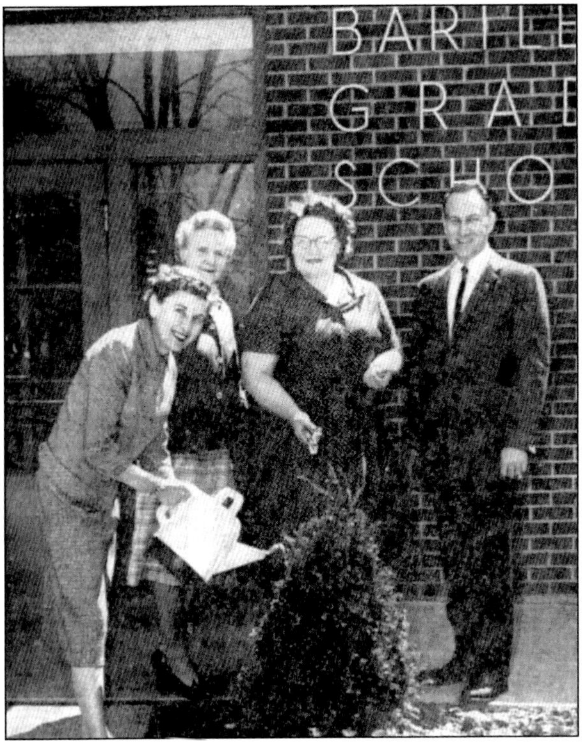

The project for the Bartlett Woman's Garden Club in spring 1961 was the landscaping of the grounds in front of the new addition to Bartlett Grade School. Shown here tending a fresh planting are Mrs. Harvey Schnadt, Mrs. Alvin Krumfuss, Club President Mrs. Fred Pierce Sr., and Principal Robert Hardt.

Bartlett seniors enjoyed coffee, dessert, cards, and good company at monthly meetings of Golden Agers, a non-denominational senior social group sponsored by the Bartlett Lions Club and the three Bartlett churches. The first meeting of seniors, 60 years and older, was held on July 14, 1964 at the "Fieldhouse," now the Bartlett Park log cabin. The club took at least one bus trip each year to dinner and a play or just a scenic trip with lunch.

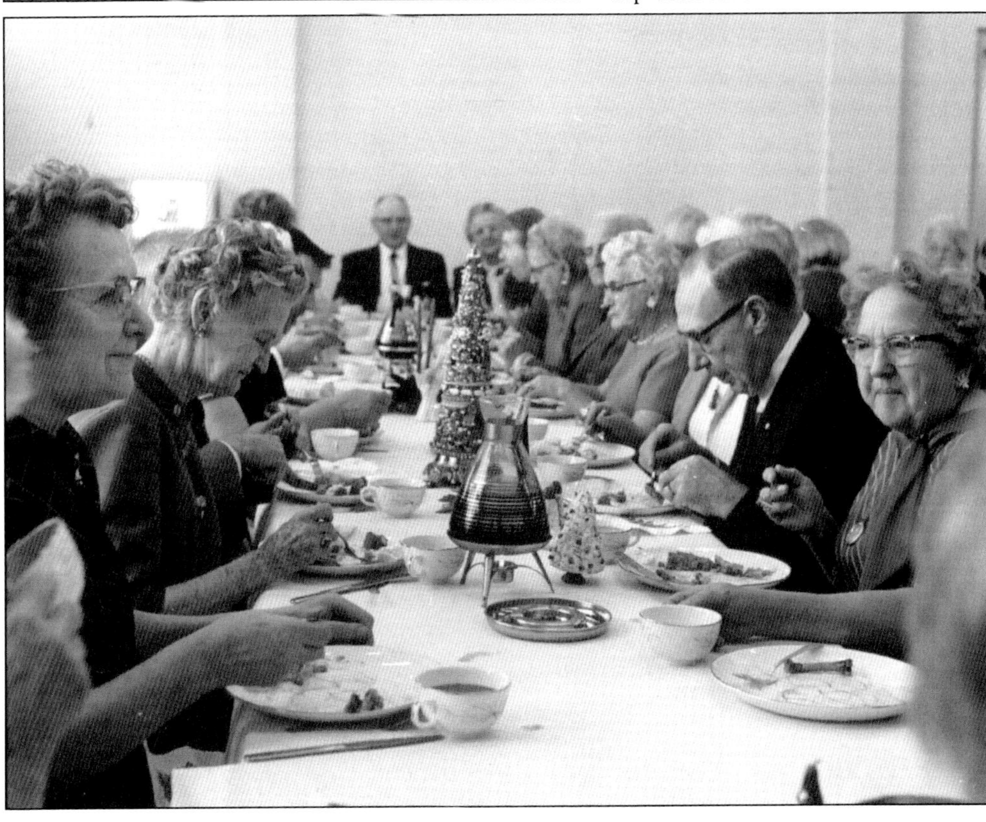

Five

SPORTS AND LEISURE

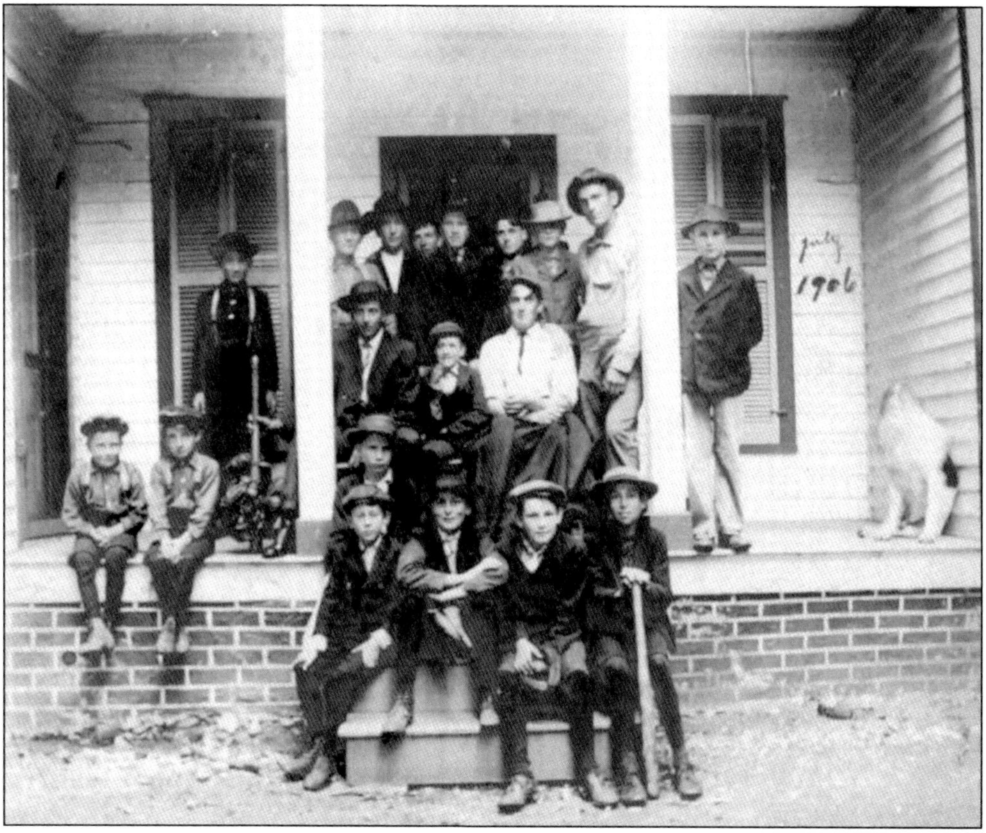

America's growing fondness for baseball at the turn of the century did not bypass Bartlett. Long before Babe Ruth homered his way to national prominence Bartlett formed an amateur league, pitting themselves against surrounding communities. This 1906 photo is the oldest known photo of a Bartlett baseball team. Bartlett's early ballplayers, shown in this picture, included Fred and Herman Wendler, Erwin Schnadt, George Schick, Fred and Henry Baxmann, Carl Markel, William Harmening, and Erv Waterman.

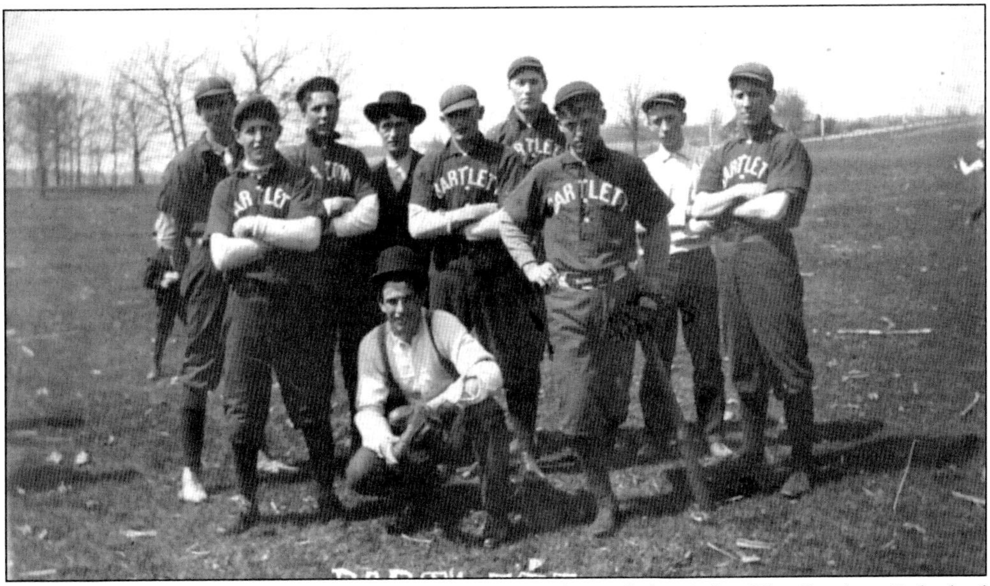

By 1908, Bartlett was fielding two full teams, the Colts and the Cubs. The Bartlett Cubs had also acquired a team sponsor in local businessman Herman Schnadt, and uniforms that mirrored the major leagues. In fact, to this day, local lore has tagged the old Bartlett Cub uniforms as the castoffs from Chicago's own hometown Cubs. For many years, the men's teams played on the Schnadt property at North and Oak, which is Bartlett Park today.

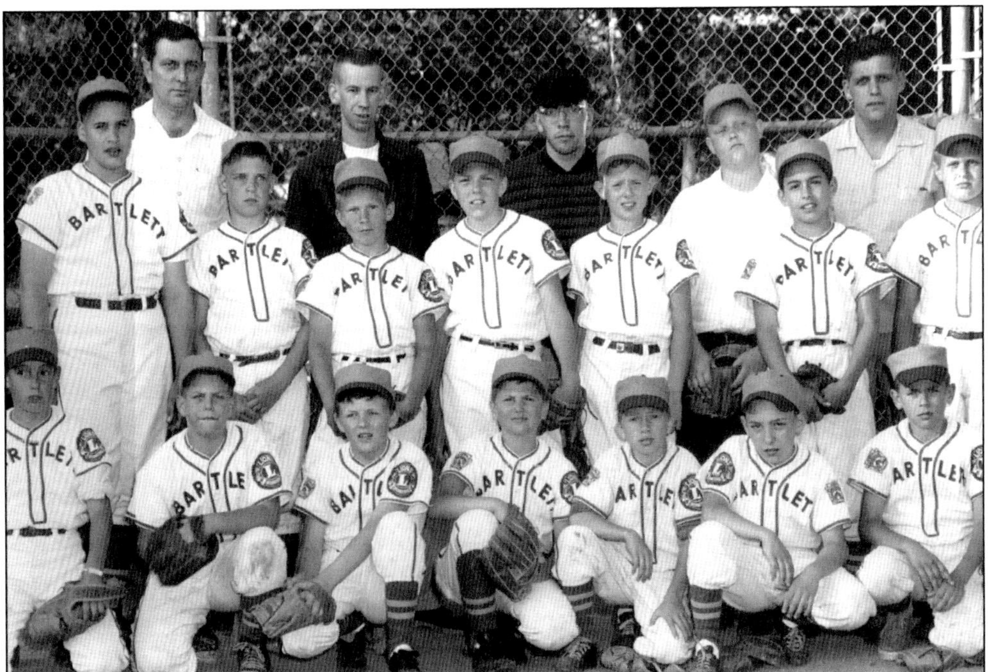

Bartlett's young boys took up bats and gloves in the late 1950s when the Bartlett Lions Club first agreed to sponsor a Little League team in town. Shown here is the 1960 team headed by (third row, left to right) Coaches George Heine and Junior Prehm, Umpire John Whitmer, Assistant Bob Kasten, and Manager Bill Jervey.

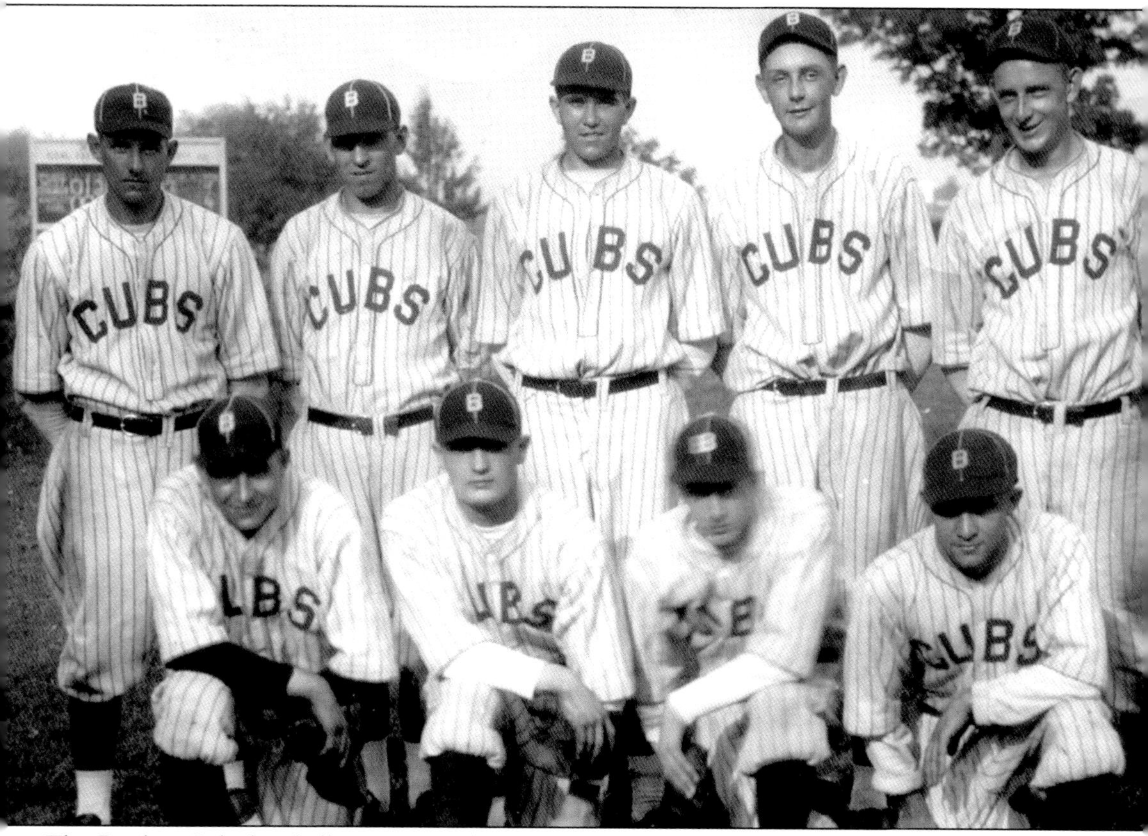

The Bartlett Cubs baseball team, *c.* mid-1930s, is pictured here. From left to right are: (first row) Walter Meyer, Wally Robins, Harvey Feurhauken, and Tony Baxmann; (second row) Bill Bock, George Wendler, John Baxmann, Ray Schnadt, and Harvey Schnadt. The team drew large crowds of fans to both home and away games, but no admission was charged. To keep costs down, Bartlett ballplayers needed to be as skilled at building bleachers and grooming the field as they were at hitting homers and striking out the opposing batters. Money for uniforms and equipment was raised by passing the hat. The $30 or $40 collected was split 60/40 between the home team and the visiting team. It was also used to pay the kids who agreed to act as ball chasers during the game and to give a token compensation to the volunteer umpire. The Cubs usually won between 12 and 15 of the 15 to 20 games they played each season.

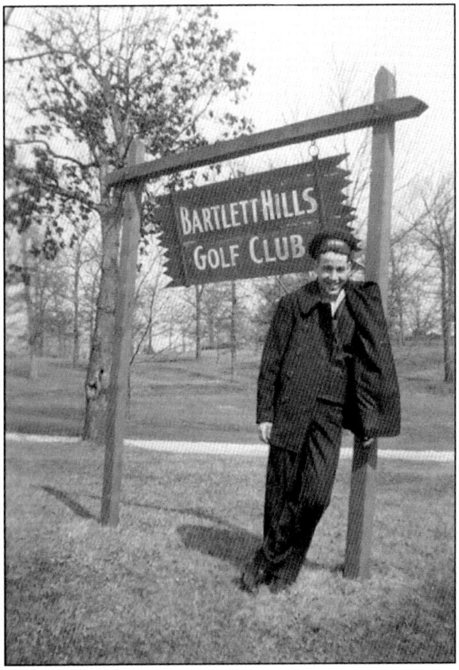

In the early 1920s, a group of Chicagoans cleared the Glos farm to make way for the Bartlett Hills Golf Club. It is speculated that builder Charles Maddox must have been an avid card player because he designed some greens in the shape of a heart, spade, diamond, and club. World War II sailor Mel Atchison was a former caddy at the Club. He was paid 60¢ for 18 holes of golf.

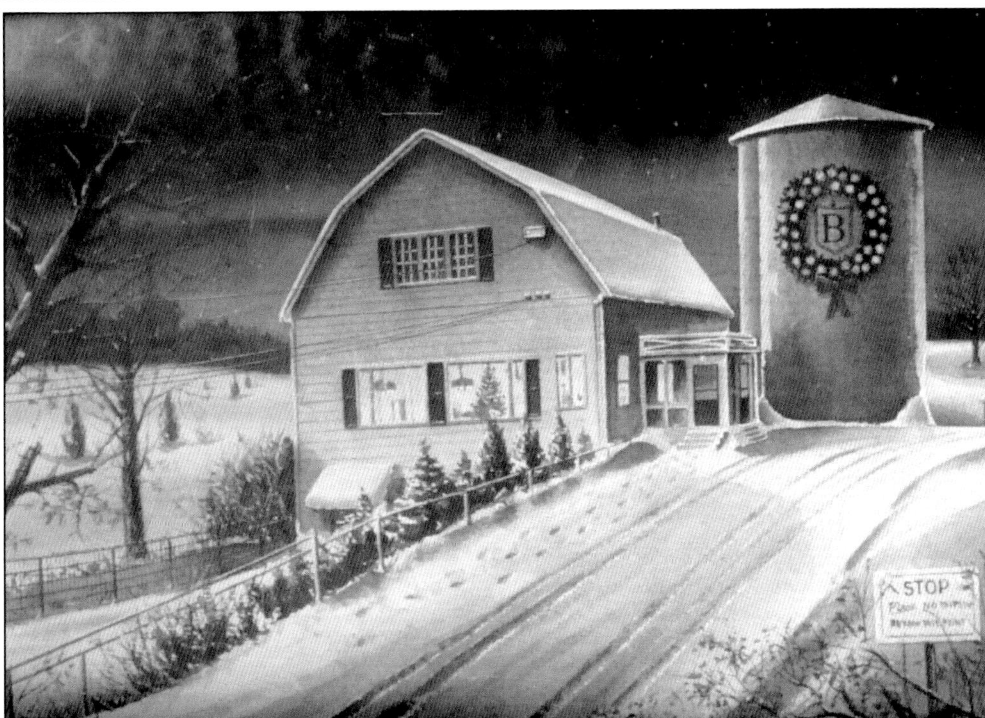

The old barn, depicted in this painting by Walter Schuster, was originally built as a stable but used as the Bartlett Hills clubhouse until 1995. The Village of Bartlett purchased the privately owned golf club in 1978. Knowing the property would be developed as a subdivision, residents overwhelmingly approved the $1.9 million bond referendum for the purchase and improvement of the course. A new clubhouse with banquet facilities was dedicated in 1996.

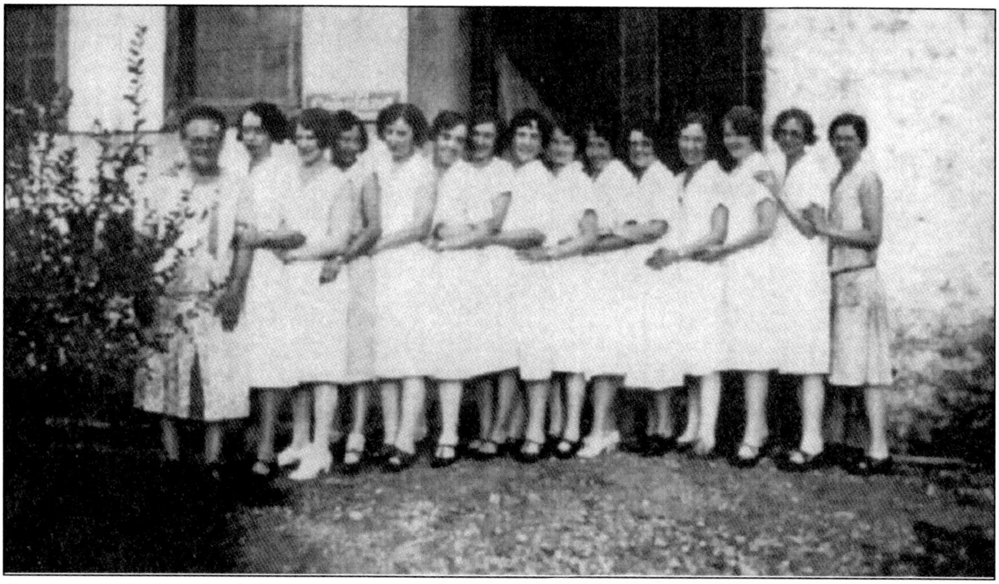

Augusta Olhaber, far left, reigned over the kitchen and this chorus line of cuties at Bartlett Hills Golf Club in this *c.* 1927 photo. Though light lunches were served daily, this larger group of girlfriends was only called to service for big bashes and special occasions. Their duties included cooking, serving, and the always dreaded after party cleanup.

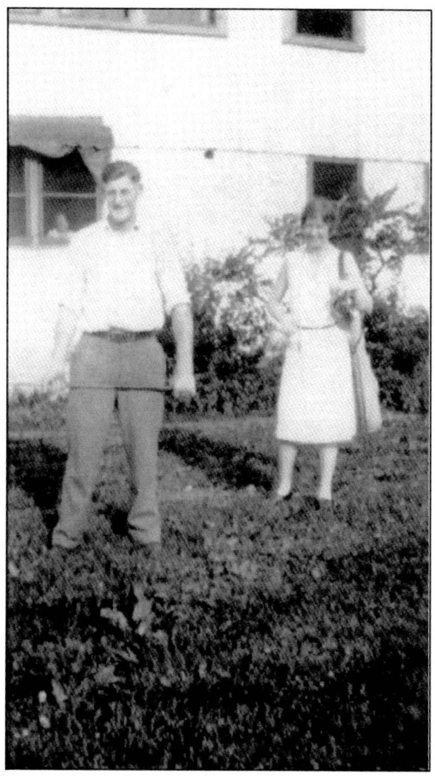

The local rules on the back of a Bartlett Hills score card from the 1930s instructed this golfing gal that "high heeled shoes must not be worn on course" and that her partner "treat his caddie as he would his son." This couple, Vi and Carl Steve, would have paid 75¢ for one round of golf played during the week or $1.25 for a Sunday spent on the course.

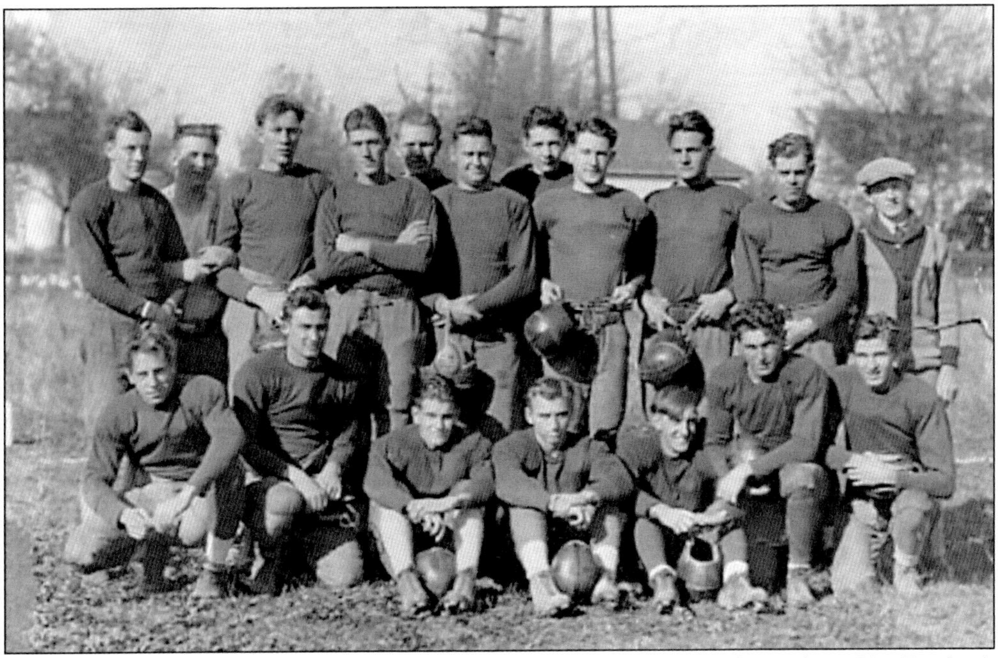

"Bear down Bartlett Bears" was the chant heard throughout town in the early 1930s. Bartlett's 19 to 21-year-old football players donned helmets, pads, and orange and black uniforms for the weekly kickoff. Games were played on the Koehler property in downtown Bartlett where Main Street Plaza stands today. Funds for Bartlett's amateur football team were raised by holding dances above the Bartlett Tavern each Saturday night.

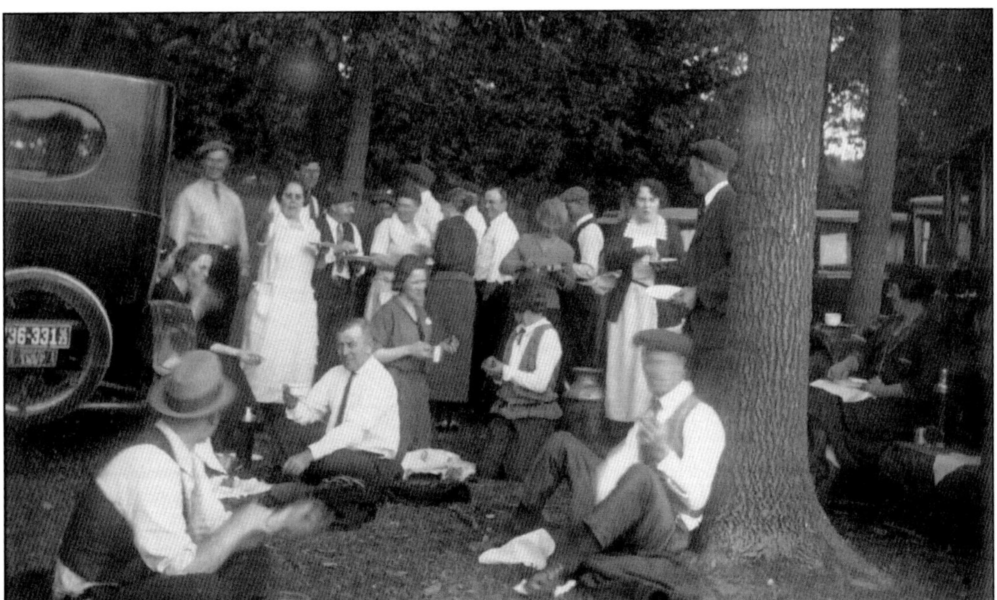

Sunday afternoon often meant a get-together in the park for Bartlett families and friends finished with a week's worth of toil. Easy picnic fare may have been on the menu, but "Sunday best" for both men and women, complete with fedoras, ties, dresses, and pearls was still the chosen attire in the mid 1920s.

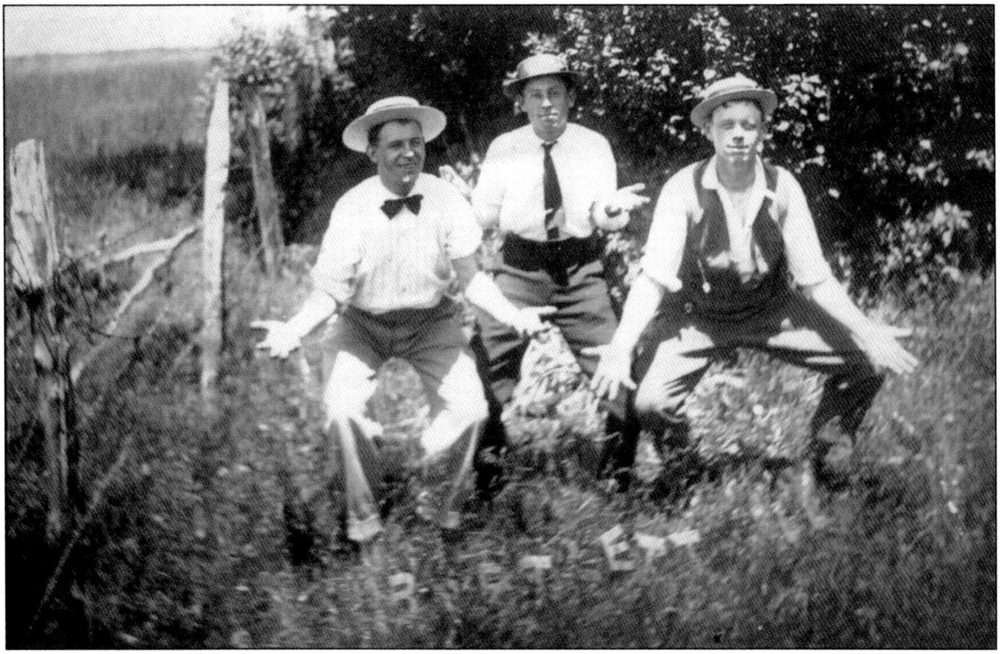

Three Stooges beware! Adolph Effinger, Herman Wendler, and Erv Schultz could out clown Moe, Larry, and Curly any day of the week. During business hours, Herman's claim to fame was as a builder and Erv was known for his service to the Bartlett Volunteer Fire Department.

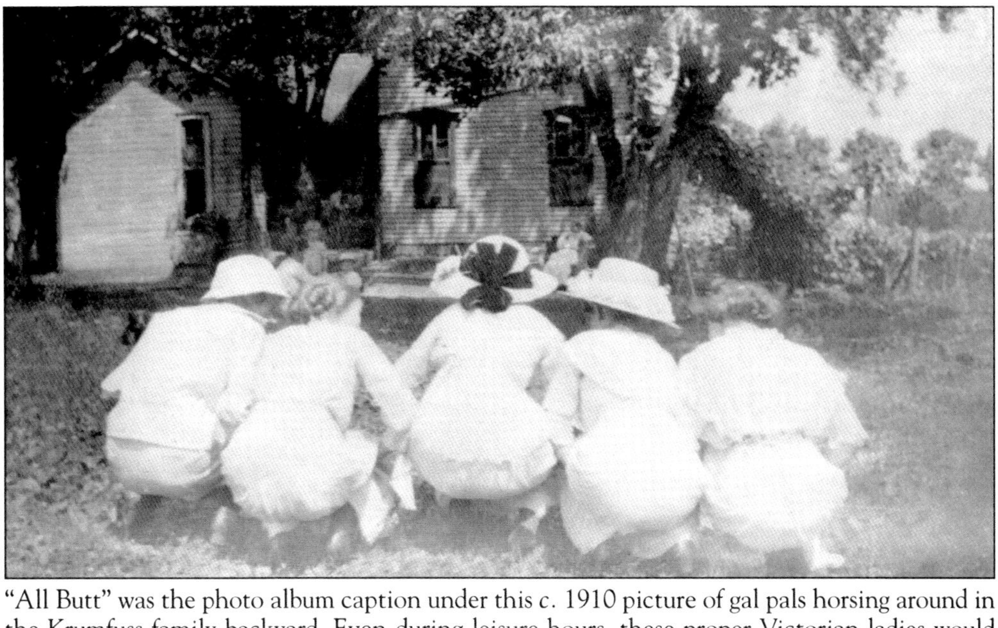

"All Butt" was the photo album caption under this c. 1910 picture of gal pals horsing around in the Krumfuss family backyard. Even during leisure hours, these proper Victorian ladies would not be seen without their chapeaus.

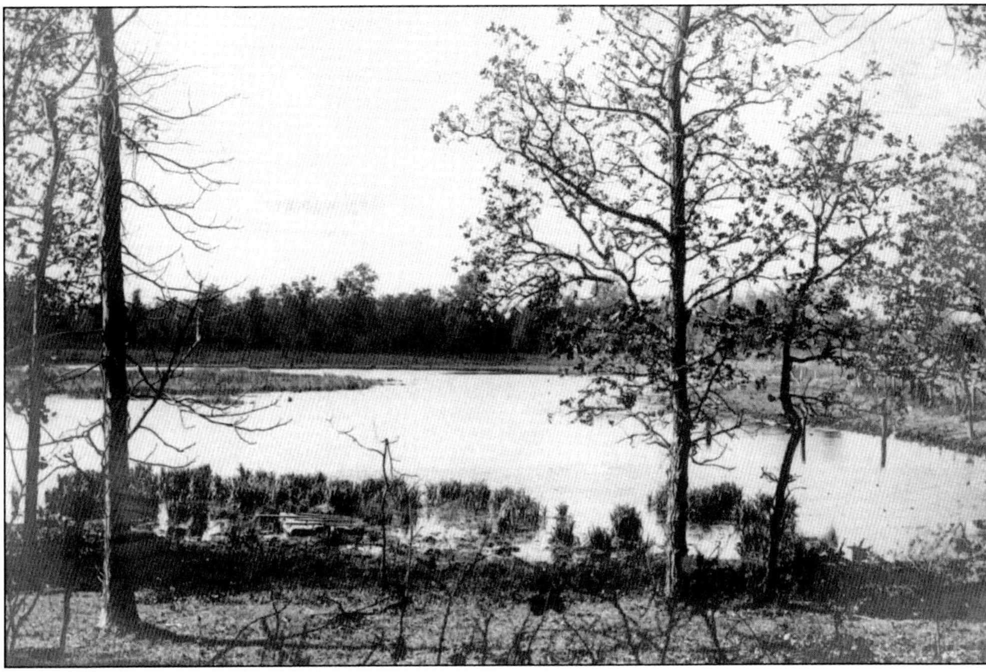

In the early 1900s, Island Lake was the all-season focus for many of Bartlett's recreational activities. Named for the floating bog in the center of the lake, the area youth frequented the locale for ice skating, sledding, swimming, fishing, and picnics. In 1929, Herrick House purchased the land for use as a campsite for children recovering from rheumatic fever and adolescent girls in need of special services. In 1939, construction of the Max Straus Summer Camp for girls and facilities for cardiac services were completed on the site. Today the West Bartlett Road property is the home of Maryville City of Youth Eisenberg Campus, a rehabilitative home for teenage girls.

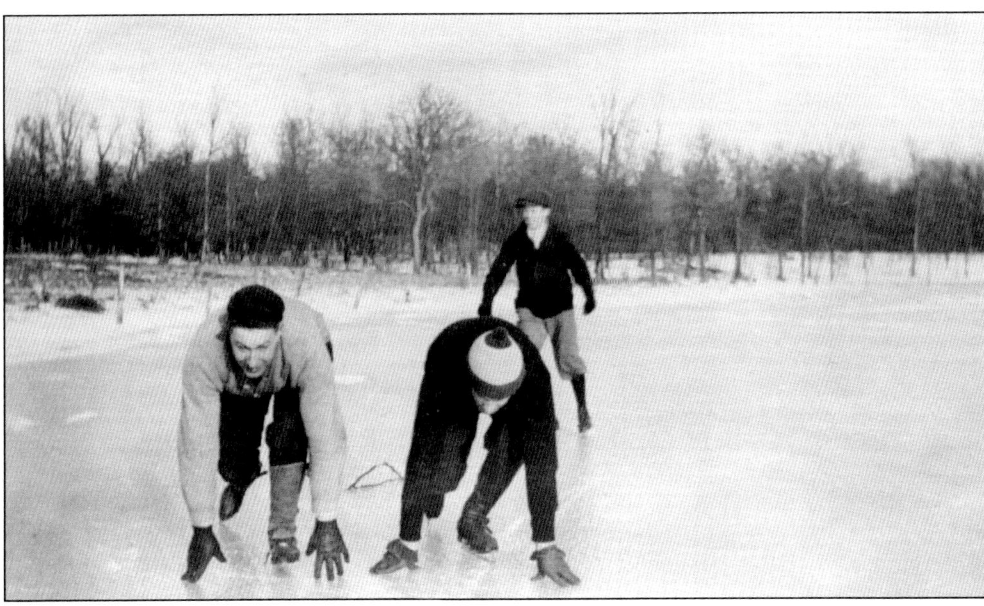

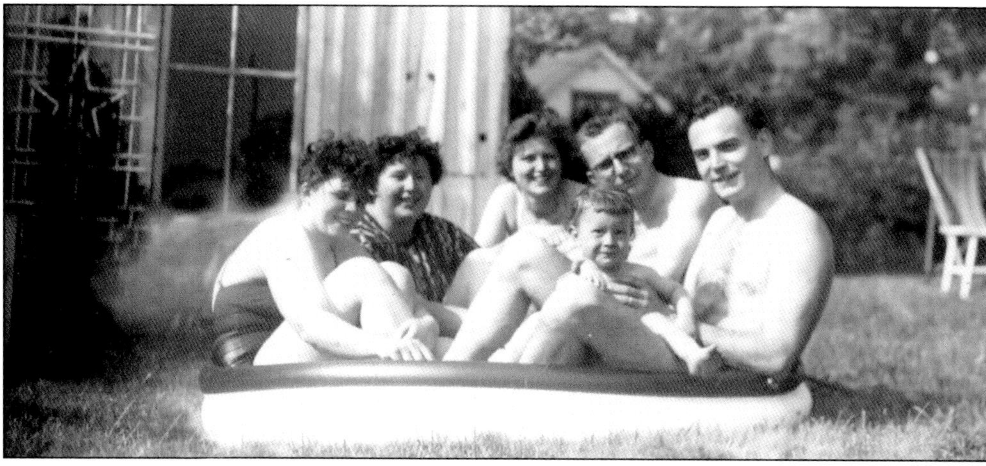

There was always room for one more when the Tappan family hosted an impromptu backyard bash. Marjorie "Button" Puffer Garner, Donna Giles Merritt, Barb Giles Tappan, Jack Ulmann, and Pete Tappan holding daughter Barbie, enjoy some splishing and splashing on a hot summer day in the early 1950s.

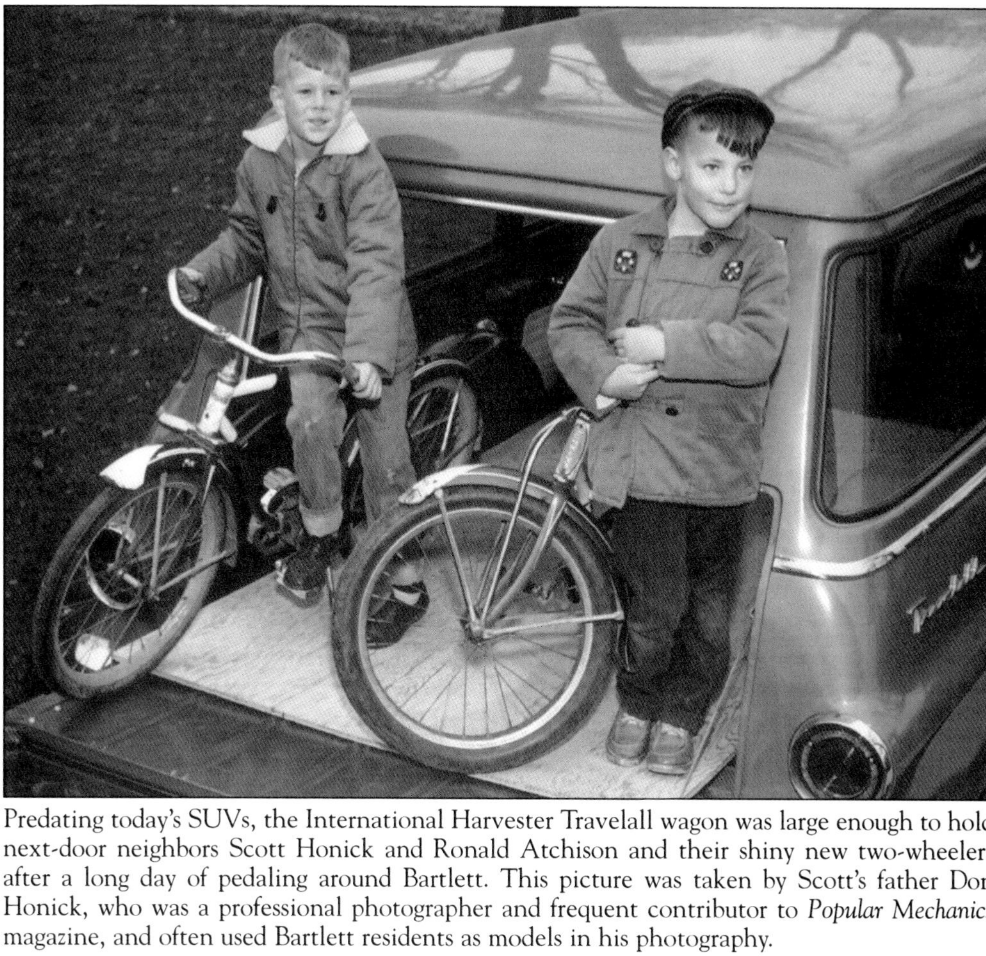

Predating today's SUVs, the International Harvester Travelall wagon was large enough to hold next-door neighbors Scott Honick and Ronald Atchison and their shiny new two-wheelers after a long day of pedaling around Bartlett. This picture was taken by Scott's father Don Honick, who was a professional photographer and frequent contributor to *Popular Mechanics* magazine, and often used Bartlett residents as models in his photography.

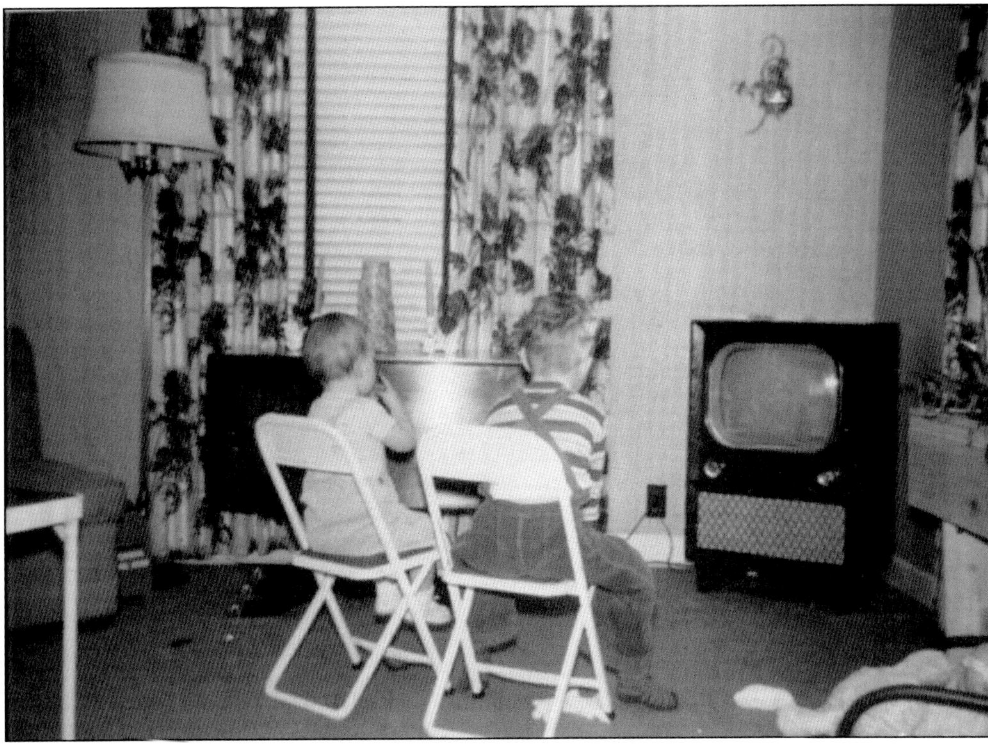

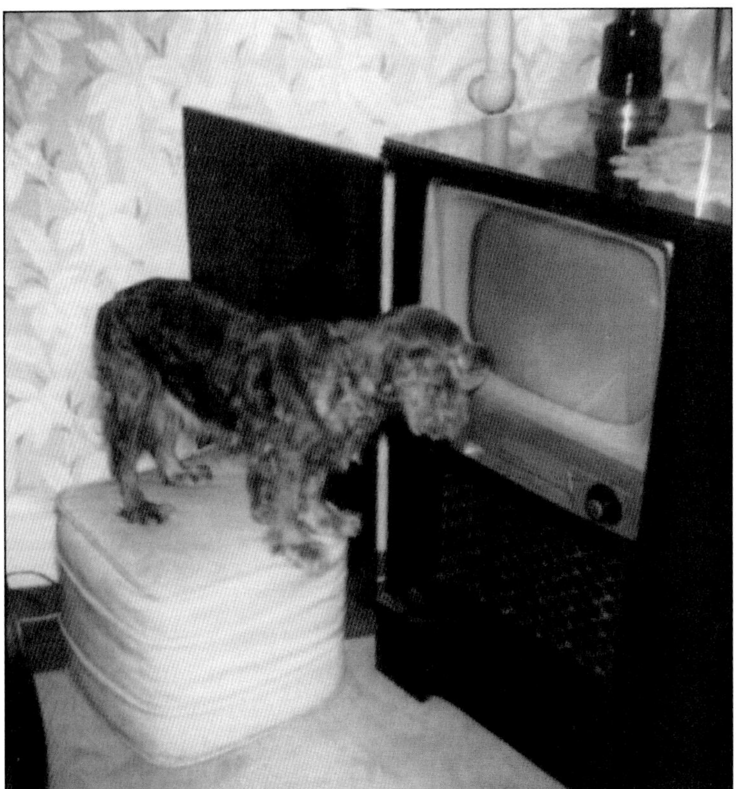

In the 1950s, a newfangled electronic device—the television—was making its way into America's homes and quickly replacing the radio. Bartlett's living rooms were no exception. Glued to the set, waiting for Howdy Dowdy or maybe the Mickey Mouse Club, Paul and Bill Peterson (above) were happy members of the brand new TV generation. Cocker spaniel Blondie Jensen Haase (at left) even got in on the new rage and took time out of her busy day to watch an episode of Lassie.

Six

Reading, 'Riting, and 'Rithmetic

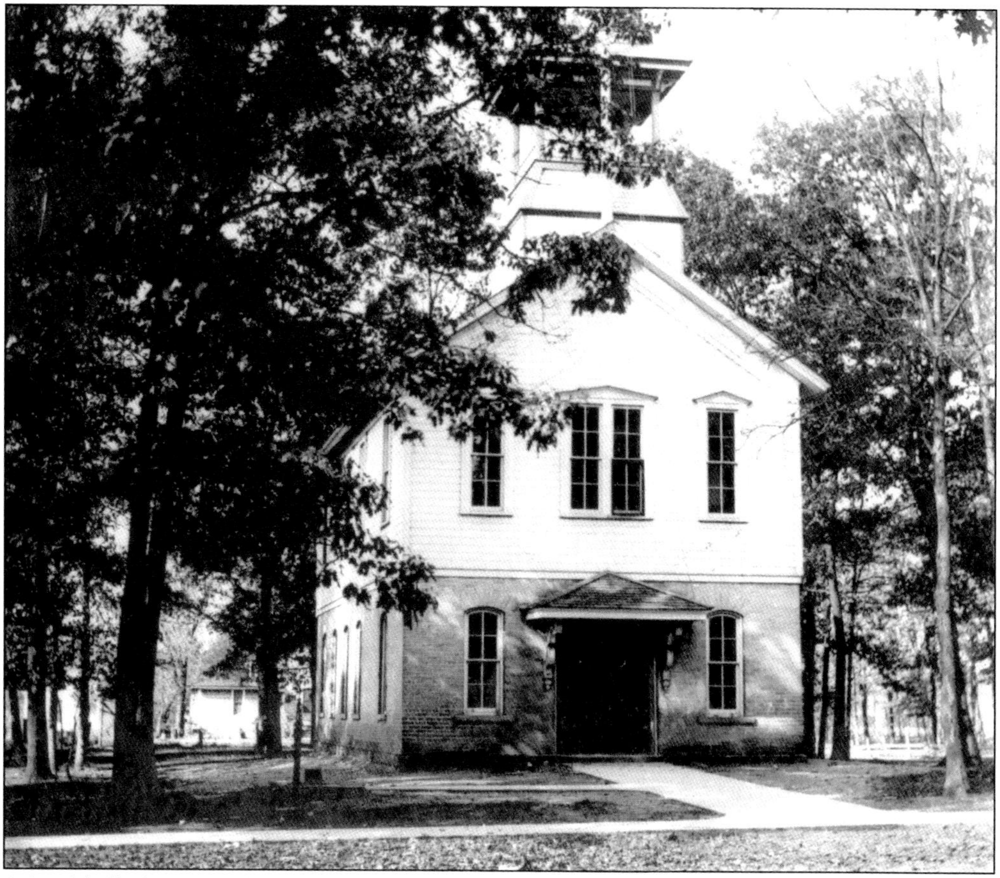

School bells first rang for "Bartlett Public School" in the 1880s. The Village's only school until 1970, Bartlett School was originally located at the southwest corner of Hickory and North Avenue. The elected Board of School Trustees of Hanover Township acted as overseers of the school. Schoolchildren shared drinks of water from a common dipper and bucket and visited the outdoor privy behind the school when nature called.

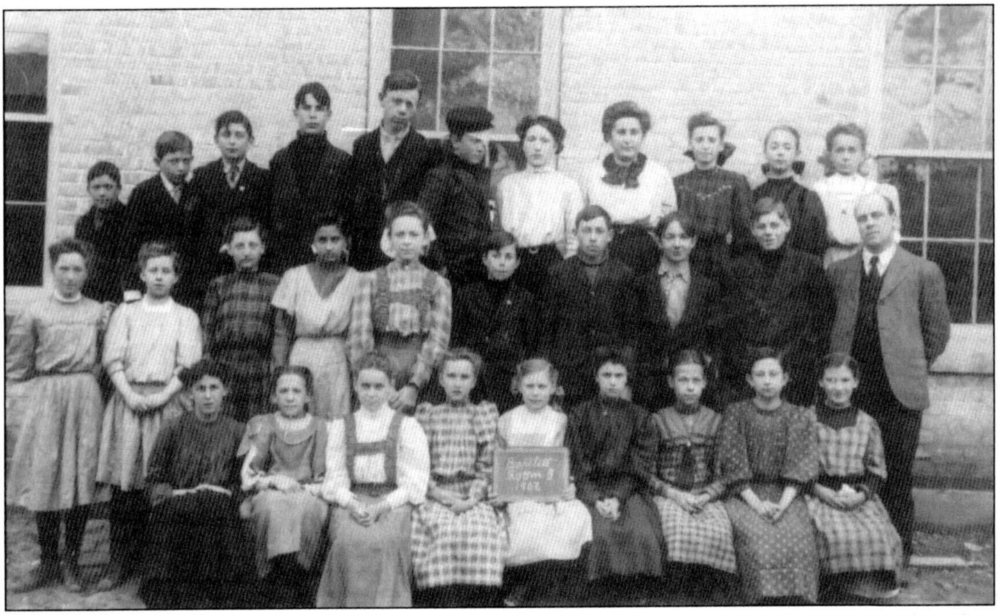

After interviewing with the school board in 1903, a young Mr. John Edman was "employed to teach the urchins and cherubs of Bartlett School." The students in this 1908 upper grade photo were some of the children that fell under his firm hand. By this time, Mr. Edman was serving as both a teacher and the school principal. In that year the school district allocated $410.47 for operation of the school.

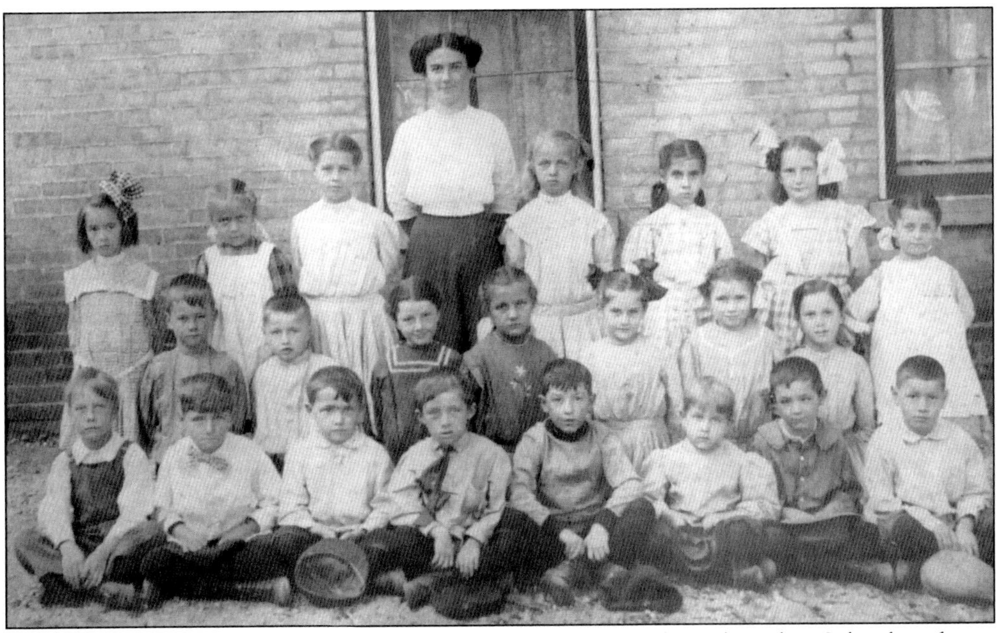

Miss Irene Kelly was the teacher of this 1908 primary grades class of Bartlett School students. When she arrived in town she boarded with the H.H. Schultz family. It was there she met her future husband Erv. The schoolyard adjacent to the building was a fine place to play. At recess time the neighborhood rang with the shouts of children playing "Duck on a Rock," "Andy, Andy, Over," and "Prisoner's Base."

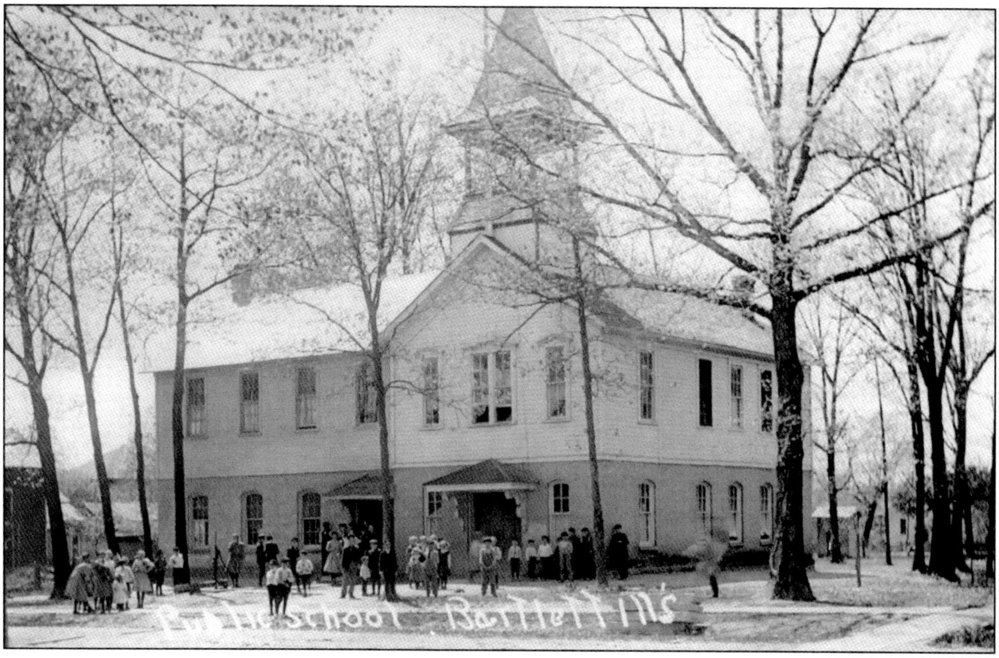

Bartlett School opened its doors a week later than usual in the fall of 1907 because a two-room addition to accommodate a student body totaling 93 pupils had not yet been completed. Bonds totaling $1,000 had been sold to fund the new construction. The larger school building and increased number of students required that additional teaching staff be hired as well.

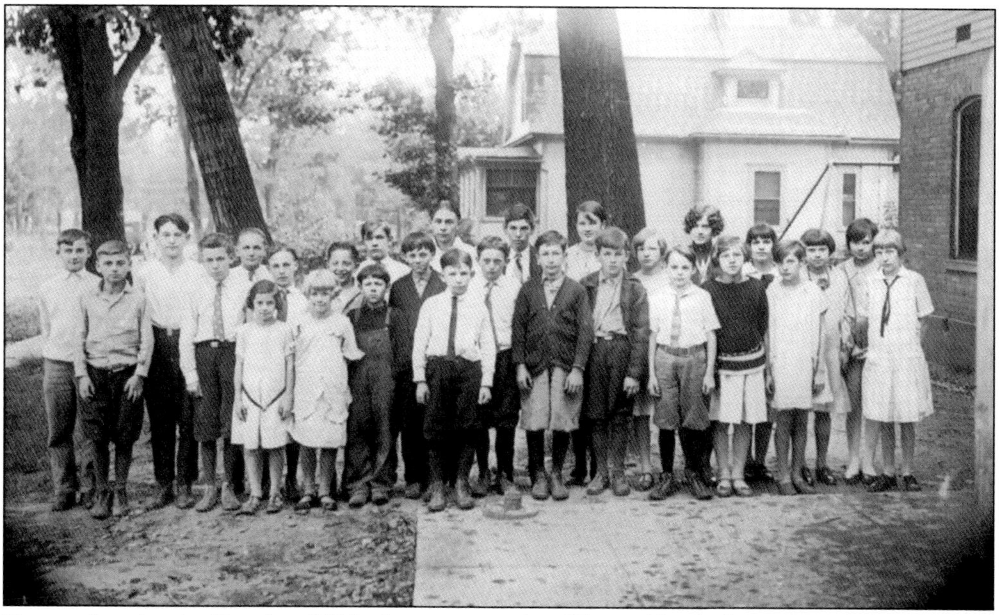

On a rainy day in October 1926, first-year teacher Elvina Ness' class stepped outside their Bartlett Elementary School classroom to pose for this photograph. The children dressed in the dominant fashion of the day. The boys wore knickers and knee-length stockings, and a few even tolerated the "Sunday best" necktie for this special occasion. The girls were miniature models of the popular flapper fashions, wearing smartly bobbed hair and the recently shortened skirts.

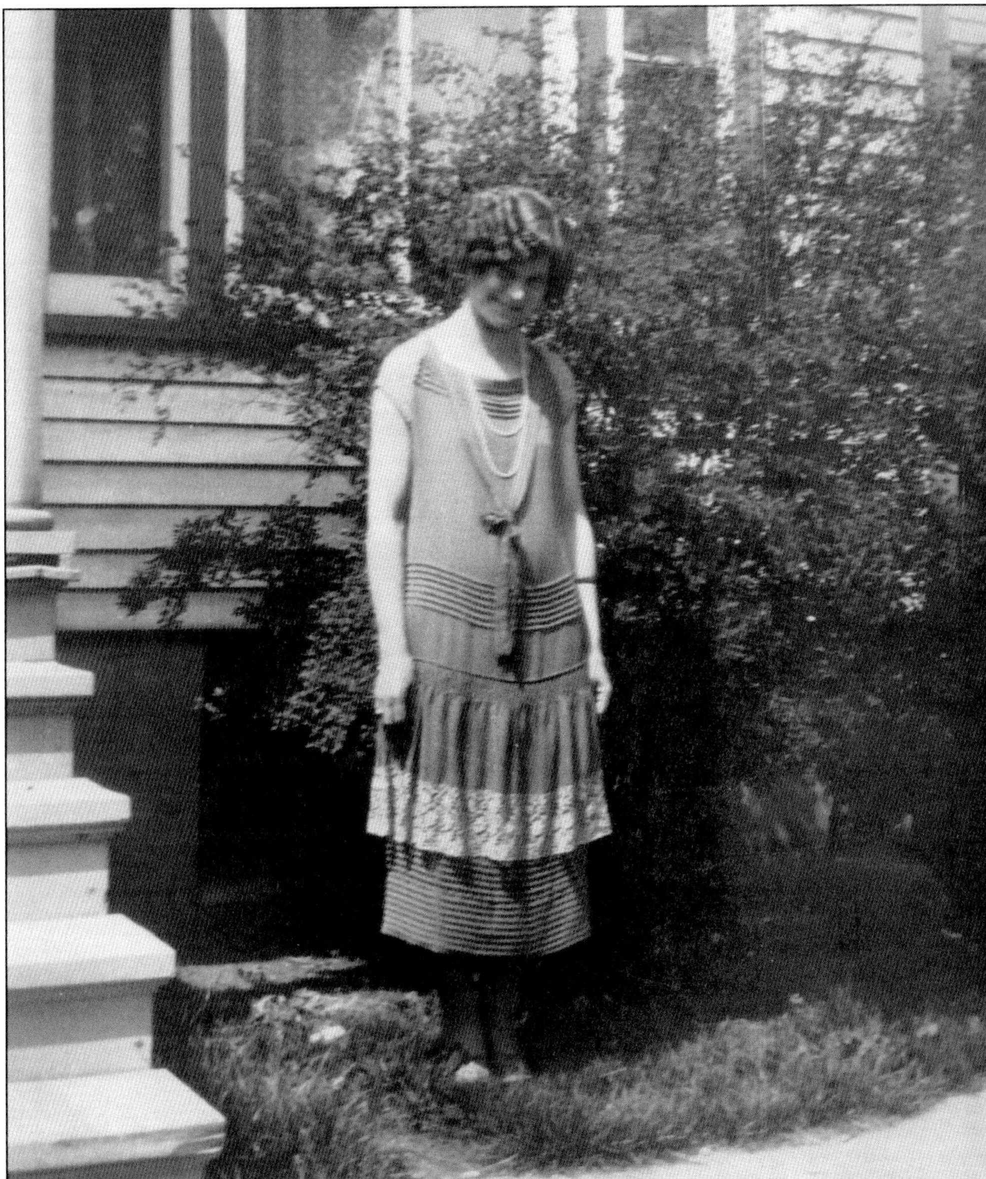

Elvina Ness Brandt came to Bartlett School as a fresh young teacher in 1926 and retired from Wayne School in 1968 as a beloved area educator, whom hundreds of former students honored with a surprise party and farewell notes. Elvina started her 47-year teaching career in a one-room school in North Dakota, where she not only taught all of the grades, but shoveled snow and coal and stoked the potbelly stove. During her 21-year stay at Bartlett School, Brandt added some new hats. She was the play director, president of the PTA, head of the Achievement Club, organizer of eighth grade graduations for all Hanover Township schools, and was appointed principal when the two-year high school housed at Bartlett School was closed in 1941. She supplemented her two-year teaching certificate and her bachelor's degree in education with additional courses at Elgin Community College and Northern Illinois University. She married lifelong Bartlett resident, railroad employee, and Boy Scout leader Harvey Brandt. Although they had no children of their own, the couple dedicated their lives to Bartlett's youth.

“C-O-O-K, C-O-O-K, COOK COUNTY, Y-E-A,” was the yell shouted at the end of each meeting of the Cook County Achievement Club. As part of the Cook County school system, Bartlett students were active in the club, which had a goal to link the school with the home and with general life outside of the classroom. Club meetings followed a formal agenda that also included time for songs, music, jokes, and socializing.

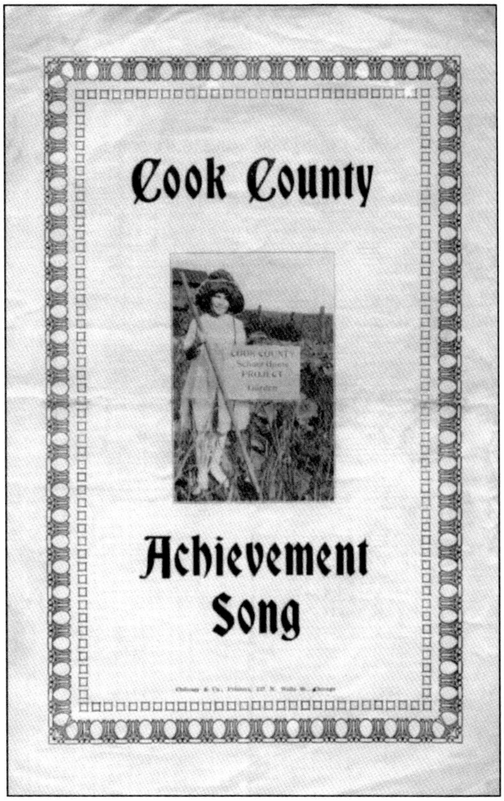

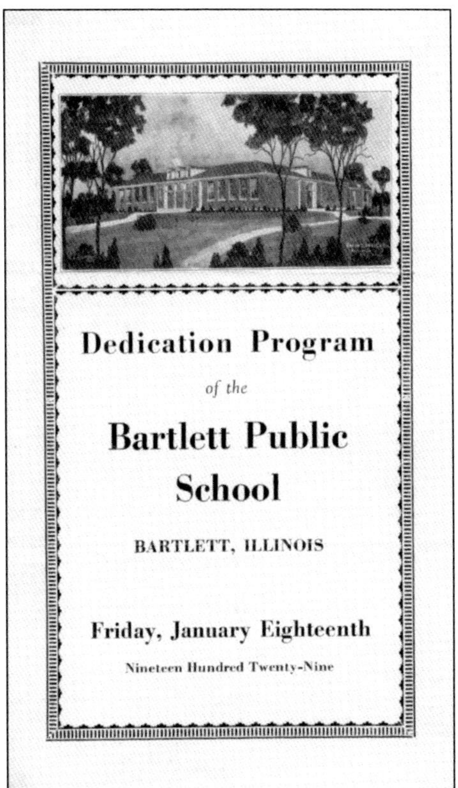

By 1929, Bartlett’s student population had outgrown the antiquated Hickory and North Avenue schoolhouse. On January 18, the community dedicated the new Bartlett Public School at North Avenue and Eastern. This “state-of-the-art” facility had four classrooms, a gymnasium/auditorium, and indoor plumbing. The old schoolhouse site was sold to the highest bidder, William C. Humbracht, for $2,465. The building was only valued at $10, but the woodshed was sold to John Kramer for $20 cash.

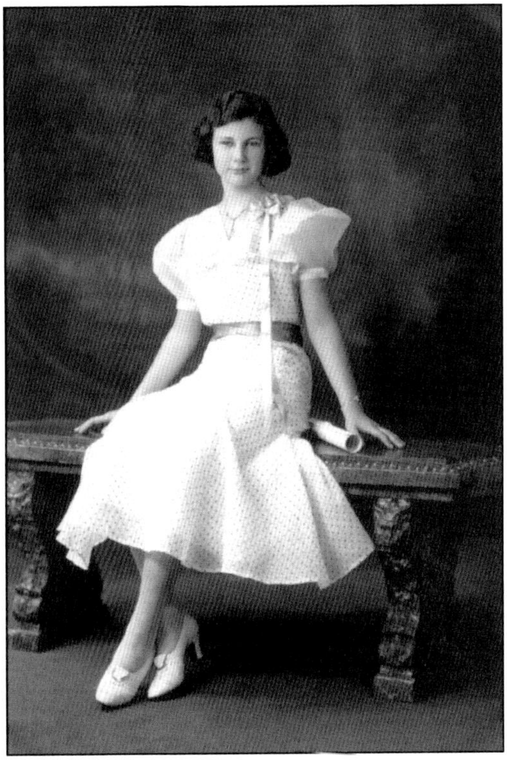

With ribbons pinned to her dress and her diploma by her side, lovely Lotta Ladwig felt all grown up at her 8th grade graduation in 1932. Each spring, Bartlett School Auditorium played host to the graduating classes of all nine district schools in Hanover Township. In addition to the presentation of diplomas, programs included class songs and poems, cornet solos, piano accordion and banjo duets, class prophecies, wills, and a benediction at the end.

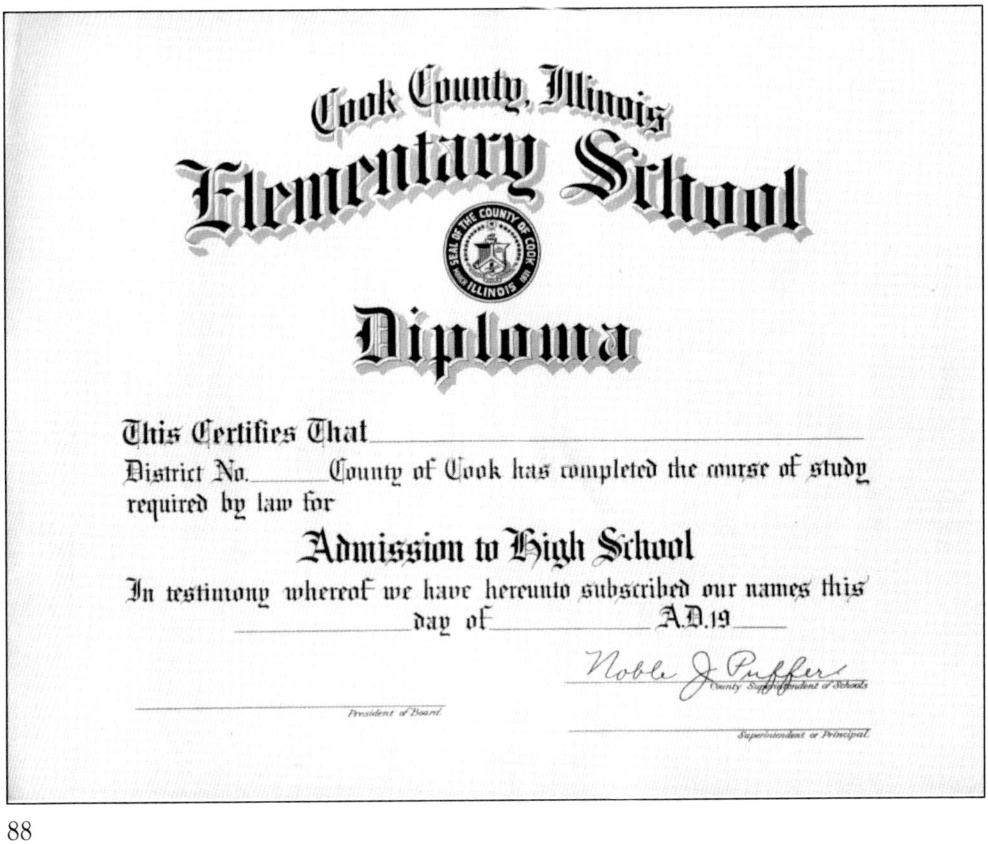

Cook County, Illinois

Elementary School

SEAL OF THE COUNTY OF COOK ILLINOIS

Diploma

This Certifies That ____________________

District No. ______ County of Cook has completed the course of study required by law for

Admission to High School

In testimony whereof we have hereunto subscribed our names this __________ day of __________ A.D.19____

Noble J. Puffer
County Superintendent of Schools

President of Board

Superintendent or Principal

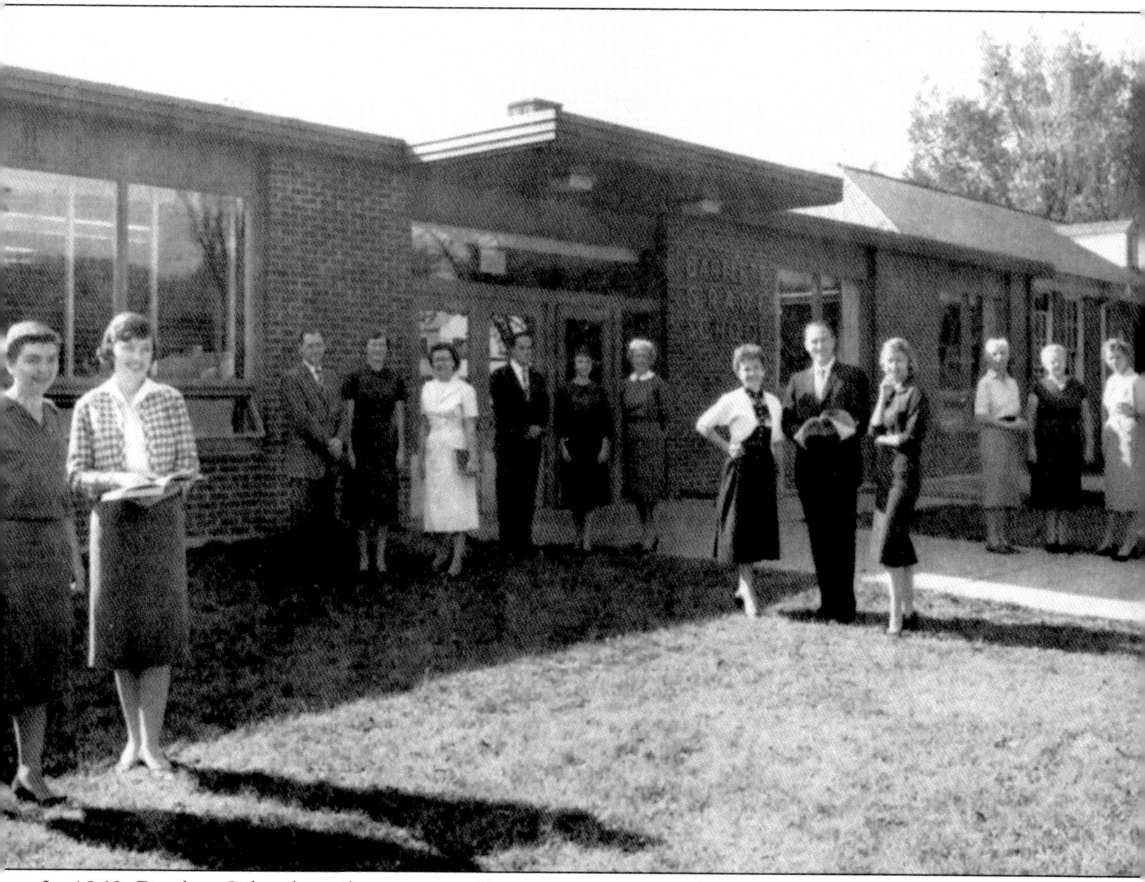

In 1960, Bartlett School teachers were still getting accustomed to the bigger and better facility that resulted from the tumultuous decade that had just ended. In order to improve the quality of education for their children, parents successfully rallied to annex Bartlett School to the Elgin U-46 School District in 1952. That fall, older children bid farewell to their small Village schoolhouse and traveled to either Ellis Junior High or Elgin High School to continue their education. In the same year, Robert Hardt (fifth from the right) was hired to act as the fifth and sixth grade teacher and new principal for the 88 kindergartners through sixth graders who remained at Bartlett School. Within five years, Bartlett School's student population had increased to 191 children and overcrowding forced Principal Hardt to partition off the old gymnasium for additional classrooms. Even parking became an issue. In February of 1957, voters went to the polls and approved a $230,000 referendum for a nine-room addition to the school. Upon Hardt's retirement in 1986, Bartlett School had grown to over 700 students and 35 teachers.

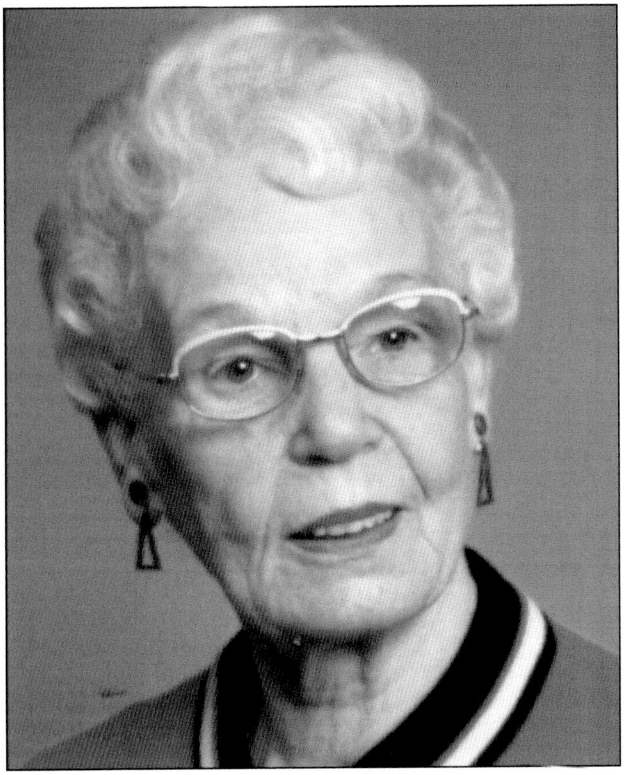

Dearly loved teacher Ruth Baxman came to Bartlett as an infant in 1906 to live with the Rev. and Mrs. William Rathmann. She attended Bartlett School through her sophomore year, graduated from Elgin Academy, and upon completing her higher education, returned to Bartlett Grade School for most of her teaching career, which spanned 50 years. Baxman's innate ability to guide children may have sprung from her own mischievous youth. In her later years, she gleefully recalled soaping windows, stealing pears, hiking up her school skirts, and other teenage pranks.

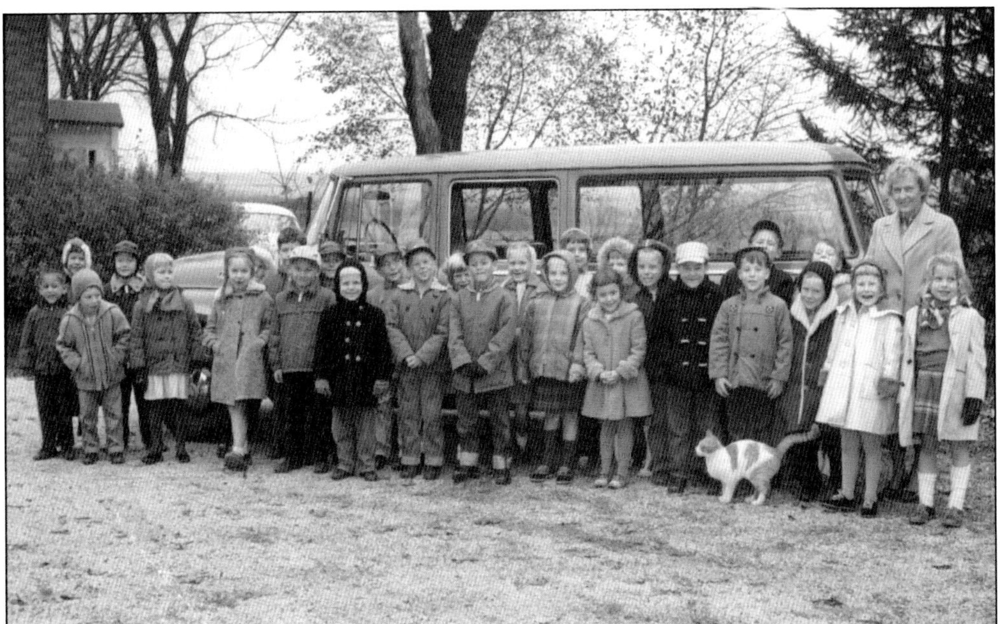

Curious staffers at *Popular Mechanics* magazine once asked how many first-grade students can you fit into the 1962 Travelall wagon. Margaret Bjorck's class at Bartlett Grade School came back with the answer. All 28 youngsters shown in this photo fit into the wagon and there were still a few empty spots in the front seat for any stray children or even the kitty cat purring for a ride here.

Since the early 1900s, the Bartlett School PTA has served as a bridge between the school and the community. The group's monthly card parties, basket and box socials, and school plays brought parents, teachers, students, and community leaders together for both entertainment and fundraising. Profits were used for needs and necessities that were not quite covered by regular operating funds, such as extra globes and maps, sports equipment, books for the library, songbooks for classrooms, a school flag, and classroom ventilators.

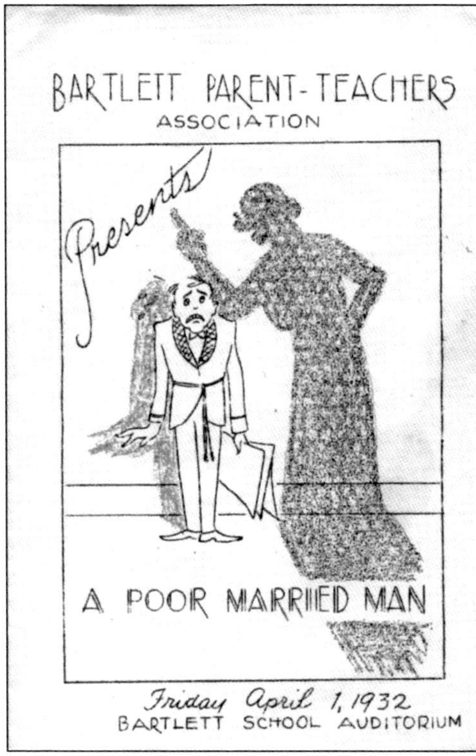

The annual school play, held in the Bartlett School auditorium, was an elaborate stage production that starred parents, teachers, and community members. Tickets were priced at 15¢ for children and 35¢ for adults and they sold out quickly.

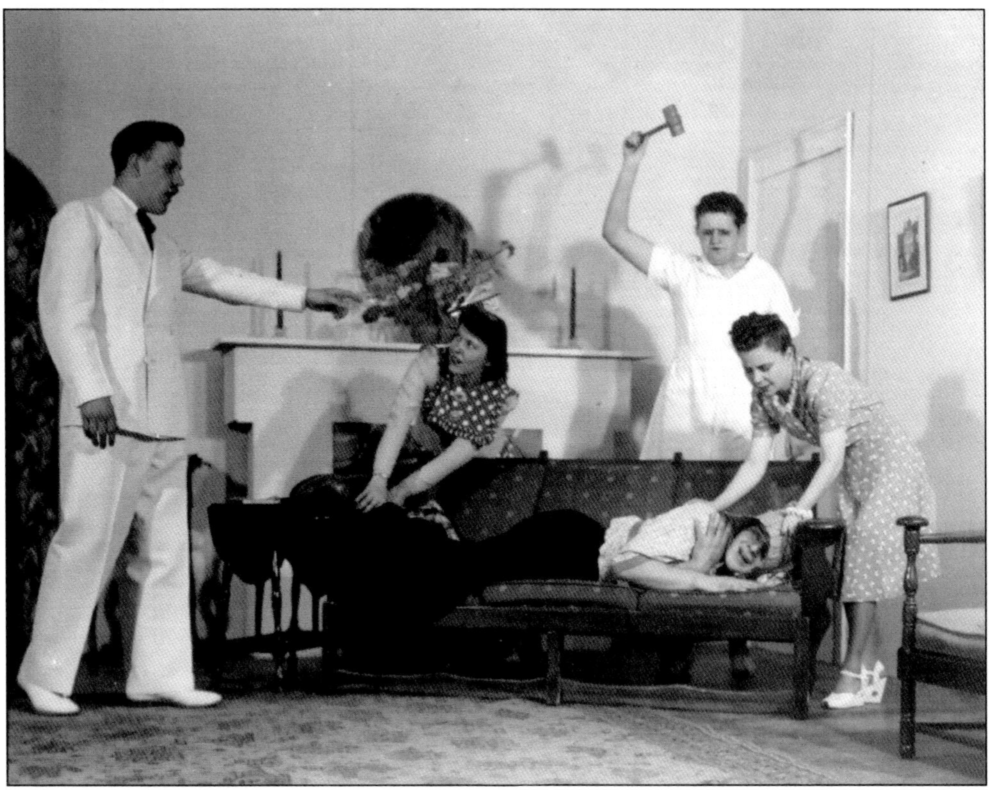

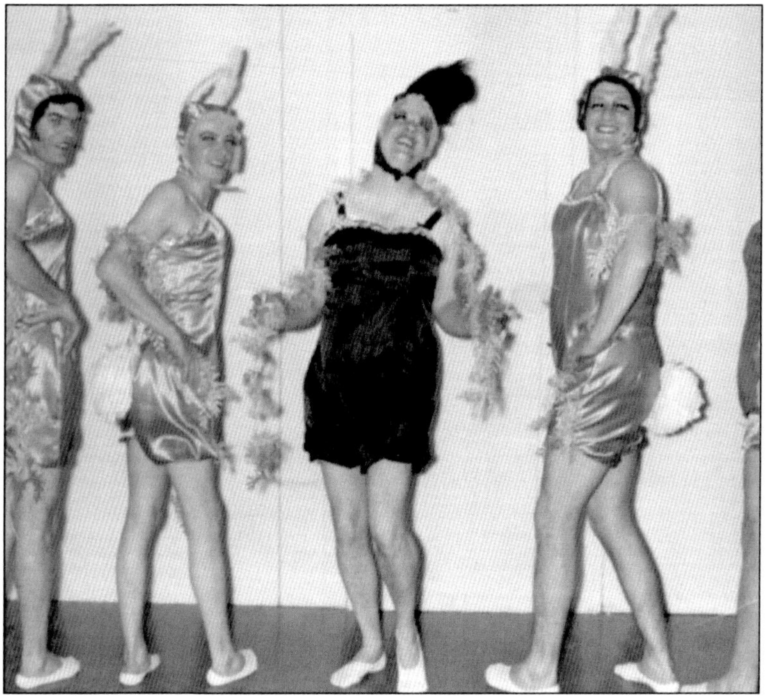

No, Hugh Hefner wasn't holding auditions at Bartlett School in 1965. These bunnies, Earl "Boom-Boom" Beckner, Ron "Flame" Semrau, Rodger "Peaches" Peterson, Matt "Electra" Bernert, and Jay "Sugar" Sinnes donned ears and tails and took center stage during the "Fungus Follies," a PTA benefit to raise money for a new theater curtain for the auditorium.

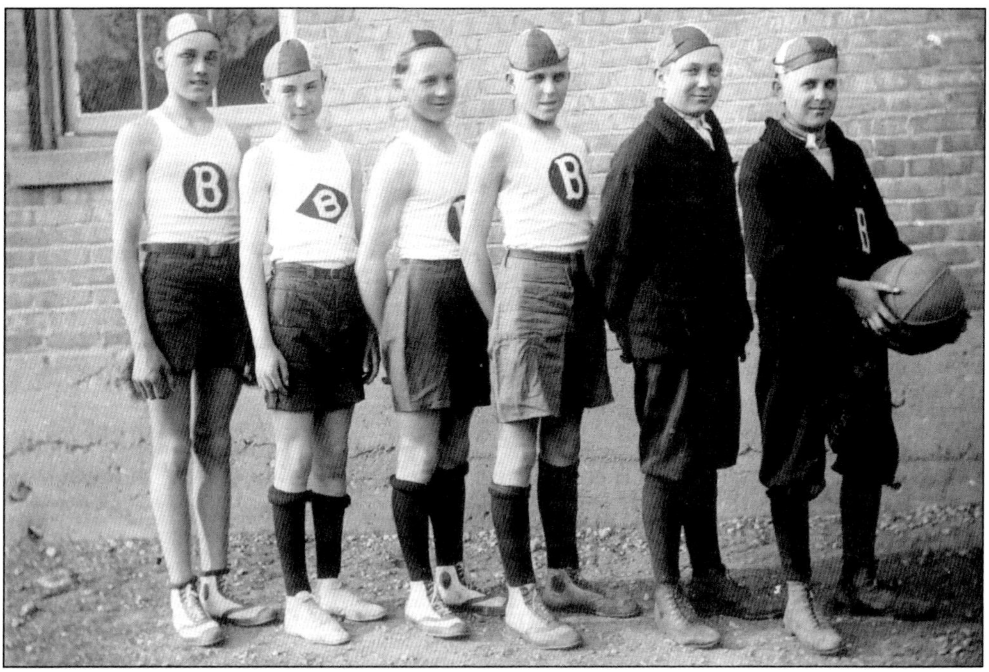

The original Bartlett High School was a two-year school that began in the 1890s and disbanded in 1941. The high school was located in Bartlett School and had a separate classroom and teacher. The lightweight basketball team of 1923-1924 wore makeshift uniforms highlighted with a Bartlett "B." Second from left is Elroy Kenneke and to the right of him is his brother Edmund. Second from the right is Walter Hoth and the letterman holding the basketball is Walter Meyer, who became the seventh Village President of Bartlett.

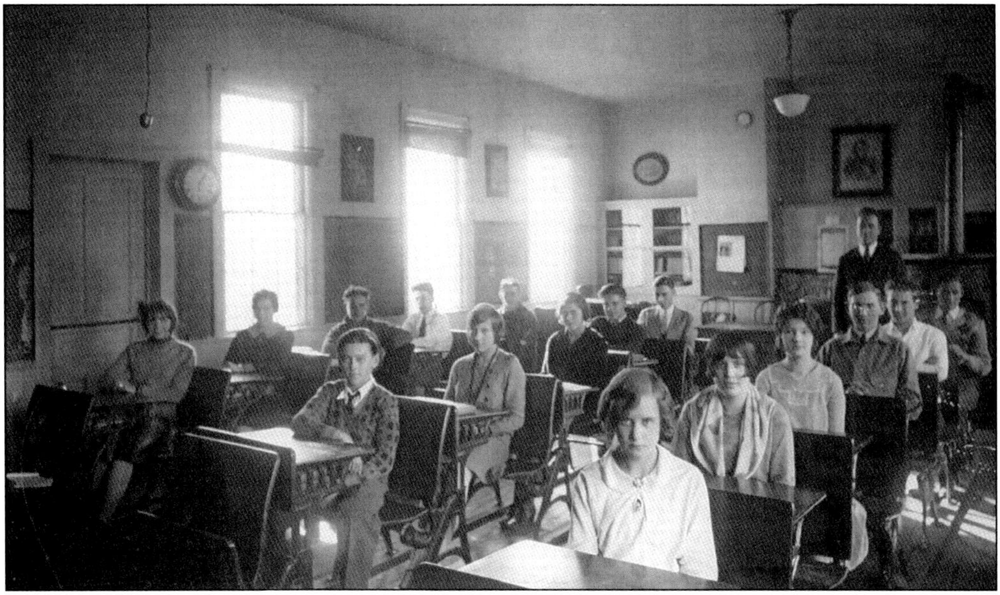

In 1928, Bartlett students learned their lessons in classrooms heated by wood burning stoves like the one in this picture behind high school teacher and principal Dallas Puffer. Ruth Harmening (middle row, second seat) recalls coming to school in the morning to frozen bottles of ink in the desktop wells. Writing assignments had to wait until after the boys brought in wood and the stove warmed up the room.

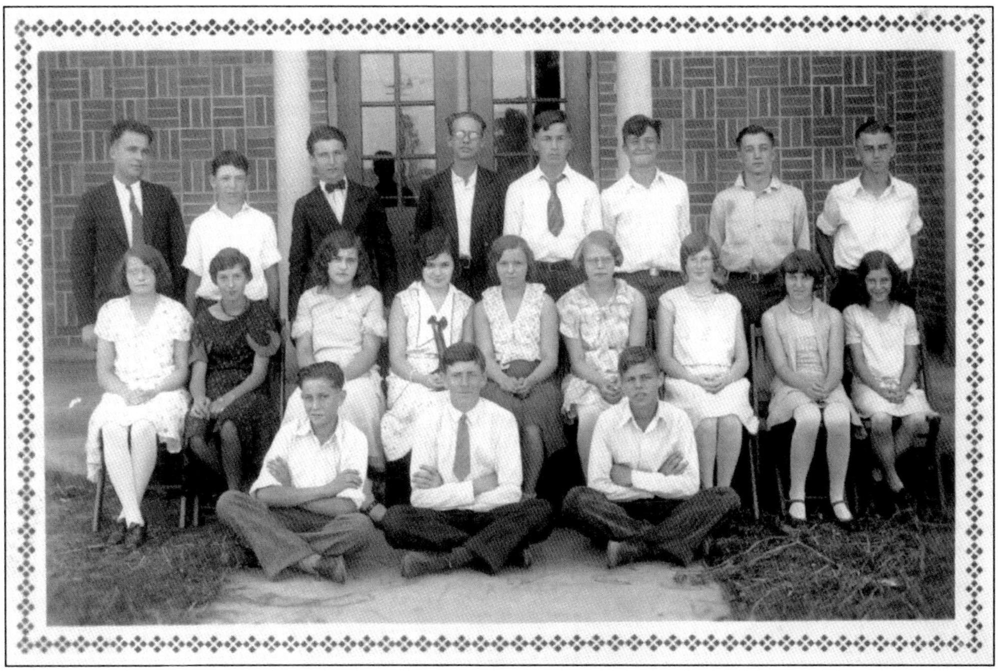

When this 1930s high school class completed the two-year program at Bartlett School, they could choose to continue their education at Elgin High, which had a 4-year program. Their tuition continued to be paid for by the Hanover Township School Board. Students traveled to Elgin High by train or carpooled in the family jalopy.

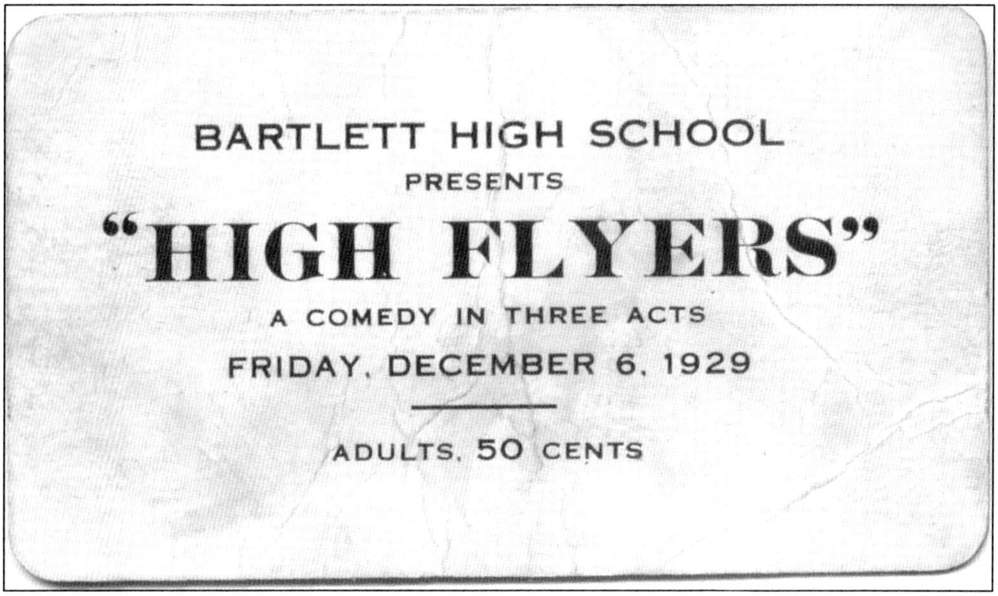

BARTLETT HIGH SCHOOL
PRESENTS
"HIGH FLYERS"
A COMEDY IN THREE ACTS
FRIDAY, DECEMBER 6, 1929

ADULTS, 50 CENTS

The high school students held separate social activities from the grade school, such as dances and plays for the community. Elaine Jensen, far left, and fellow thespian classmates take a final curtain call in this 1939 "high society" production.

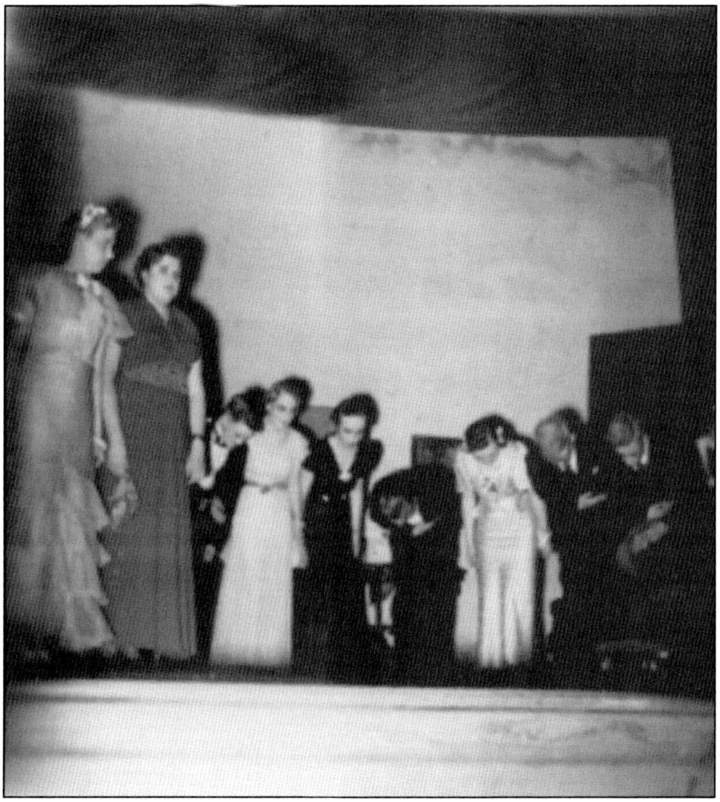

Seven

HEARTH AND HOME

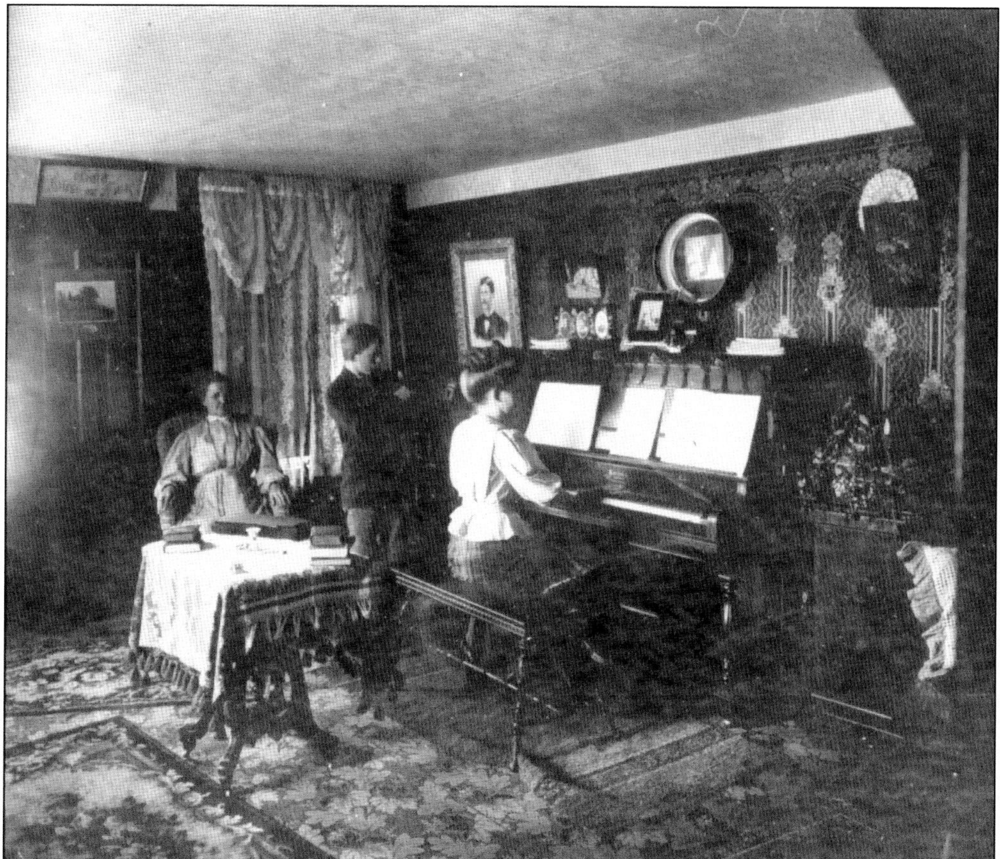

Occupying much the same role as today's home entertainment center, the focus of the proper turn-of-the-century parlor was a piano. Della O'Brien, accompanied by younger brother Earl on the violin, plays an after-supper tune for their mother Sophia in the family's home on Railroad Avenue, where Ameritech stands today.

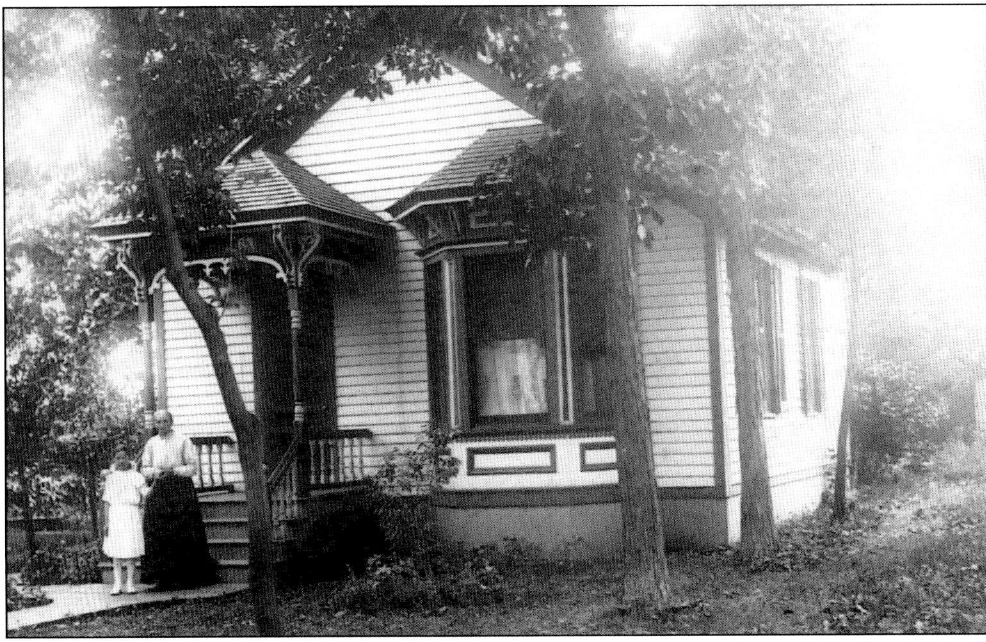

Grandma Bauermann and granddaughter Edna Goldenstein stand in front of the family's little painted lady at 226 S. Oak Avenue around the turn of the century. Even though it was not as large as the traditional homes of the era, the quaint architectural details on the porch brackets and stairway spindles, and the multi-color trimwork reflect the style of the Victorian period. The home still stands today.

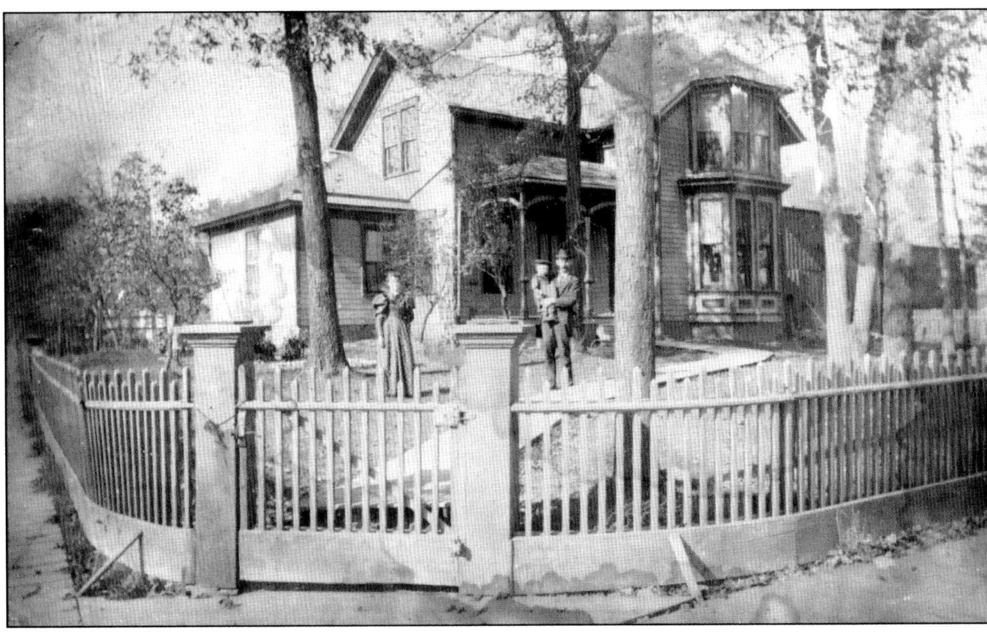

This house at the northwest corner of Oneida and Oak was the residence of the Stumpf family in the early 1900s. Today it is more readily known as Candy! Candy! Candy!, a favorite stop for children walking home from Bartlett Elementary School. The Stumpf's purchased the home in May of 1893 for $1,800. After the death of his wife, Mr. Stumpf sold the home for $3,600.

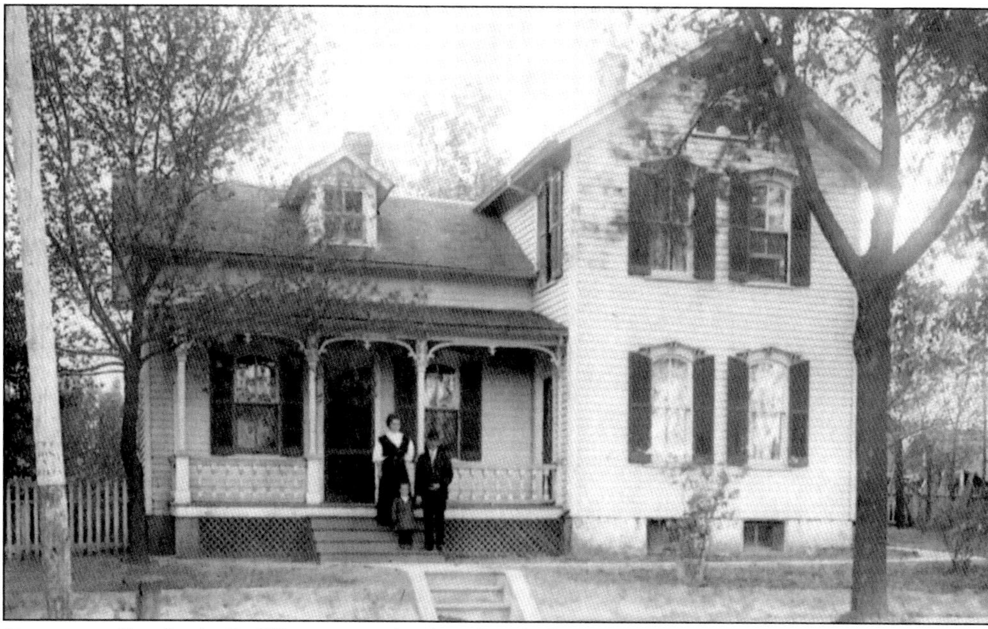

Carpenter Friedrich C. Watermann built a family home at 211 Railroad in the 1880s. The structure was built in a gable-front-and-wing style, which was typical of the expanding Midwest during this time period. Friedrich's daughter Clara, shown here with husband Herman Bartlett and son Elmer, lived in the home briefly after her marriage. Today the building is home to Banbury Fair, a craft and antique store.

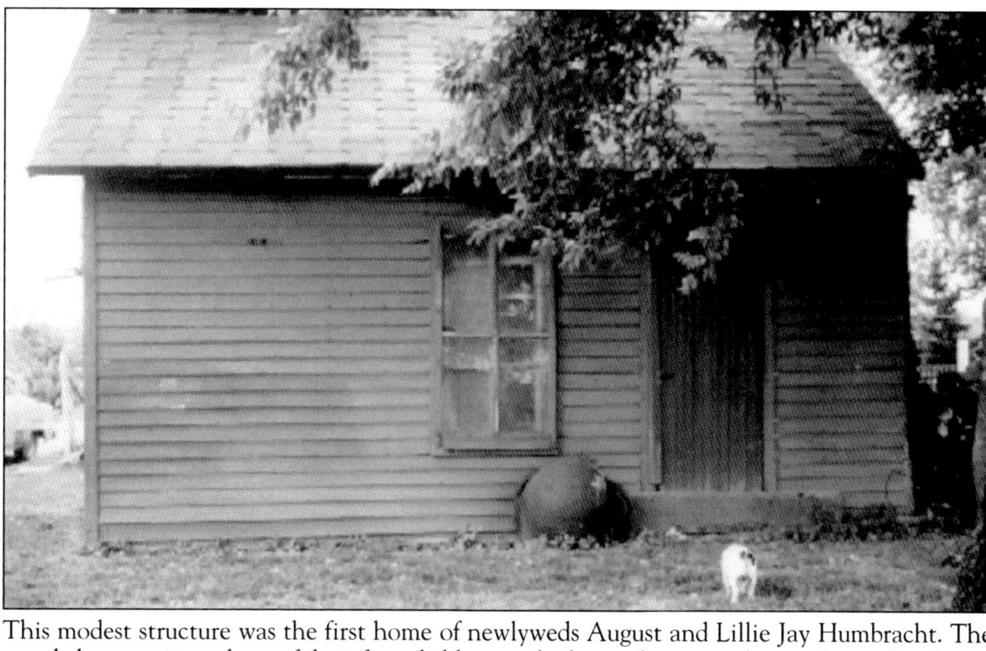

This modest structure was the first home of newlyweds August and Lillie Jay Humbracht. The couple began raising three of their four children in the home, but moved into a larger farmhouse on the same property prior to the arrival of their only daughter Jane Humbracht Ping. This building was then converted into a chicken house complete with plaster walls. Today, Jessica Lane runs through what was the entrance to the family farm.

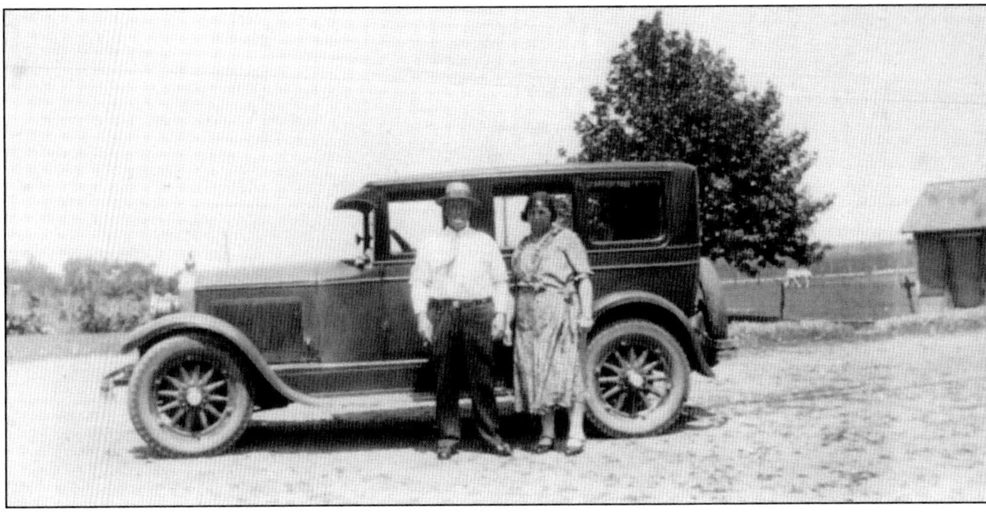

Louis and Martha Oltendorf, standing by their 1926 Buick, owned this farm at 27 W 651 Stearns Road from 1912 to 1974. Aside from the original 40 acres that made up Bartlett proper in the early 1900s, much of the surrounding countryside consisted of family farms such as this one. The Oltendorfs raised grain, dairy cows, and three lovely daughters, Elvira, Elta, and Edna, during their 62 years on this farm, which was known throughout the area for its landmark windmill. Today, the site is part of the DuPage County Forest Preserve District.

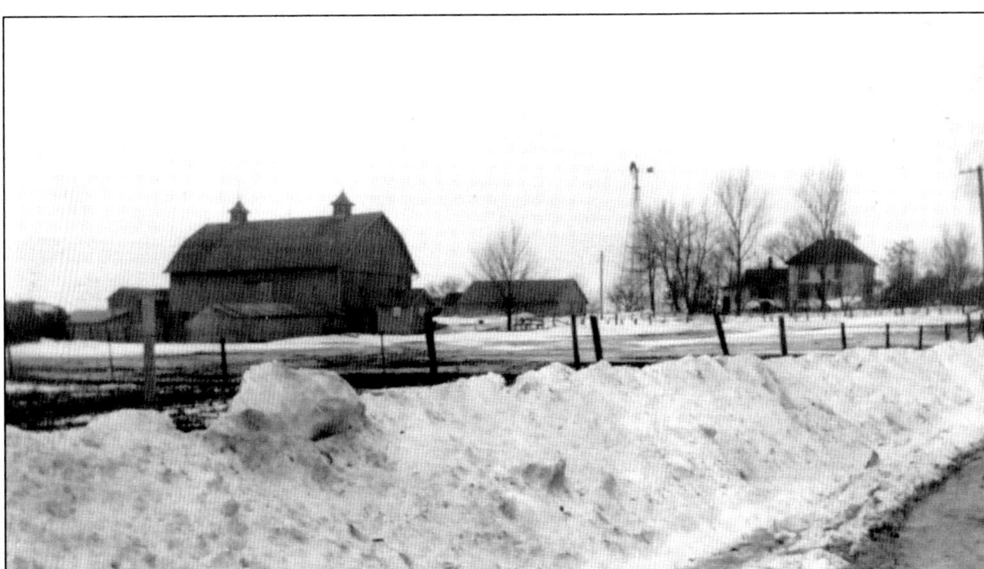

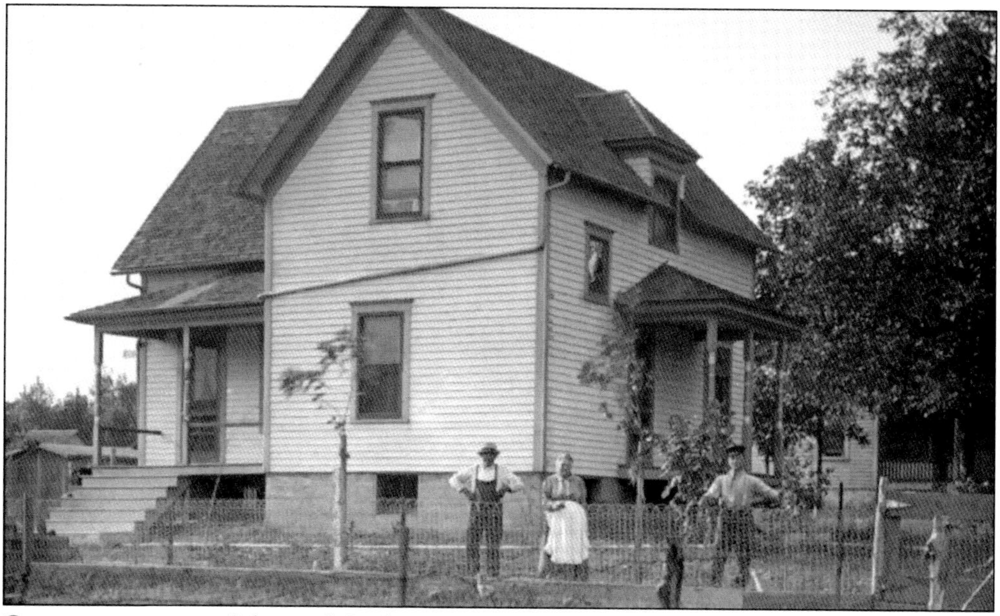

German immigrants John and Sophia Detrich Schultz outside their Bartlett home, which still stands today at 244 S. Hickory. John was a dealer in hides and manufactured grease and fertilizer. He returned to Germany three times, bringing young men back to America to live a better life. Sophia was the first president of the Frauen Verein (the Ladies Aid Society of Immanuel Evangelical Church). The Schultz family moved to Elgin in 1917.

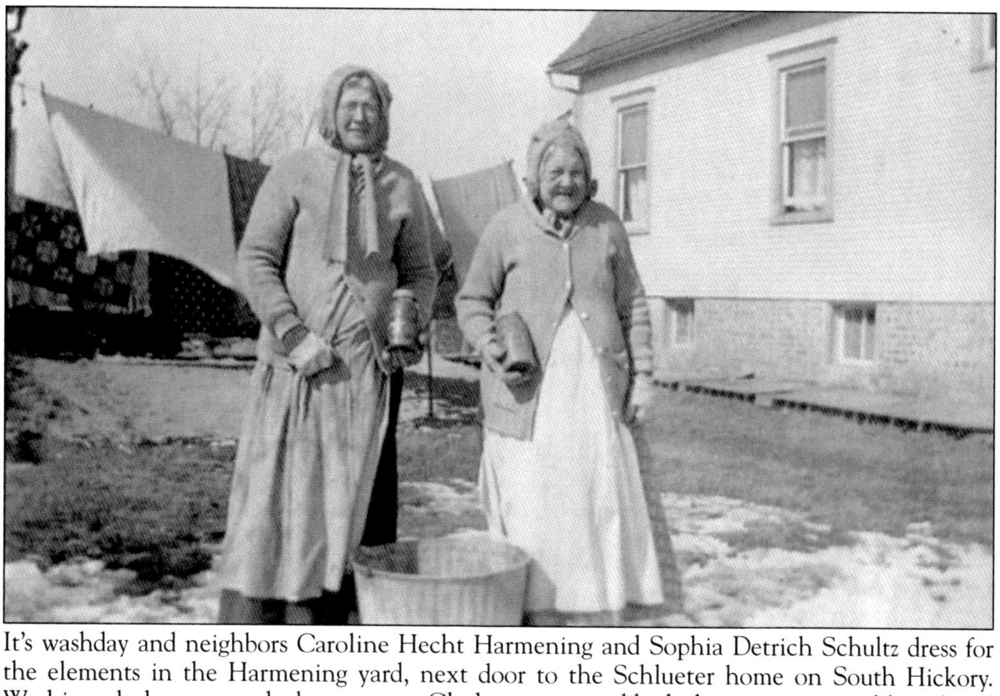

It's washday and neighbors Caroline Hecht Harmening and Sophia Detrich Schultz dress for the elements in the Harmening yard, next door to the Schlueter home on South Hickory. Washing clothes was a daylong event. Clothes were scrubbed clean using a washboard and cranked through a wringer to press the water out. Afterwards, the women hung the clothes to dry in the sun. Pickling and canning were also chores of the day.

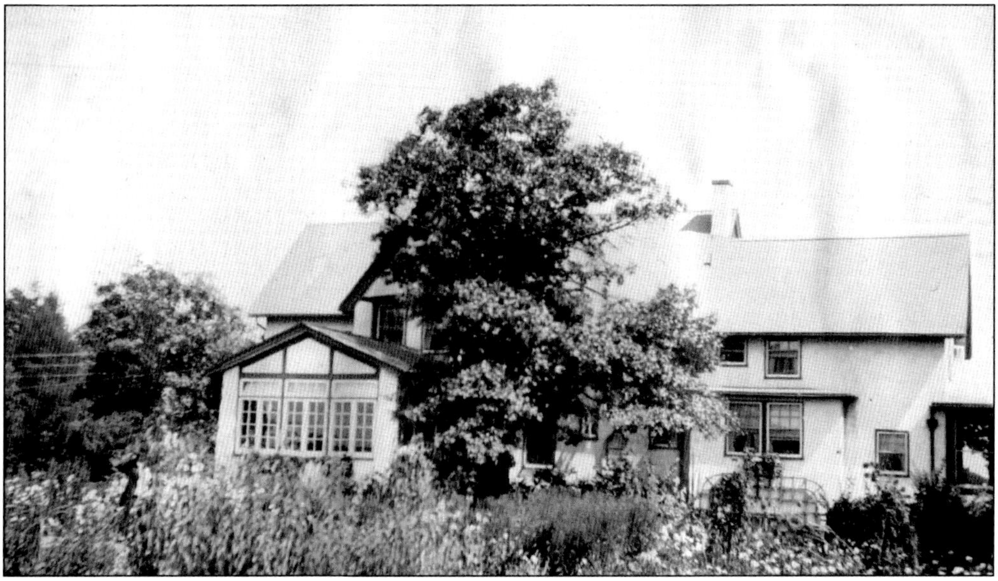

In 1915, colorful Chicago attorney Charles Erbstein purchased more than 200 acres on Lake Street in Hanover Township. The Villa Olivia estate, named after his daughter, was the family's own private paradise and included a 16-room mansion, Olympic size swimming pool, cabanas, riding stables, 18-hole golf course, and later a well-listened-to radio station, WTAS. After Charles' death in 1927, his widow converted the property into a country club, which she managed until 1953.

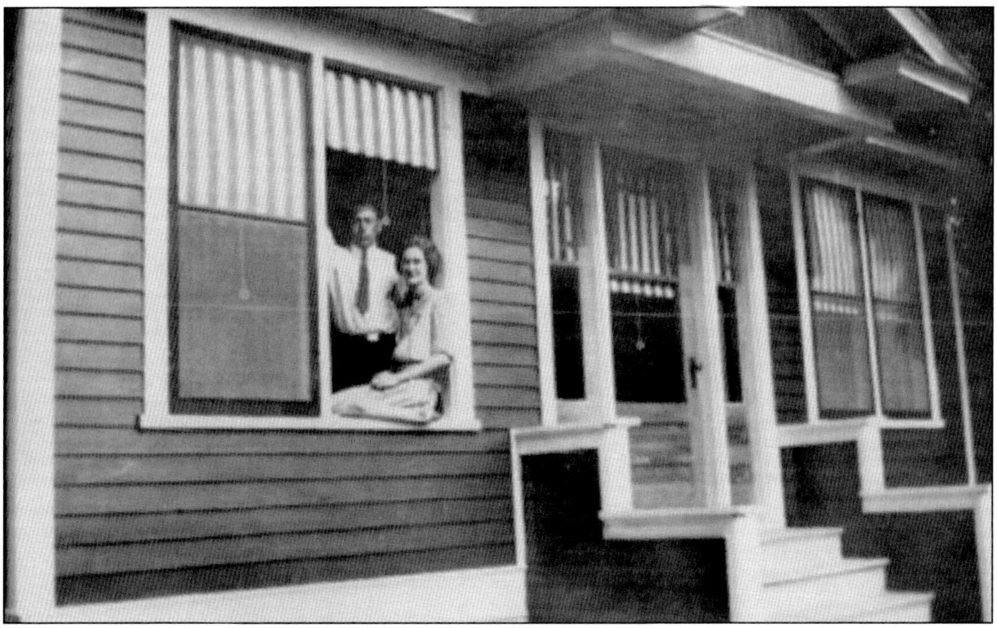

Building contractor Herman Wendler and his wife Amelia look out the window of their first home at 129 N. Hickory. The house was originally built on Western Avenue in October 1893 to serve as the German school for Immanuel United Church of Christ and the church's large German congregation. Herman moved the structure in 1921 and remodeled it into the family home for $750.

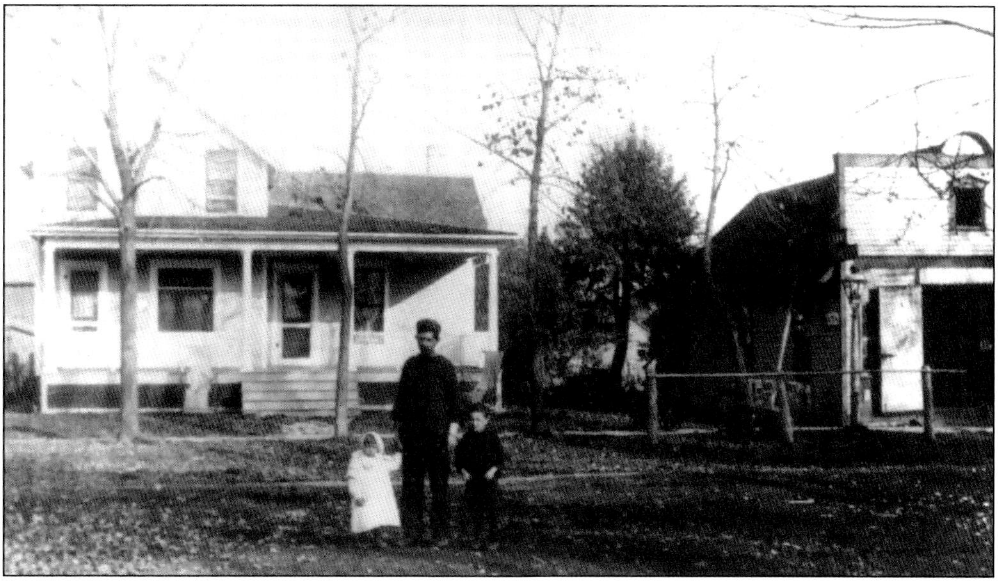

Henry C. Marxen, a pioneer resident of newly incorporated Bartlett, operated this blacksmith shop next to his home on South Oak Street for 50 years. When the neighborhood children heard clinking on his anvil, they ran to get rings made from nails. Marxen also served the Village as a trustee for 20 years, beginning in 1934. Henry is shown here with two of his 13 grandchildren, Alex and Henry R. Marxen.

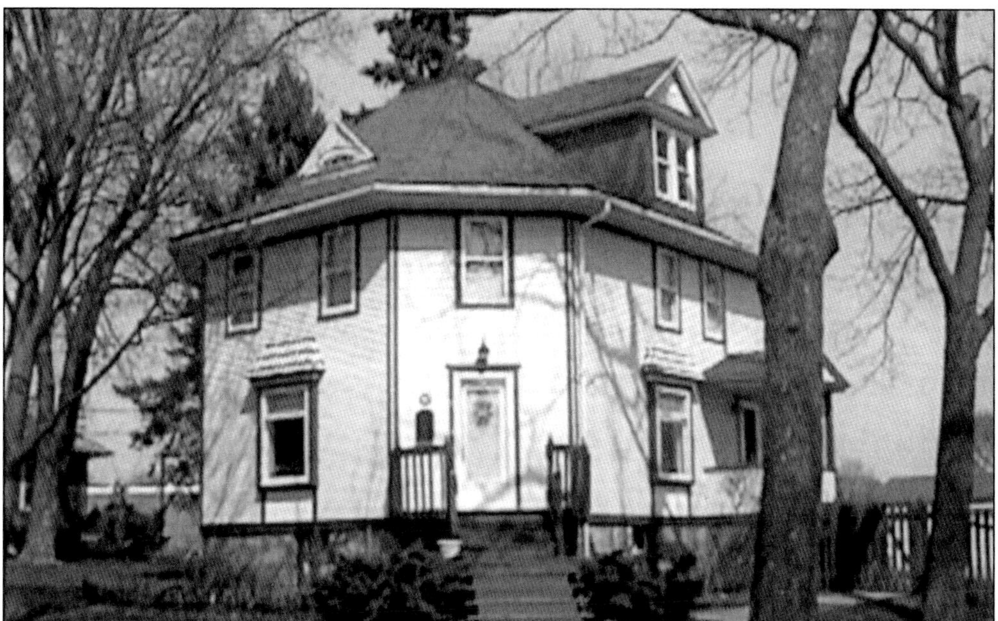

Rob Cagann and wife Felicia Stanczak have no trouble finding the perfect exposure for their houseplants because they have their choice of eight different views. The Bartlett couple owns one of the rare octagon homes still remaining in Illinois today. The clapboard house at 139 S. Eastern was built by Henry Hothan around 1913, was briefly converted into apartments, and is now being restored to its original façade.

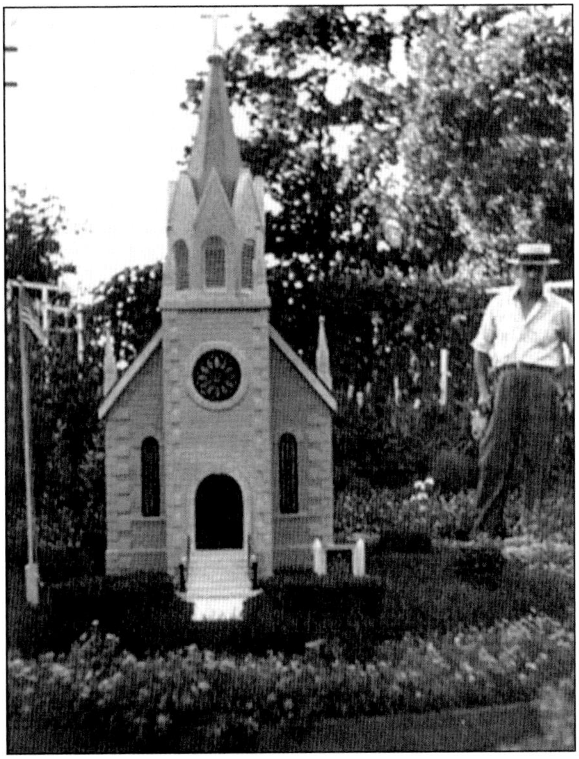

What brought 4,231 people to rural Bartlett in 1939, when the town itself only had a population of 608? It was the Little Stone Church in the Garden, located in the backyard of Martin and Grace Leiseberg Johnson at 210 W. Morse Avenue. Carpenter and master craftsman Martin built the beautiful, 6-foot tall replica of the 1860s-style church, along with a school and blacksmith shop, and opened the garden gates for all to enjoy his miniaturized hamlet.

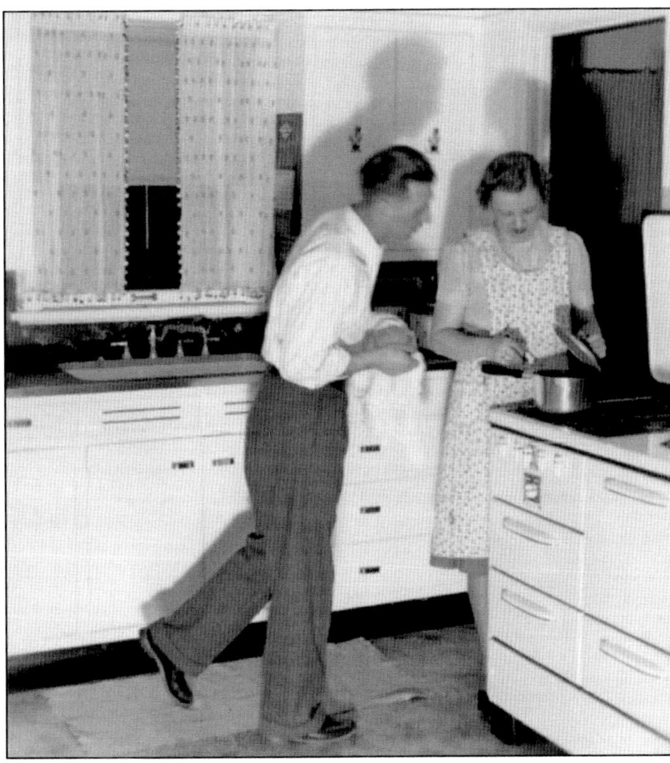

"What's cooking?" young Fred Benicke asks his aproned wife Vernetta in the kitchen of their 1939 custom-built Tudor residence at 143 N. Eastern Avenue. Bartlett business owner and volunteer firefighter "Fritz" and lifelong Bartlett resident Vernetta selected the plans for their dream home from a house and garden magazine.

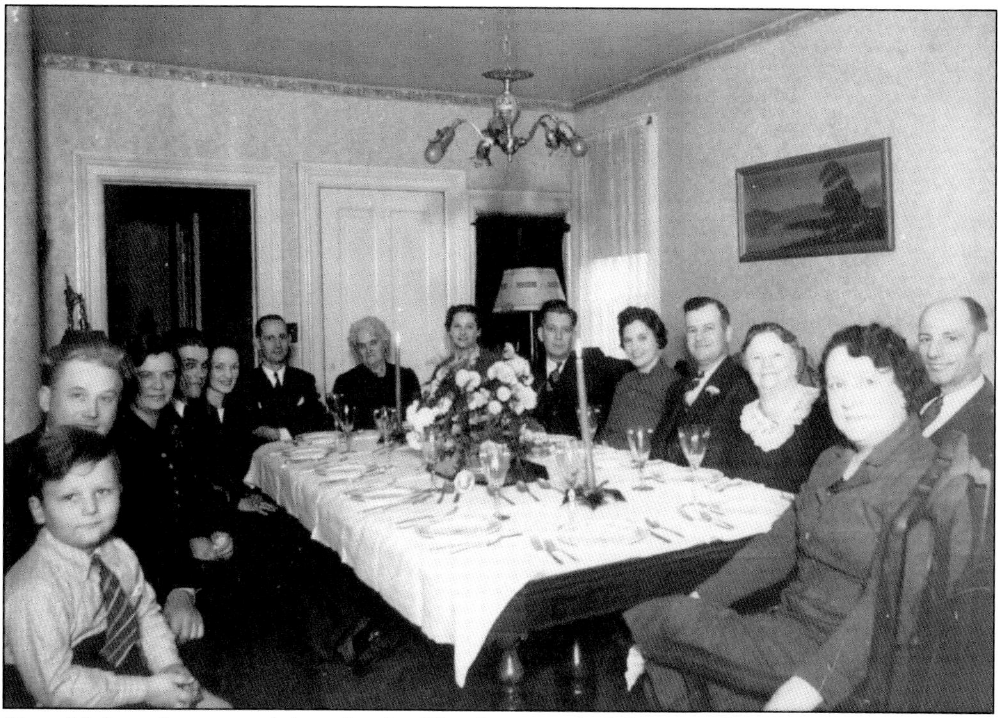

Grateful for relatives and friends, the Thanksgiving holiday was the one time of year that the Baxmanns always set aside for gathering around the table at the family homestead at 400 Oneida Avenue. The house originally belonged to Fred and Anna Baxmann and their nine children. The couple lived their entire married life in the home that still stands today.

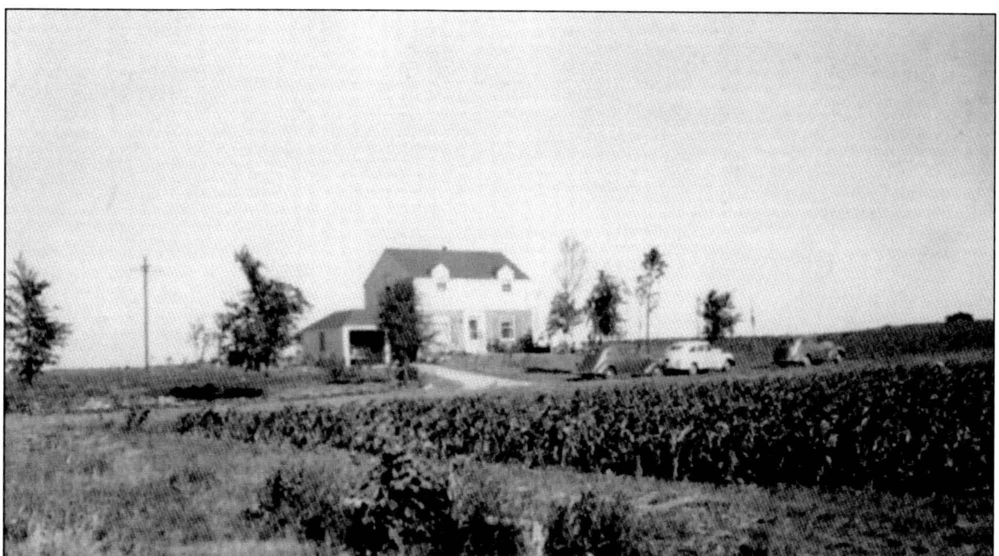

It would be another 25 years before the Giles house, shown here in 1945 shortly after it was built, would be swallowed up in 1971 by new construction for the Bartlett Green subdivision. The home of Tom and Ruth Giles still stands today, among many neighbors, at the corner of North Avenue and Berteau.

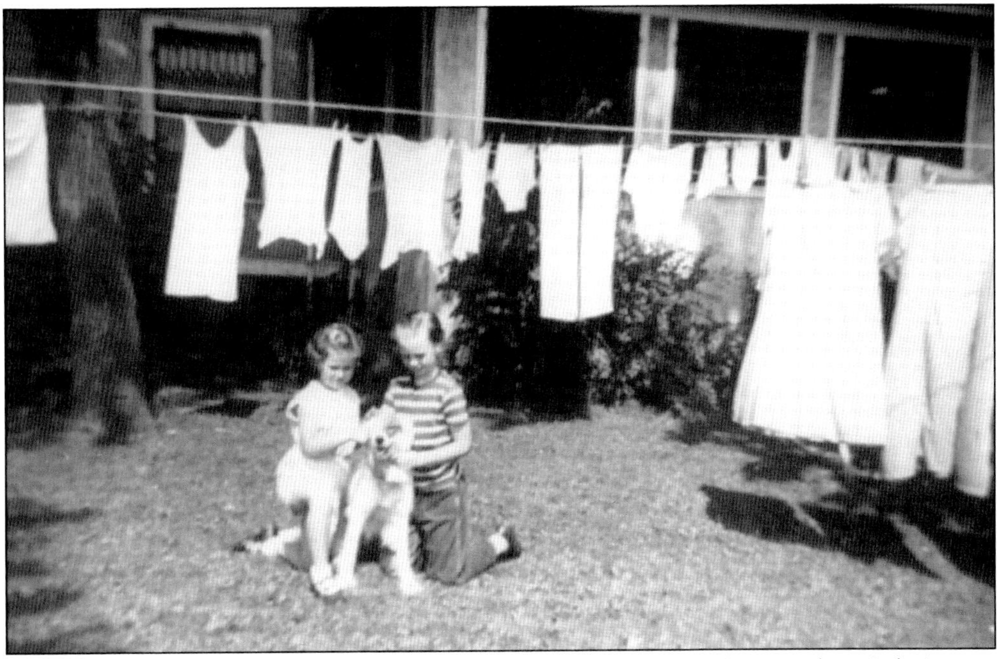

The Ping daughters, Sandra Kay and Jean Ann, collar Spot in their front yard on Oak Avenue before he gets into the family laundry. Bartlett homemakers relied on sunshine and outdoor breezes instead of dryer sheets to give their clothes that just washed freshness.

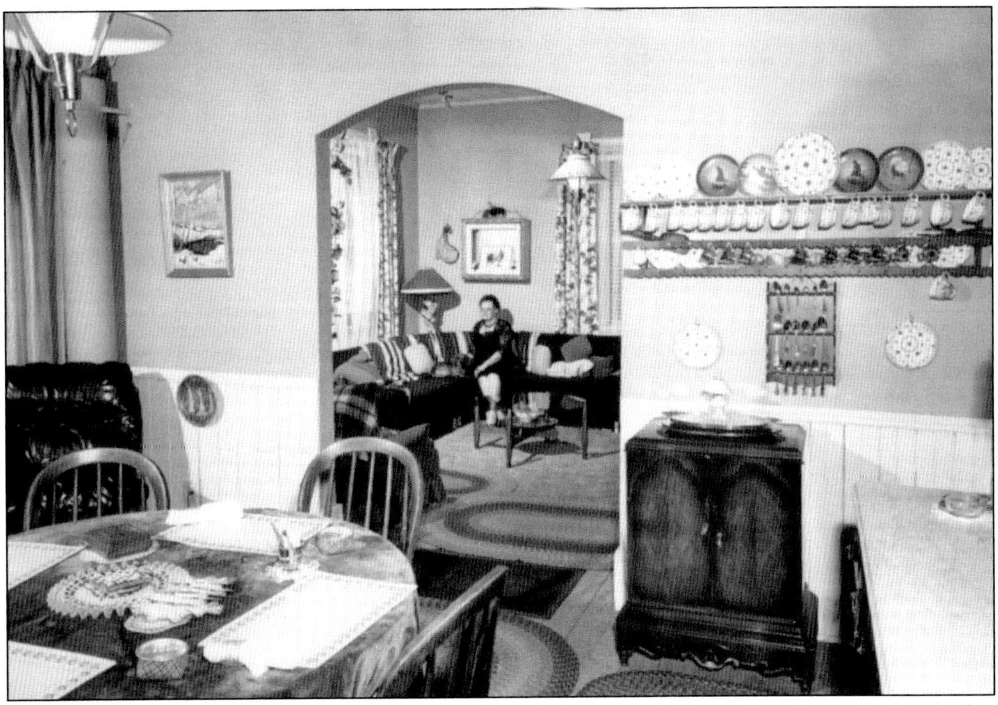

Blue Delft china from her native Norway and braided rugs said "home" at the end of each day to Serena Jensen according to this 1963 photo. Serena only needed to make a short trek from the family-owned Bartlett Tavern to the residence at the rear of the building.

Eight

PRIDE AND PATRIOTISM

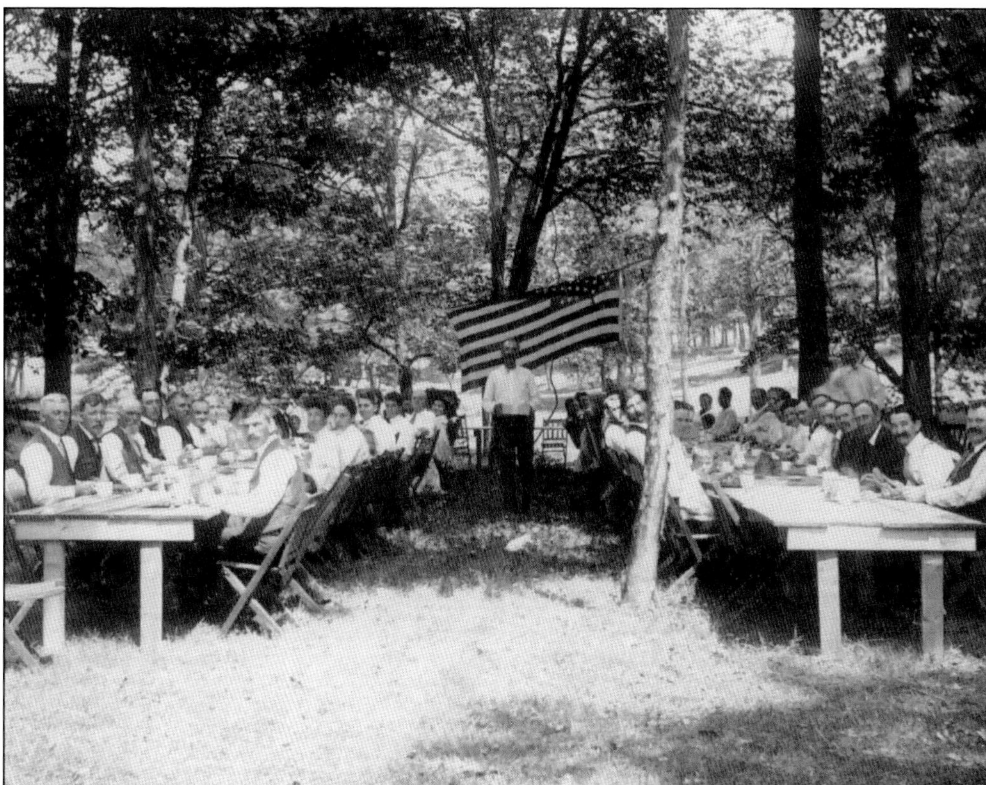

The Fourth of July has always been a holiday for freedom, family, friends, and festivals in the Village of Bartlett. At the turn of the century, Bartlett residents gathered at this popular picnic ground near the downtown depot. An Independence Day picnic would not have been complete without Old Glory at the center of the celebration.

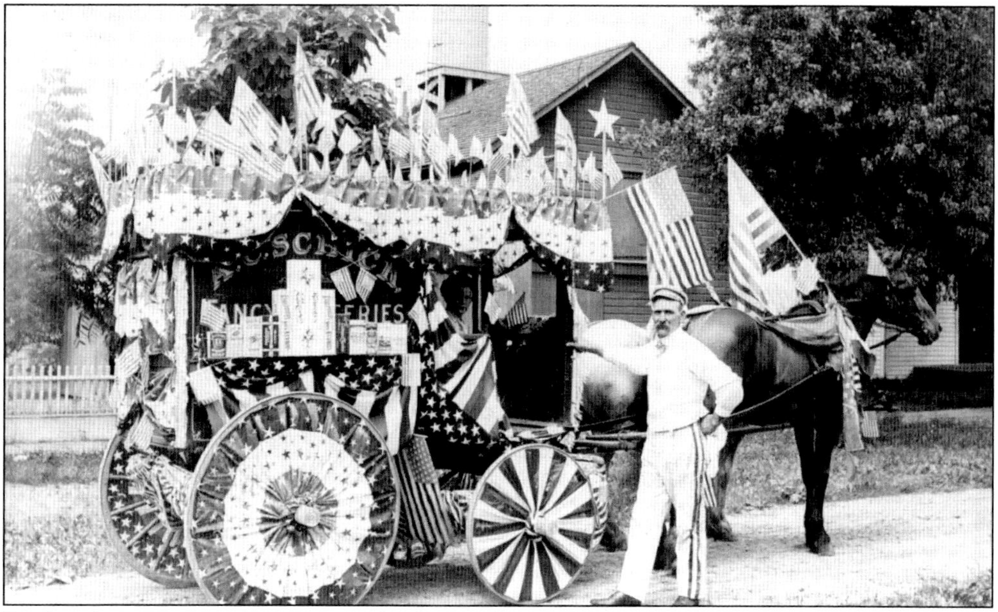

Bartlett businessman August C. Schick proudly displays his delivery wagon festooned with bunting and American flags for an annual Fourth of July parade. Schick was a grocer who ran a general store and was also active in the community. He was elected to serve as a Village Trustee, was a Hanover Township Supervisor and was the first Fire Chief of the Bartlett Volunteer Fire Department in 1898.

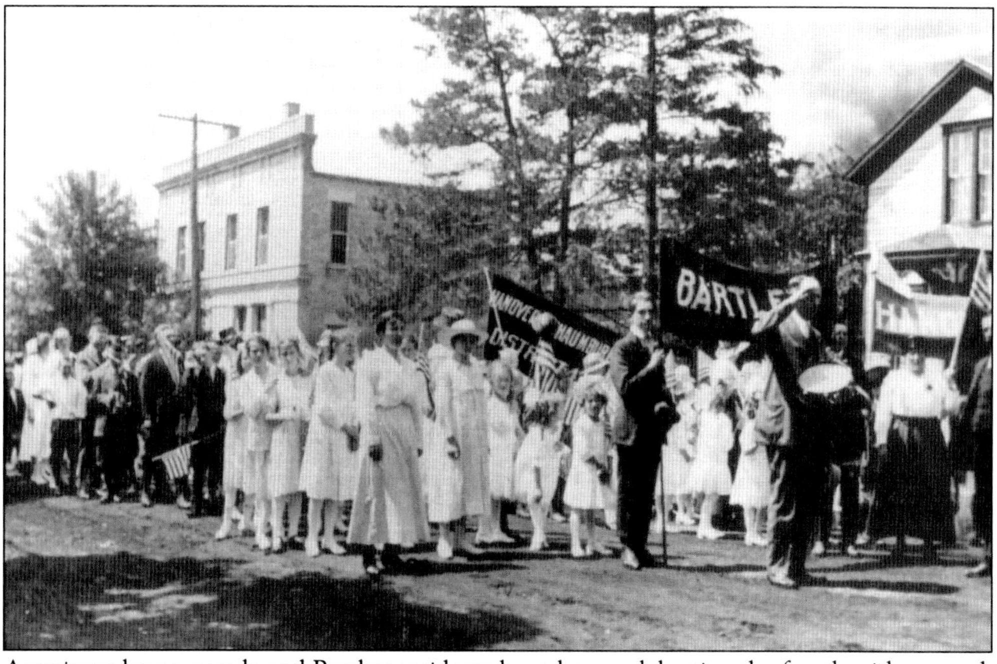

Americans love a parade and Bartlett residents have been celebrating the fourth with a grand, old-fashioned parade since the early 1900s. Marchers would gather at the town hall early in the morning and the local band would lead them down Oak Street to what is now Bartlett Park. An afternoon of food, music, and prominent speakers would cap off the holiday.

In 1868, the 30th of May was designated for the purpose of "strewing with flowers or otherwise decorating the graves of those who died in defense of our country." Early Bartlett residents observed "Decoration Day" by marching in one body to the cemetery and laying bouquets of flowers at the markers of our departed veterans. Today we continue the tradition with our annual Memorial Day Remembrance Walk.

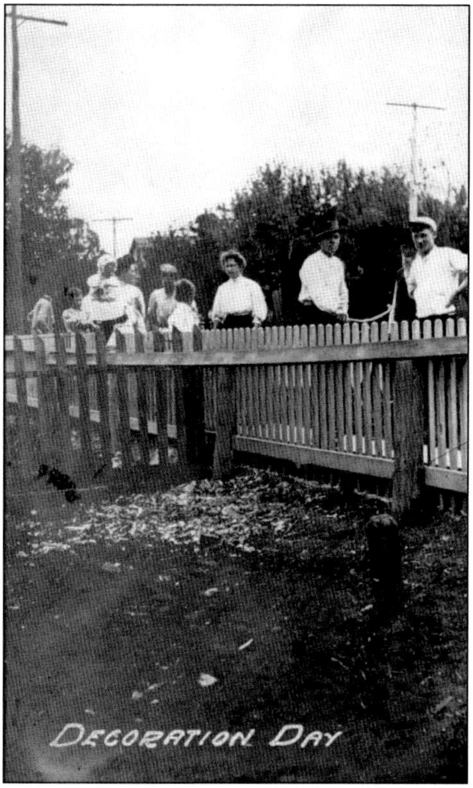

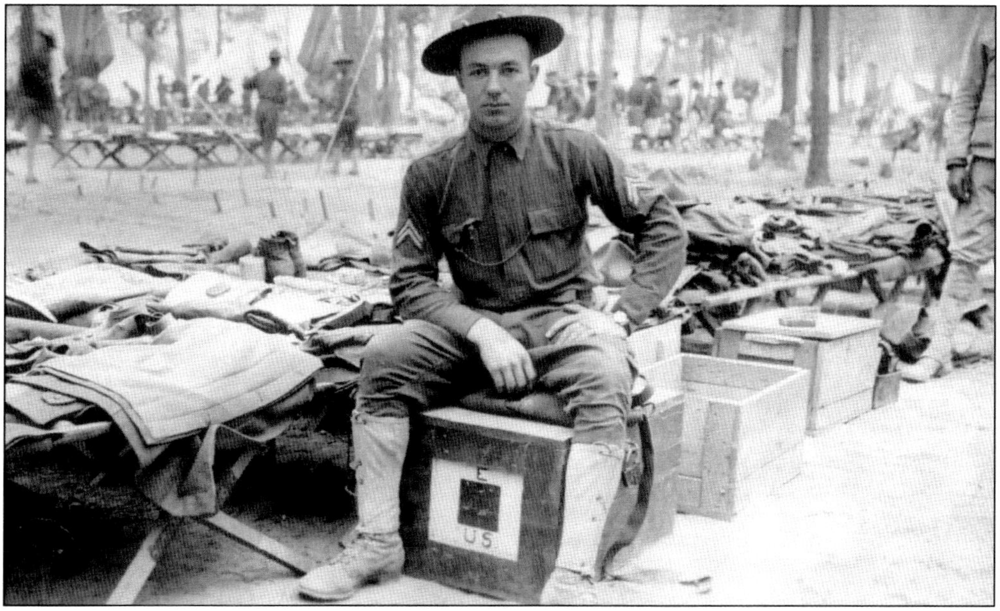

It was with the start of World War I that Bartlett's true patriotism was tried, when many of the town's favorite sons were sent to camps, near and far, to proudly serve our country. Corp. Fred C. Staib, the son of town physician Otto Staib, was stationed at Camp Logan near Houston, Texas. Originally a National Guard Camp, it was turned into an emergency training center during the war.

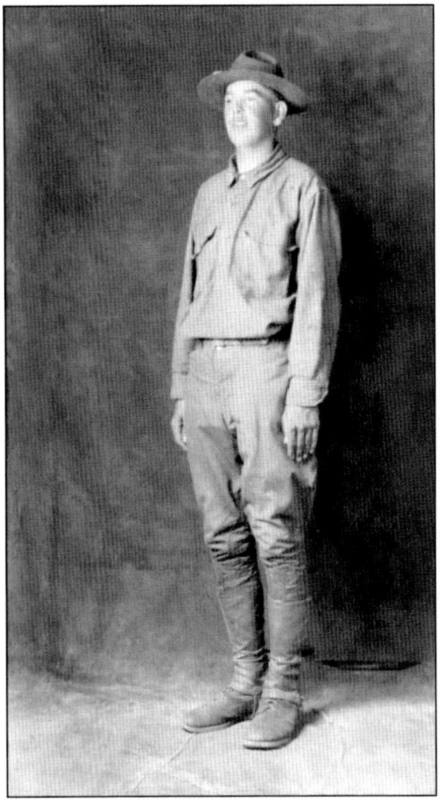

George was just one of the three Wendler brothers who was called to duty during World War I. He was stationed at the Army base in Waco, Texas along with his brother Herman. Fred served in the Navy. After the war, George returned to Bartlett to serve his community as Fire Chief and Village Trustee.

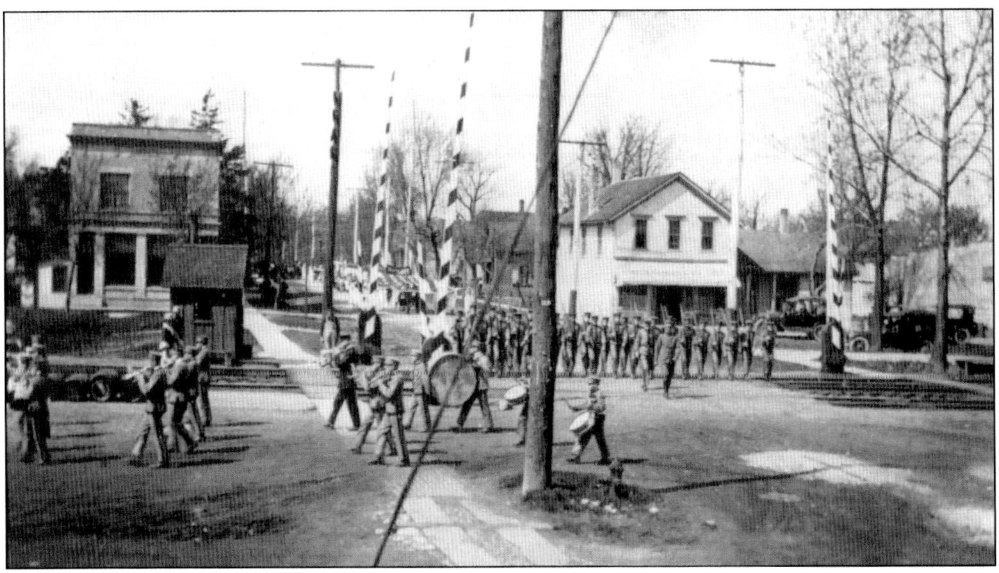

In 1918, on the 11th hour of the 11th day in the 11th month, America celebrated the end of the war and the signing of the armistice. Armistice Day was named in 1926, around the time of this Bartlett Armistice Day parade. If the hope had been realized that World War I was "the War to end all Wars," November 11 might still be Armistice Day rather than Veteran's Day. War soon broke out again in Europe.

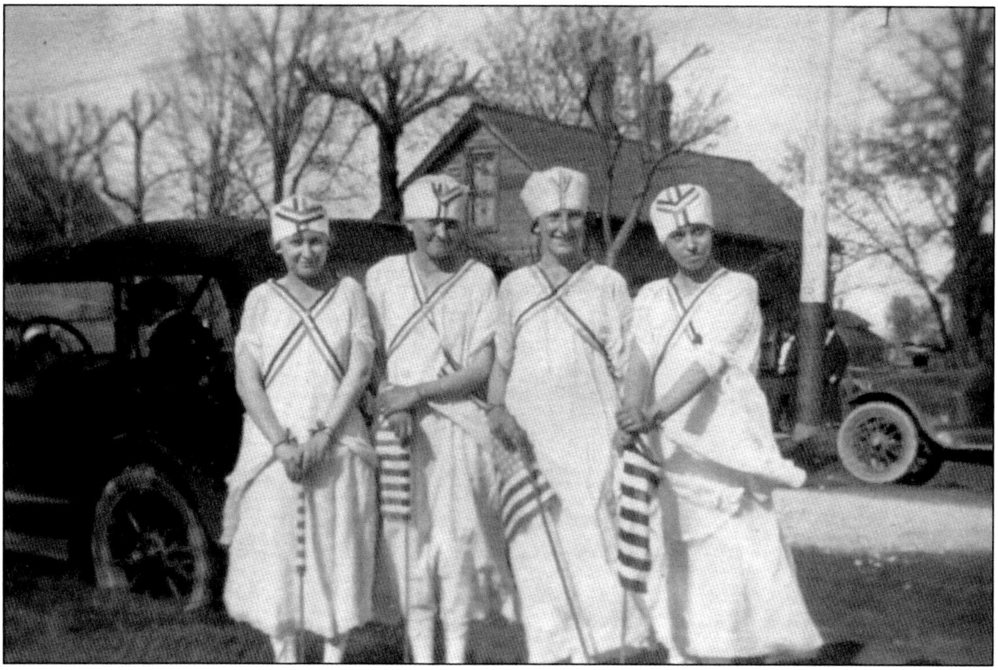

Patriotic pals, Grace Leiseberg, Esther ?, Estella Schnadt, and Clara ?, garbed in red, white and blue stand ready to unfurl their stars and stripes to celebrate the dedication of the new American flag in town.

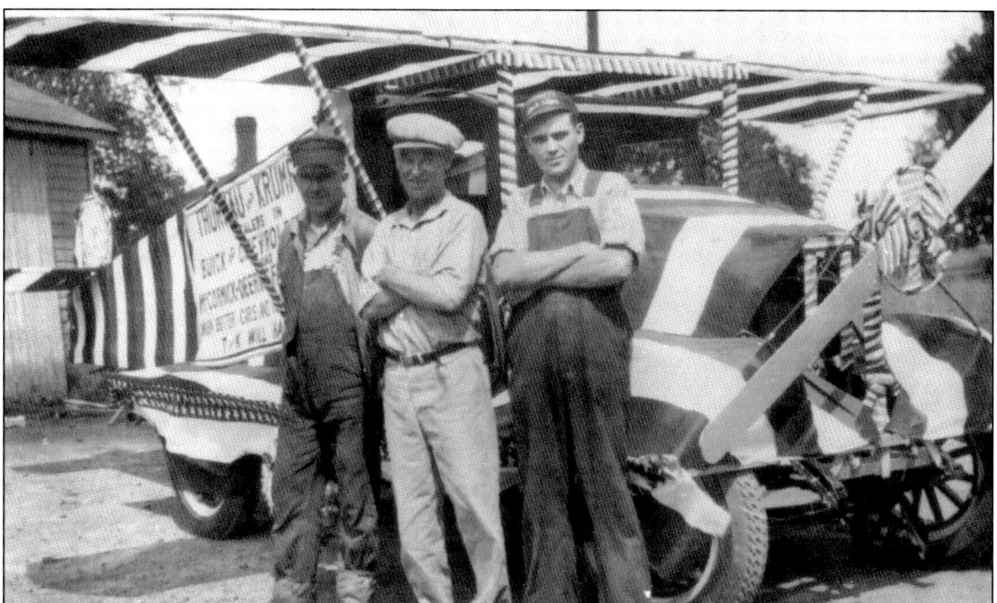

Businessmen Edward D. Thurnau and Edmund G. Krumfuss hoped the all-American "Spirit of Bartlett" would encourage residents to "fly over" and visit their car and farm implement dealership located on Main Street, after the year's Fourth of July festivities ended.

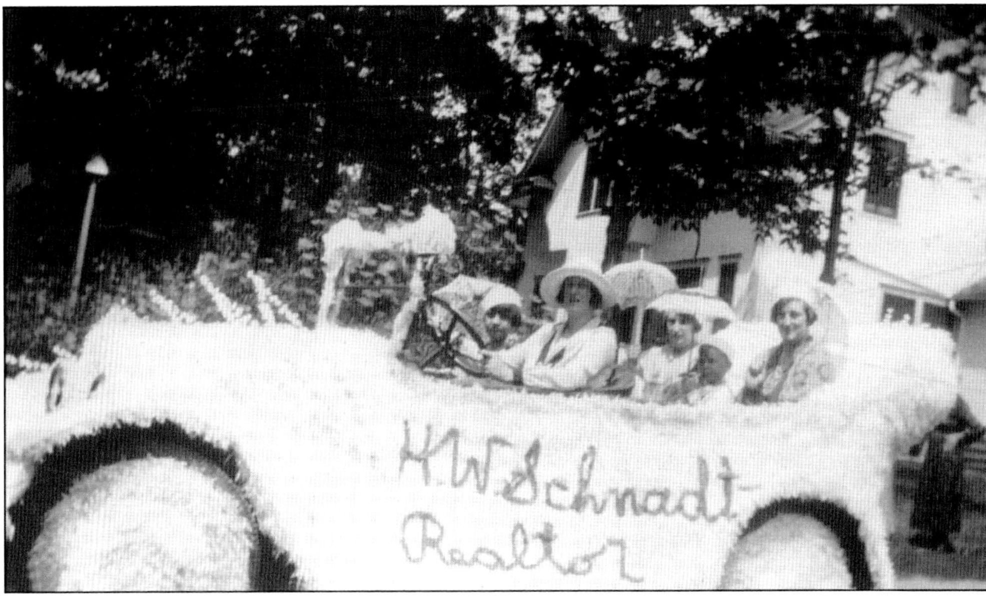

The three Schnadt daughters and their young companions were proud to steer this first prize winning "roadster" along Bartlett's Fourth of July parade route in 1926. Father Herman's realty office was located on Oak Avenue. Lace parasols and wide-brimmed hats shielded the young ladies from the hot summer sun.

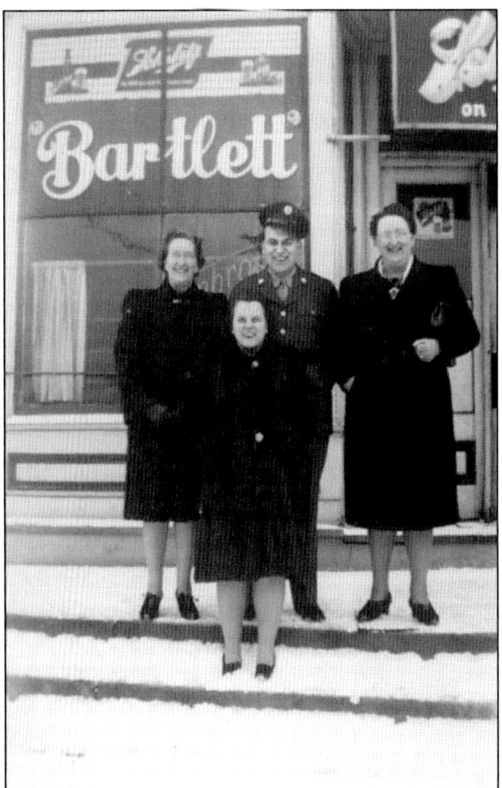

Earl Humbracht was the first man to be drafted into the Armed Forces from Bartlett in 1941. He and brother Paul Heinberg were two of the more than 25 young men from the Village to serve. A technical sergeant in the Army, Earl was in the European Theater and was discharged in 1946. Home on furlough, Earl visits with aunt Estella Schnadt, stepsister Dorothy Heinberg, and aunt Luella Schnadt Lange at the Bartlett Tavern.

Best buddies Gerald Faber and Arthur Atchison went to the enlistment office together to sign up for the Navy during World War II, claiming their spot among "Bartlett's Greatest Generation." After the war, Gerry returned to Bartlett to join his father in the family business, Faber Construction Inc. He also served as a trustee for the Fire Protection District and the Village.

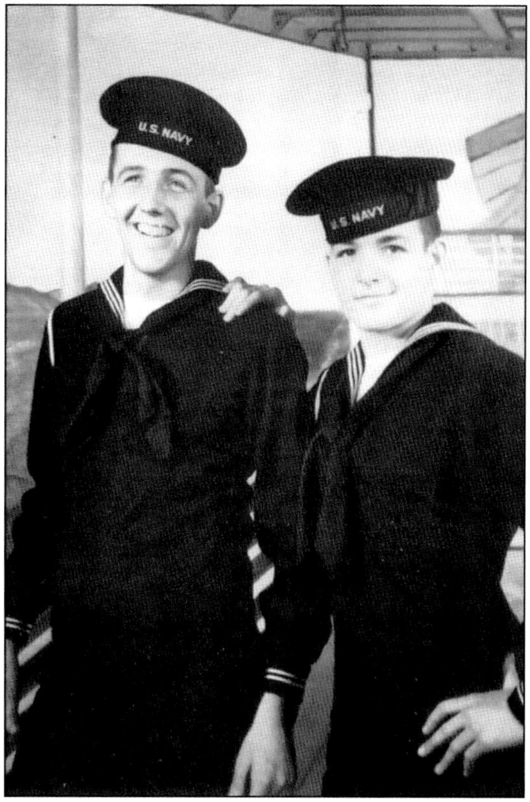

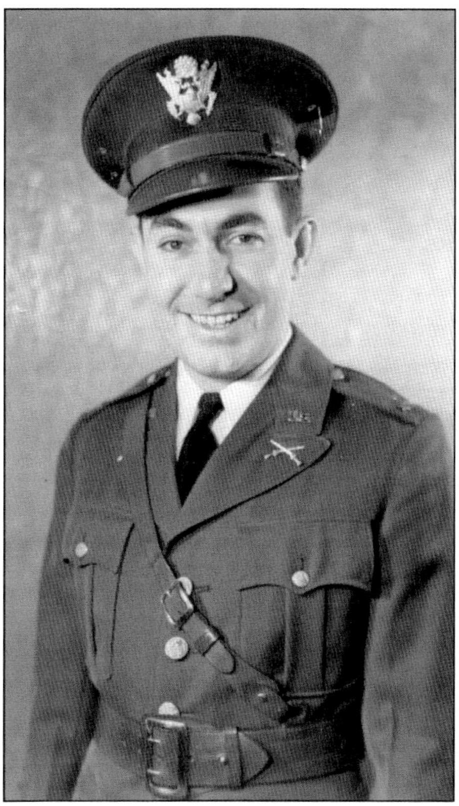

Lt. Alfred Regenburg was awarded several Purple Hearts and the Bronze Star for bravery during World War II. He was in the Invasion of Normandy, Battle of Bastonne, and the Battle of the Bulge. He returned to Bartlett with shrapnel remaining in his leg. He went on to head the Bartlett Plan Commission and served as president of the Lions Club from 1949 to 1950.

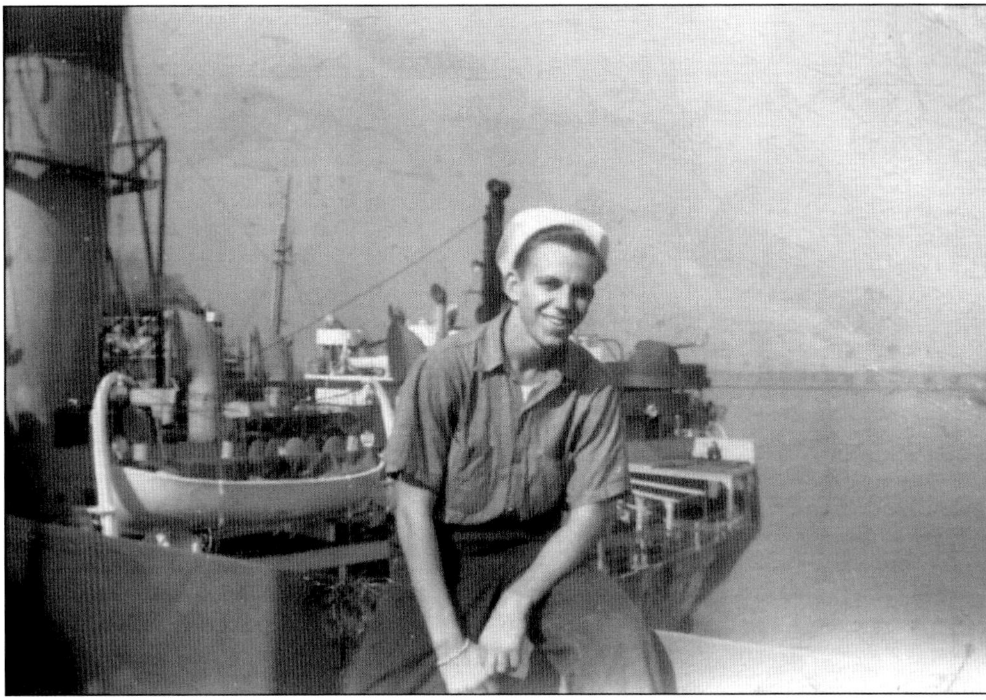

His original enlistment papers were stamped 4F because he was missing fingers after a work-related accident, but that didn't deter young Wally Vlasak from serving his country during World War II. Wally hid his disability and joined the Merchant Marines. Brothers Edward and George served in the Army. Wally returned home to volunteer as a Bartlett firefighter for 20 years.

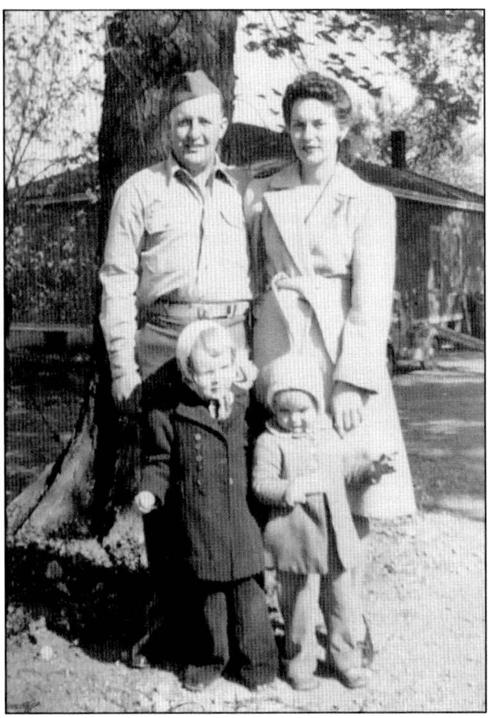

World War II was a war that not only called our young sons and brothers but also our heads of households, our husbands, and fathers. Lifelong Bartlett resident Frank Danner left his wife Dorothy and daughters Deanna Gail and Barbara Sue to serve in the U.S. Army Air Force from 1944 to 1946. He returned to Bartlett to work for a hometown company, Flexonics. He and Dorothy were blessed with four grandchildren.

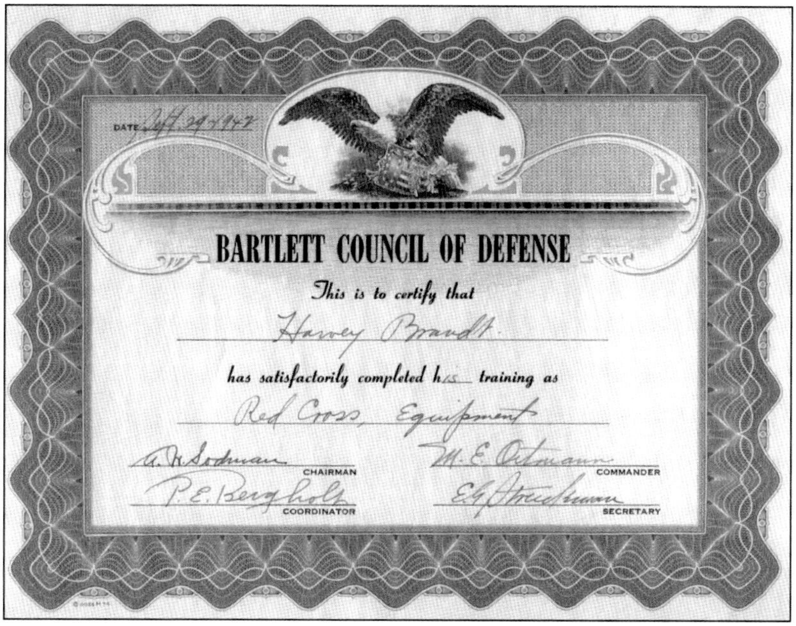
DATE Sept 29 1942

BARTLETT COUNCIL OF DEFENSE

This is to certify that

Harvey Brandt

has satisfactorily completed his training as

Red Cross, Equipment

A. W. Sodman — CHAIRMAN

COMMANDER

P. E. Bergholz — COORDINATOR

SECRETARY

On November 17, 1941, A.W. Sodman, President of the Village Board, called a meeting of representatives of the various civic, fraternal, and religious organizations of Bartlett to organize, under state law, a local chapter of the National Defense Council. The Bartlett Council of Defense recruited and trained more than 70 residents to conduct rubber scrap drives and to lead the preparedness effort by acting as auxiliary firemen and policemen, air raid wardens, messengers, rationing board members, and volunteers in the local chapter of the Red Cross. Defense helmets, gas masks, and night sticks were issued in preparedness for an enemy attack on our soil. The Village Board also established an emergency defense fund in the amount of $50, authorized blackouts and air raid protection, moved to instruct the local citizenry on the handling of incensing bombs, and passed a victory garden ordinance.

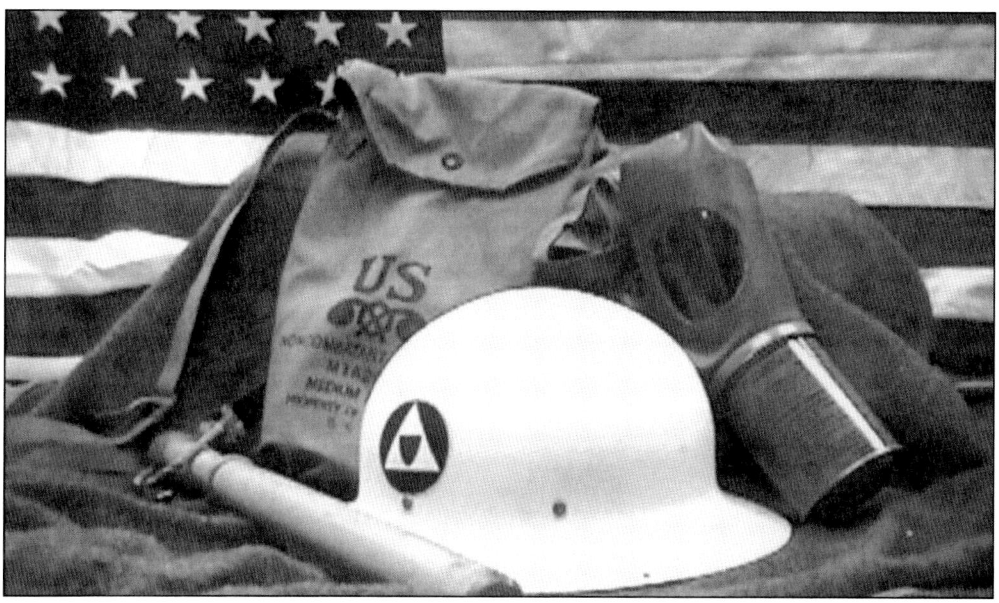

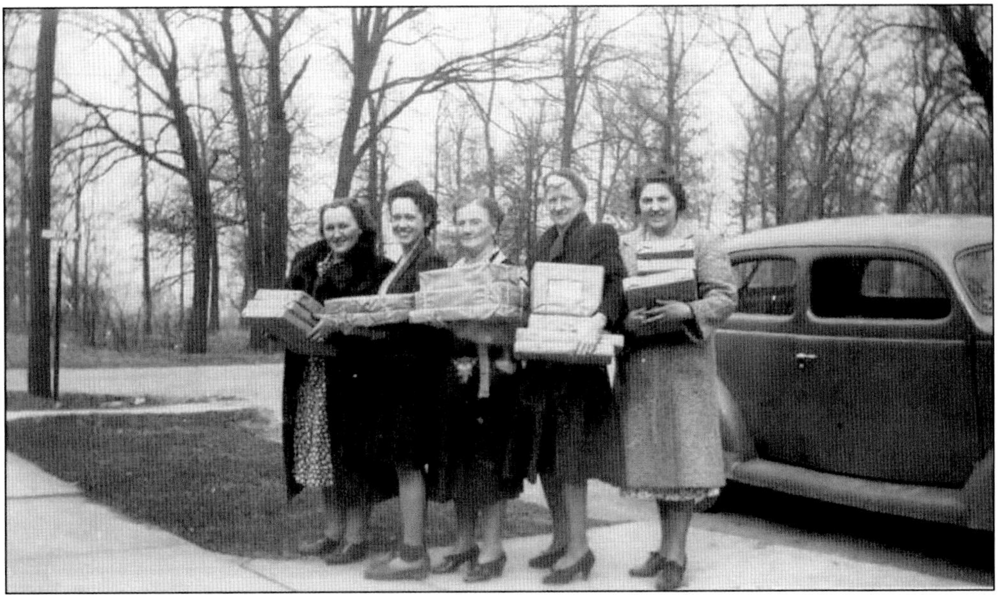

While Bartlett boys endured the hardships of war, their friends, families, and neighbors supported them with prayers, letters, and care packages. The Bartlett Woman's Club (above) was quick to help with the war effort. In 1941, they held a tea with "a bundle for Britain" as the admission fee. By 1942, the club was purchasing war bonds and packing boxes for overseas. "Cookies, candies and smokes made an attractive box." Every small deed counted, whether it was rolling 900 surgical dressings, rationing sugar, sharing "war recipes, or saving tin cans and worn hose.

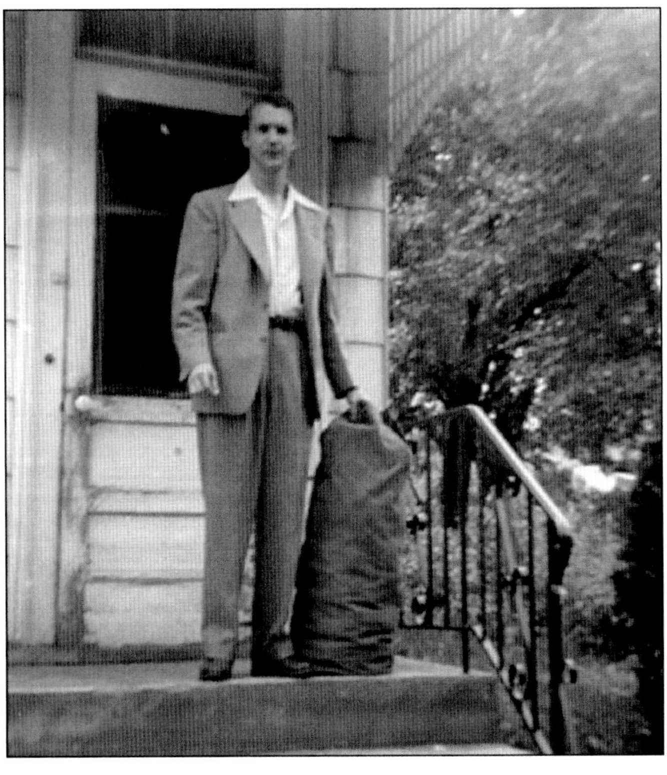

World War II Petty Officer Eugene Haase came home from the Pacific long enough to marry his wartime sweetheart Violet Jensen before being recalled by the Navy in 1951 to serve during the Korean conflict. For the third time in less than 50 years, Bartlett watched its best and bravest pack their duffel bags and ship out to perform the ultimate act of duty for their country.

Nine

Worship and Remembrance

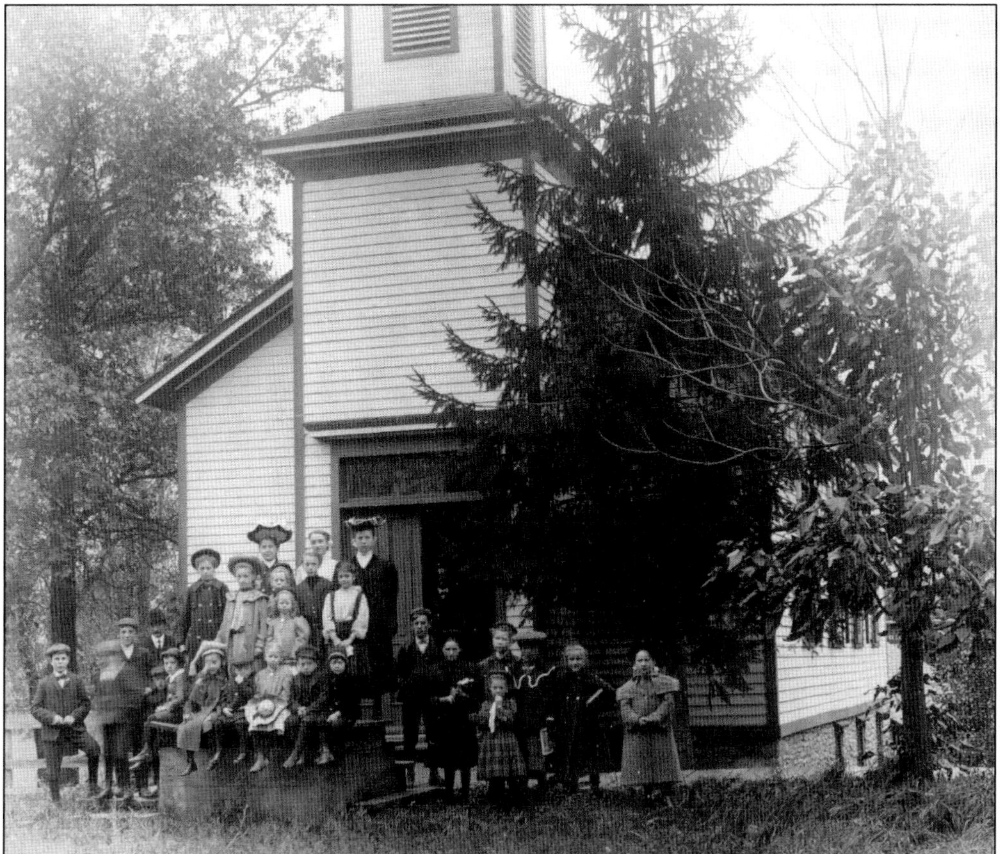

Town founder Luther Bartlett took care to set aside land for the basic foundations of a new community—a school and a church. Religious services were originally held above Sayer's store. In 1879, the church of Wayne Center was abandoned and the building itself was moved to Oneida and Hickory, the site donated by Bartlett. By the early 1900s, the Congregational Church was disbanded due to the large influx of German immigrants who established their own congregation.

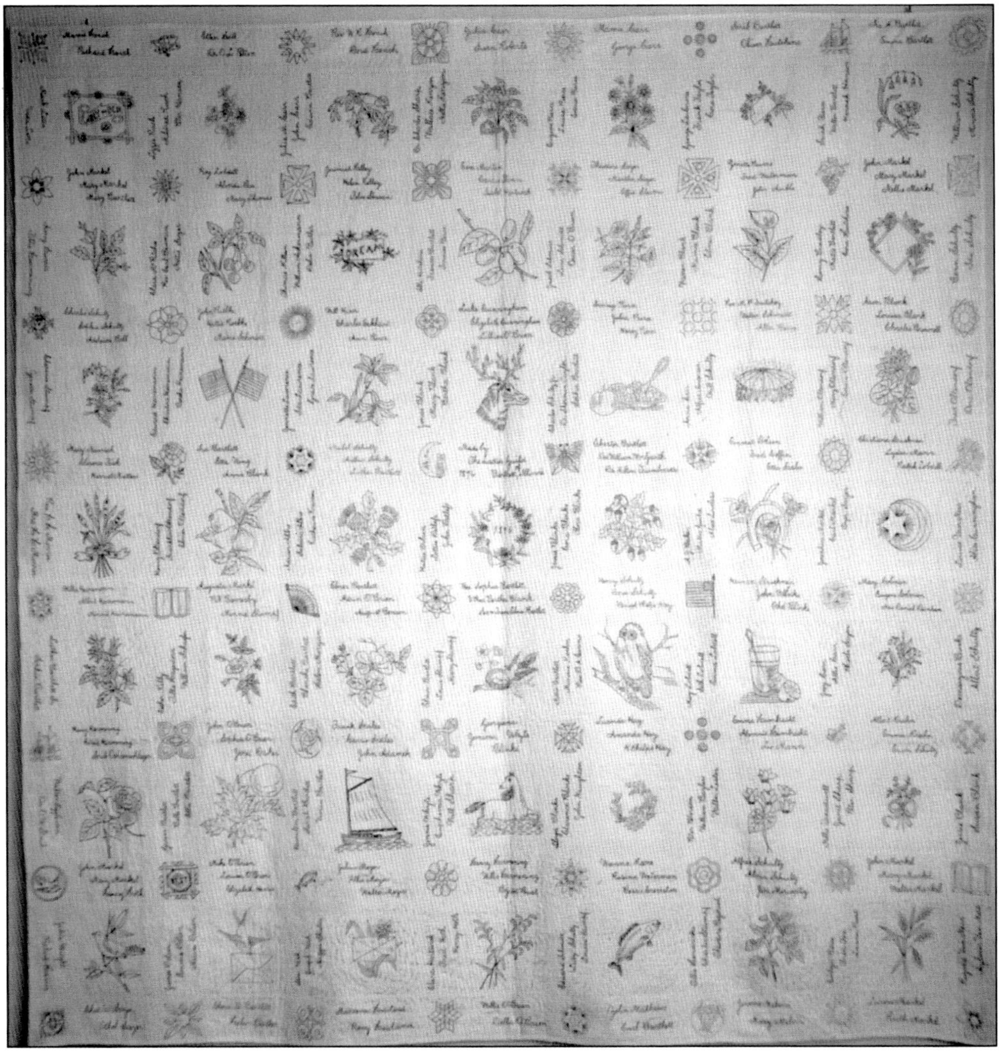

When the Ladies Guild of the Congregational Church of Bartlett began stitching a fund-raising quilt in 1896, little did they know that it would one day hang among the Picassos, Dalis, and Monets at the Art Institute of Chicago. The Bartlett Album quilt bears 49 names, many of them from Bartlett's founding families, who donated one dollar each to have their surnames sewn into the fabric. Wisconsin Latin teacher Alice Petracchi, daughter of the church's minister, Rev. R. M. Merritt, had kept this wonderful piece of folk art in a cupboard drawer and only used it when a Bartlett friend came calling. Petracchi donated the red and white quilt to the Art Institute where it was part of a permanent exhibit during the late 1970s and was labeled as follows: American, Illinois, Bartlett, Bedcover, 1896, cotton, plain weave; embroidered; quilted; backed with cotton, plain weave, 204.2 x 200.4 cm, Gift of Mrs. Luigi Petracchi in memory of The Reverend and Mrs. Robert F. Merritt, 1978.335. photograph © 2002, The Art Institute of Chicago, All Rights Reserved.

Immanuel Evangelical Church, today known as Immanuel United Church of Christ, is Bartlett's oldest continuing congregation. Since they had no church of their faith in Bartlett, the German-speaking people appealed to Pastor Gustav Hagemann of Ontarioville (now Hanover Park) to assist them in organizing a local congregation. Planning began in earnest in August and September of 1891. Mr. August C. Schick, one of the charter members of the congregation, accepted the contract to build the 32 by 50 foot church for the sum of $1,825.

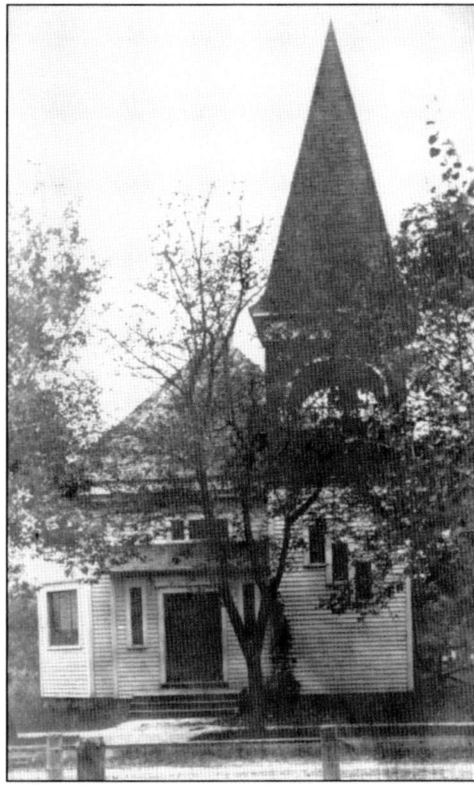

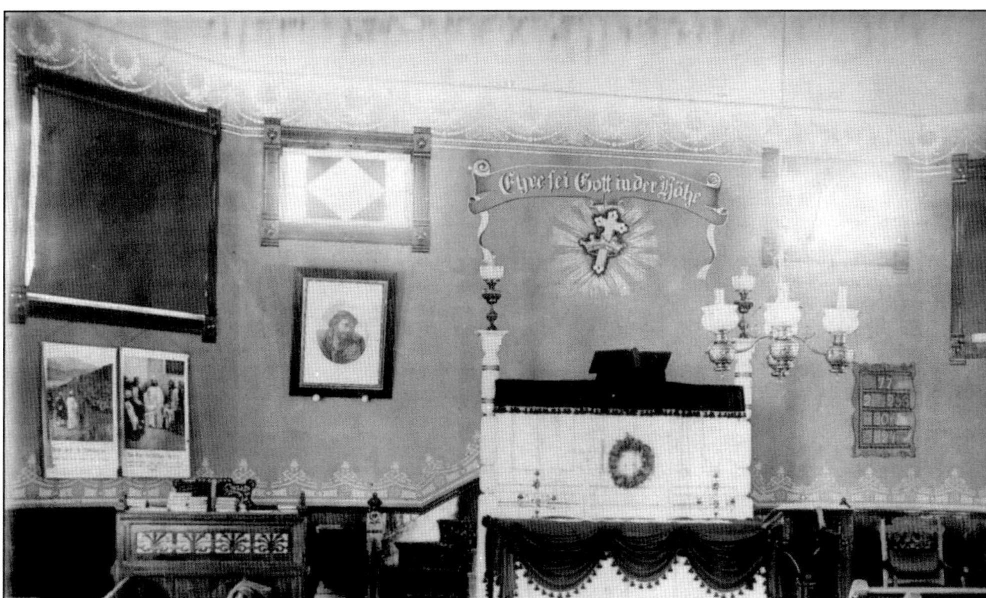

Incorporation papers were taken out by the congregation on September 21, 1891 and on October 1, the cornerstone of the new house of worship was fittingly laid by Pastor Hagemann. In 1893, the Frauen Verein (Ladies Aid) furnished the church and purchased a 609-pound bronze bell. The painted banner over the alter translates from German to read "Glory to God in the Highest."

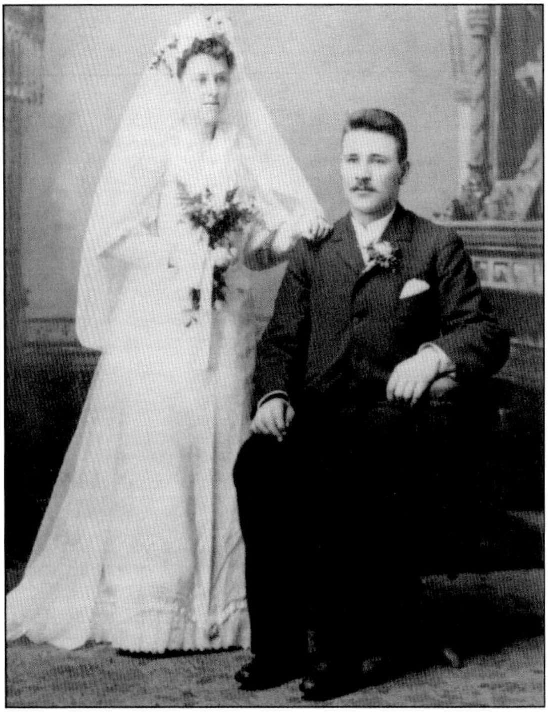

Gottlieb (George) Schick and Ida Tatge were the first couple to be married at Immanuel Evangelical Church on February 9, 1893. It wasn't until the mid 19th century that the all-white wedding dress such as Ida's became fashionable. Up until then a bride simply wore her best dress, regardless of its color. The young couple welcomed their first child George Christoph Fritz August Schick on May 2, 1895.

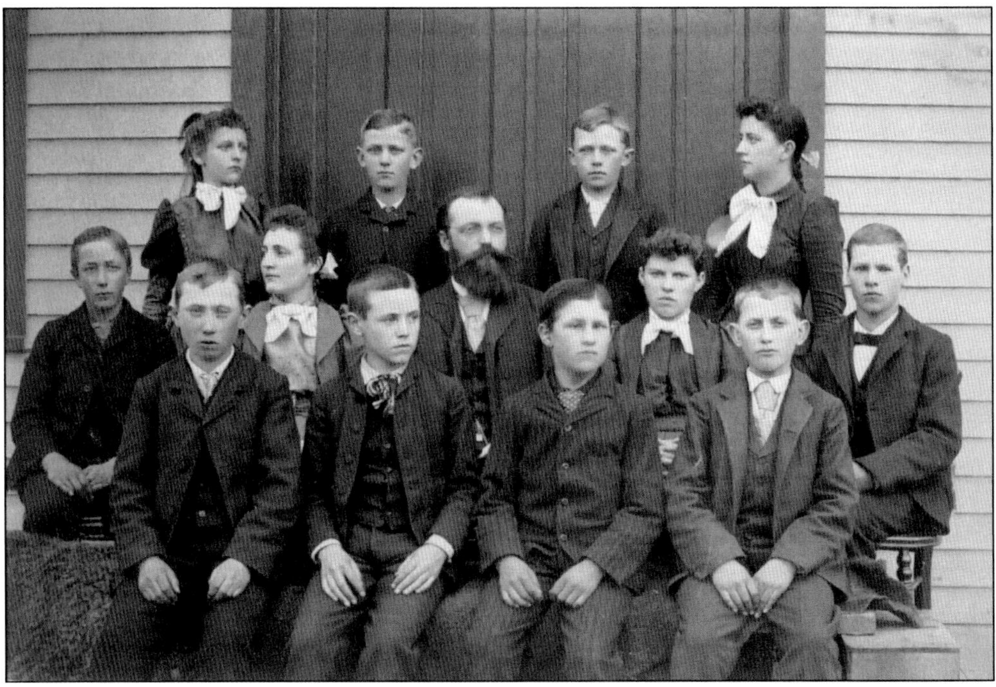

Pastor Carl Baumann of Texas came to service as the second minister of Immanuel Evangelical Church in 1892. This is the first class of young people to be confirmed under his tutelage on April 9, 1893. The congregation developed rapidly under Baumann's capable leadership. He organized a Sunday school, dedicated the parochial school, and built a parsonage adjacent to the church in 1899. The congregation reluctantly accepted his resignation in 1913.

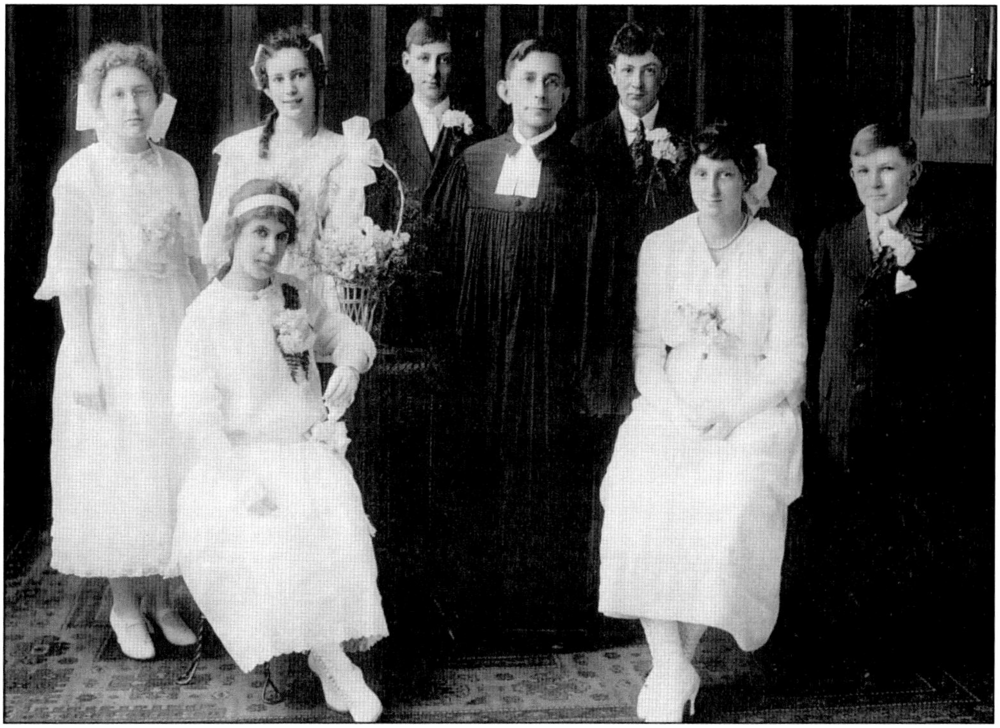

For many Bartlett families, the church was a truly essential part of their lives from the cradle to the grave. Immanuel Evangelical was the church that played this important role in Gracie Leiseberg's life, shown standing on the far left in this 1917 confirmation photo. Gracie Alvina was baptized at Immanuel Evangelical in 1901, married Martin Johnson of Elgin there on October 31, 1925, and was laid to rest by her church in 1996. She was active in the Ladies Guild and was a member of the Golden Agers, who met at the church. Major life events were beautifully documented by church records such as Gracie's marriage certificate shown below.

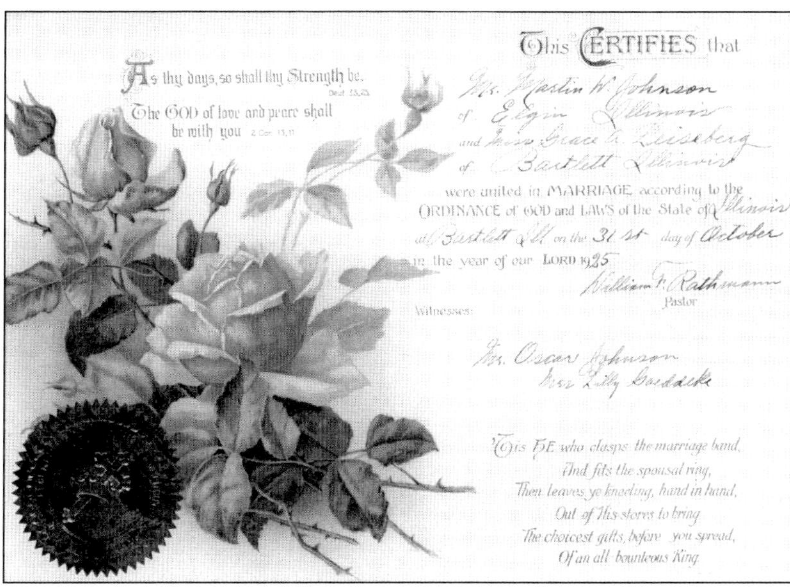

As thy days, so shall thy Strength be. Deut. 33.25

The GOD of love and peace shall be with you 2 Cor. 13.11

This CERTIFIES that
Mr. Martin W. Johnson
of Elgin Illinois
and Miss Grace A. Leiseberg
of Bartlett Illinois
were united in MARRIAGE according to the
ORDINANCE of GOD and LAWS of the State of Illinois
at Bartlett Ill. on the 31st day of October
in the year of our LORD 1925
William F. Rathmann
Pastor

Witnesses:
Mrs. Oscar Johnson
Miss Lilly Goeddeke

'Tis HE who clasps the marriage band,
And fits the spousal ring,
Then leaves ye kneeling, hand in hand,
Out of His stores to bring
The choicest gifts, before you spread,
Of an all-bounteous King.

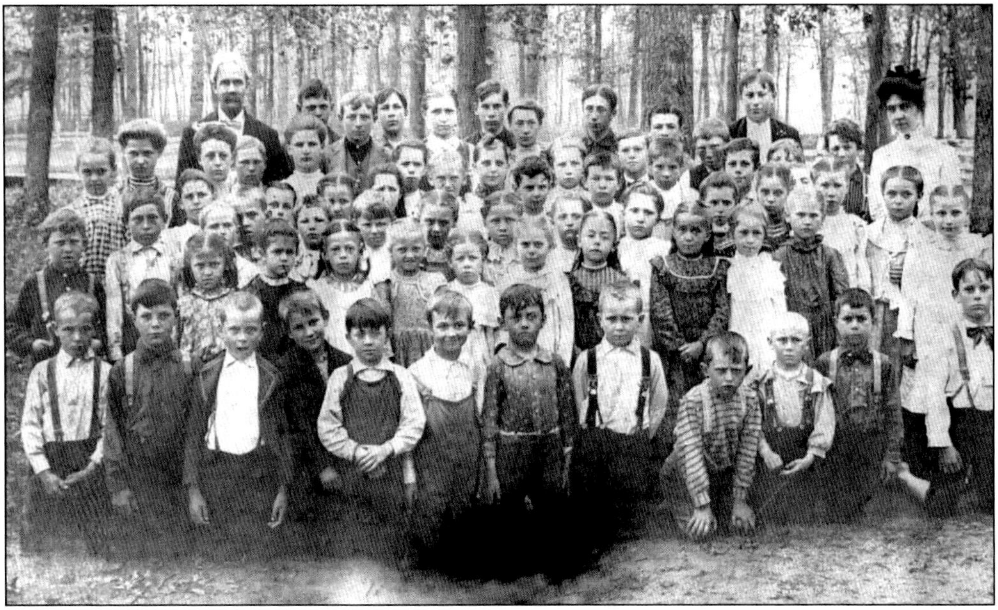

By 1900, 73 percent of the residents of Bartlett were either natives of the old country or children of German-born parents. Immanuel Evangelical Church leaders decided to build a parochial school in 1892 to address the particular needs of their congregation. In addition to religious instruction, the children received German language and heritage lessons in order to keep the old world culture alive in the next generation.

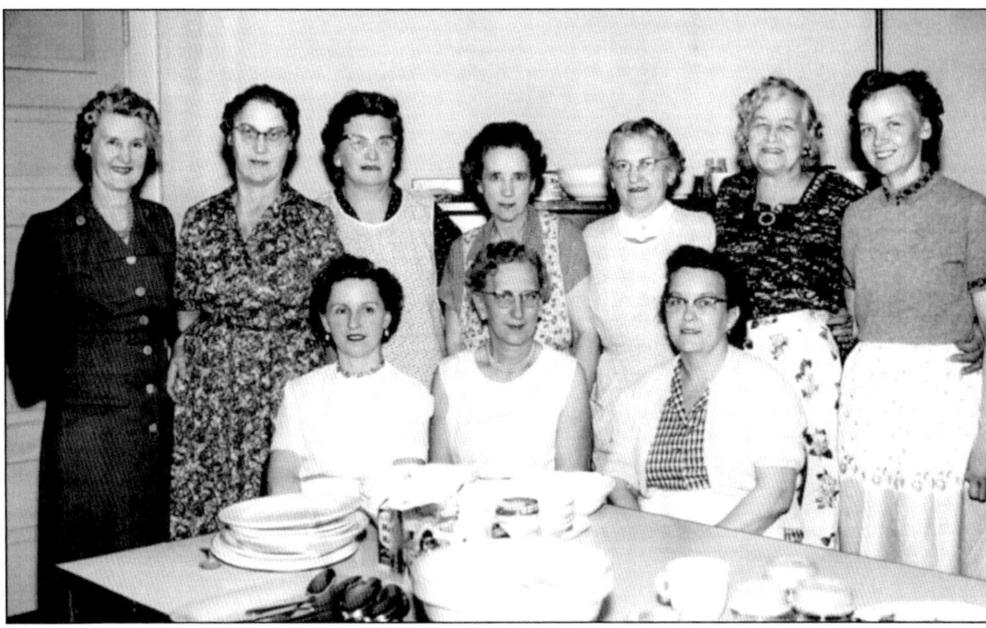

In September 1891, nine ladies came together to organize the Ladies Aid for Immanuel Evangelical Church. They were the charter members of the group whose purpose it was to provide Christian fellowship, instruction, inspiration, and cooperation in service to the local church and community. Their spirit of dedication was passed from mother to daughter through the Eisenhower era, shown here, and continues to exist today.

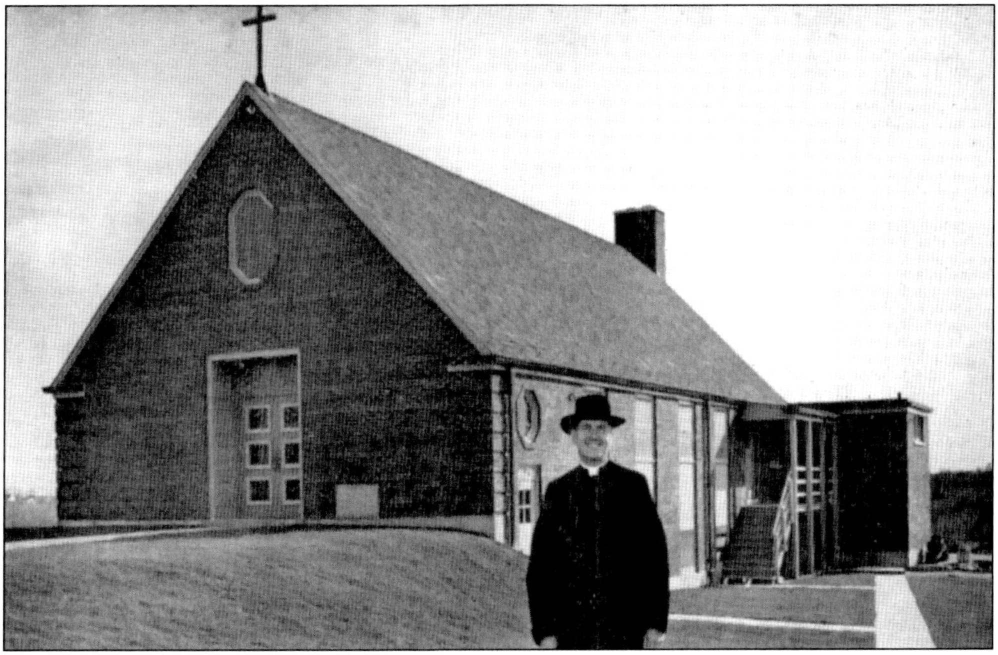

There was a Catholic presence in Bartlett for many years before the cornerstone was laid on May 30, 1950, for the "Little Church," the first church building of St. Peter Damian Parish at North Avenue and Crest. In 1929, a small group of Catholic women founded Our Lady of Victory Sodality to combat anti-Catholic prejudice fostered by the reported activities of the Ku Klux Klan in town. But the first Catholic Mass was not said in Bartlett until June 14, 1942 when Rev. Peter Gall celebrated Mass for 53 people in the home of Mr. and Mrs. Albert Buerger. Weekly Masses continued in the Buerger home for almost a year, until he completed a chapel (shown below) within the factory later known as Setko Fasteners Inc. In 1949, Rev. Thomas B. Horne was sent to form St. Peter Damian Parish and act as the first pastor. Father Horne (pictured above outside the "Little Church") guided the congregation for almost 24 years, retiring in 1973.

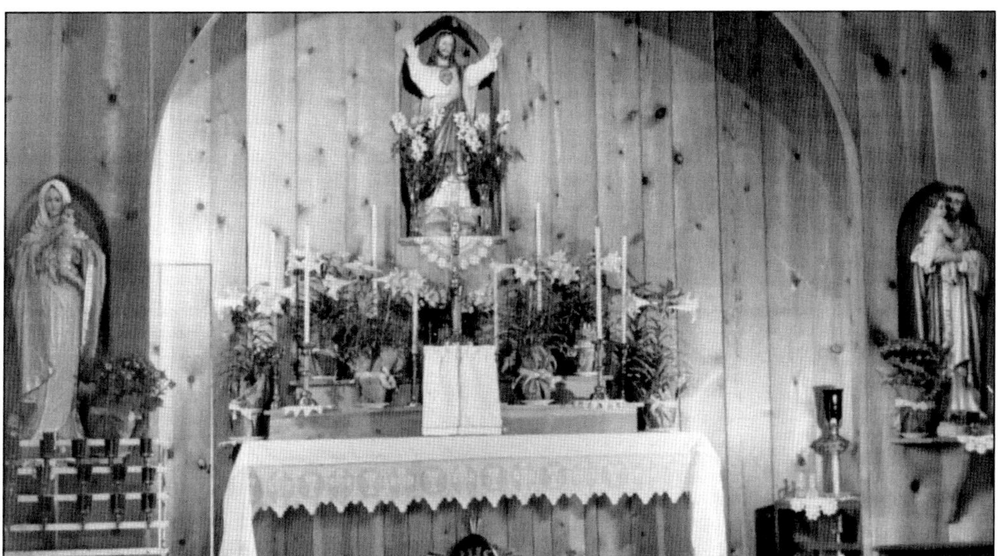

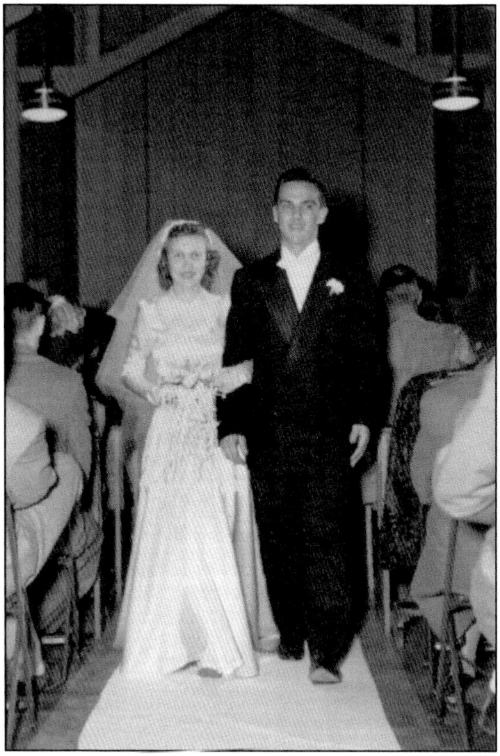

St. Peter Damian Church was not yet completed when Leona Hinz and Robert Mydill were the first couple to be married in the new church building on October 14, 1950. For lack of pews, guests at the wedding sat in folding chairs. As the story is told, Father Thomas B. Horne took a break from landscaping duties to perform the ceremony and came into the church with mud and grass clippings still clinging to his shoes.

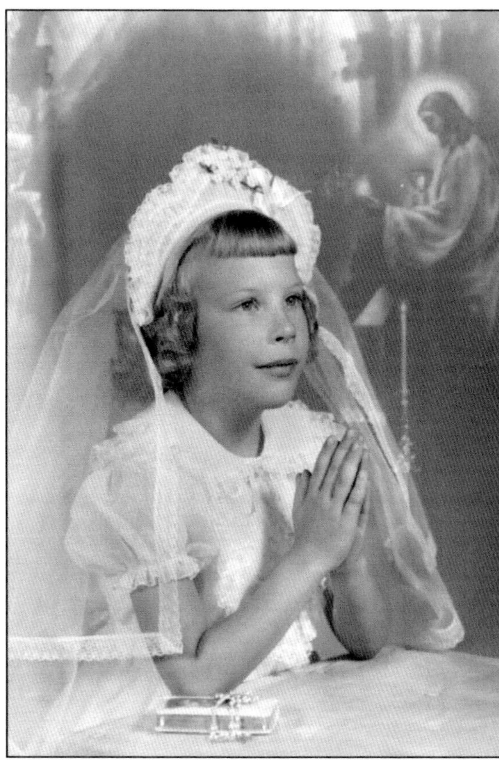

On May 13, 1956, Theresa Rauhut Stickling dressed in the traditional white dress and veil and was ready to receive First Holy Communion with her Catechism classmates at St. Peter Damian's Little Church. Because the parish population was still growing, this joyful sacrament was not administered annually, so Theresa's younger sister Janis also received Communion the same year.

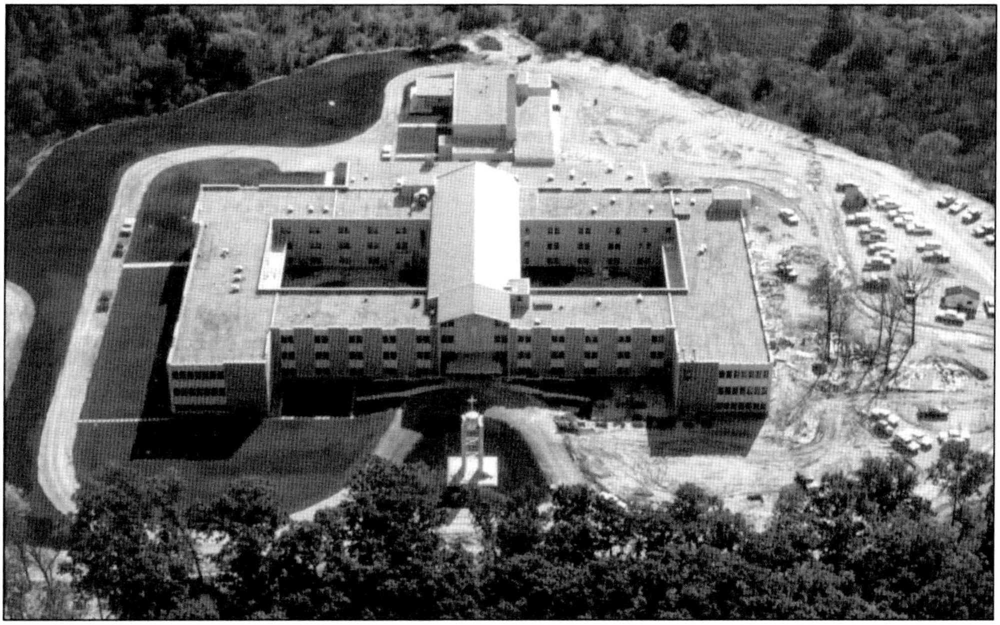

The Congregation of the Sisters of St. Joseph, Third Order of St. Francis transferred its motherhouse and Sister Formation, where young nuns were educated, from Chicago to Bartlett in 1963. The congregation moved into a new convent on a 100-plus acre site on West Bartlett Road, east of Route 59. When the college was dissolved in 1968, that portion of the facility became the Bartlett Learning Center for handicapped children.

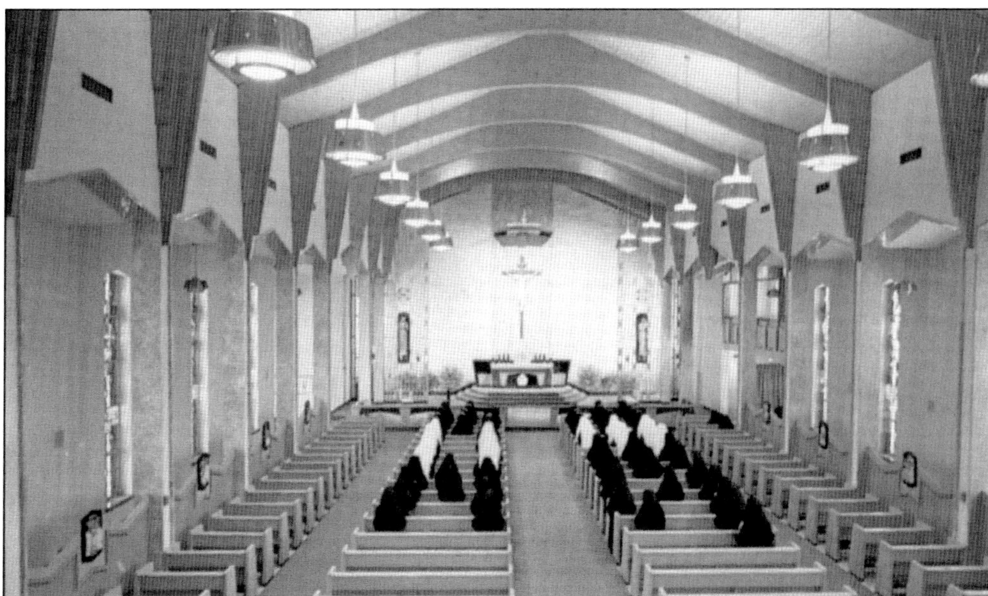

This view of the Sisters of St. Joseph chapel shows members of the convent community in meditation and prayer. The convent campus was home to nearly 400 sisters, novices, postulants, and aspirants to this teaching order. In 1989, an addition was made at the south end of the Immaculata Convent grounds and Francis Hall Infirmary was completed to serve the aged and infirm sisters.

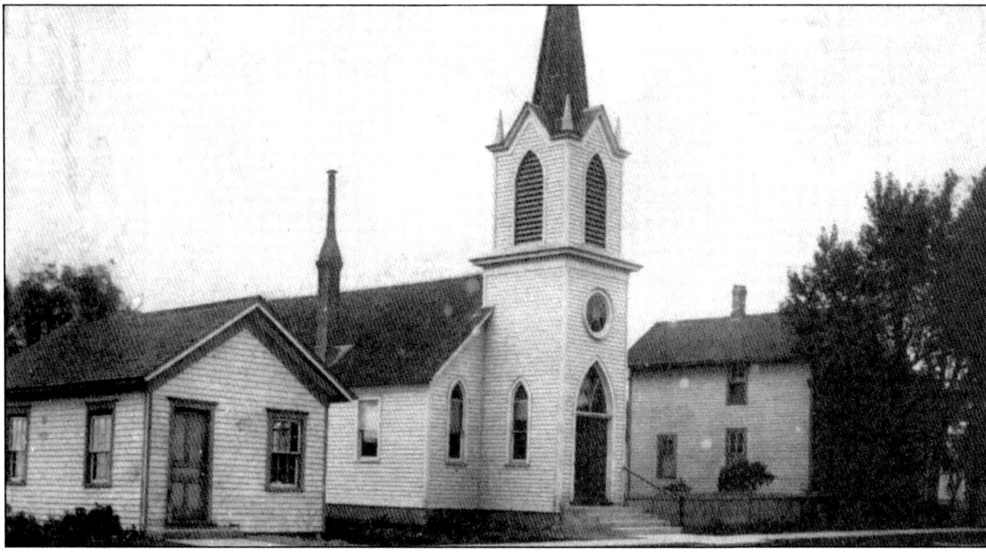

Immanuel Congregation, originally organized as a Lutheran Society, held its first worship service on January 1, 1871 in a church in Bloomingdale Township. In 1876, the church building was placed on logs and moved to Ontarioville. Immanuel joined the Lutheran Church-Missouri Synod in 1899. On Christmas Eve 1959, because Immanuel's membership had outgrown the old church building, the congregation began holding worship services at Set Screw & Mfg. Co. in Bartlett. This temporary location was made possible by company president and Immanuel member Calvin Brown. Shown in this 1964 photograph taken in front of the alter of the Set Screw factory church are Immanuel's communicant members for over 40 years, many of them descendants of founding church members.

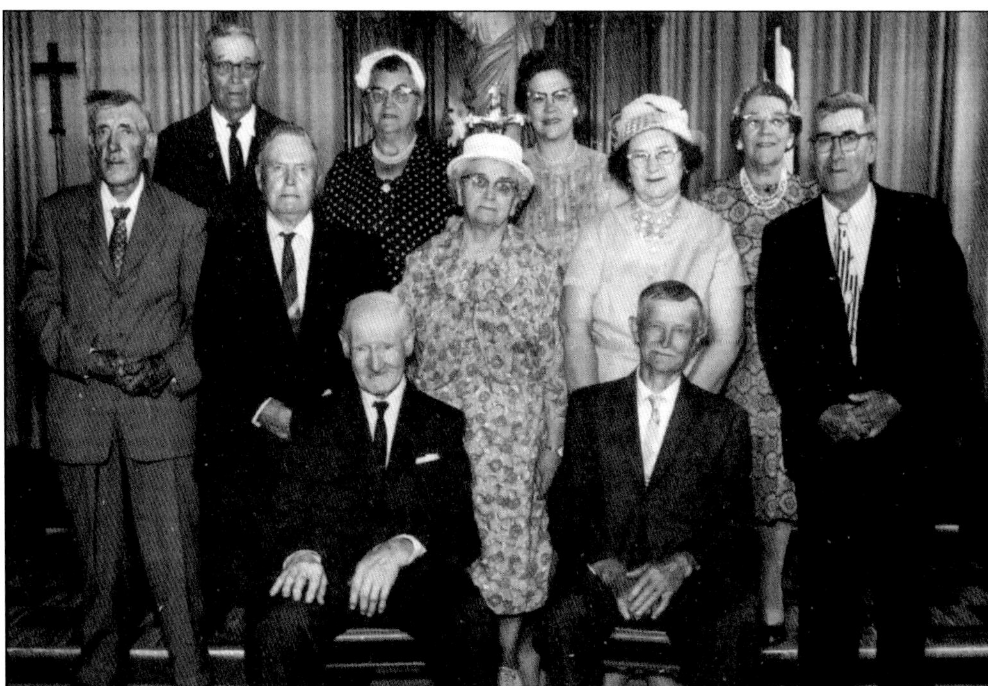

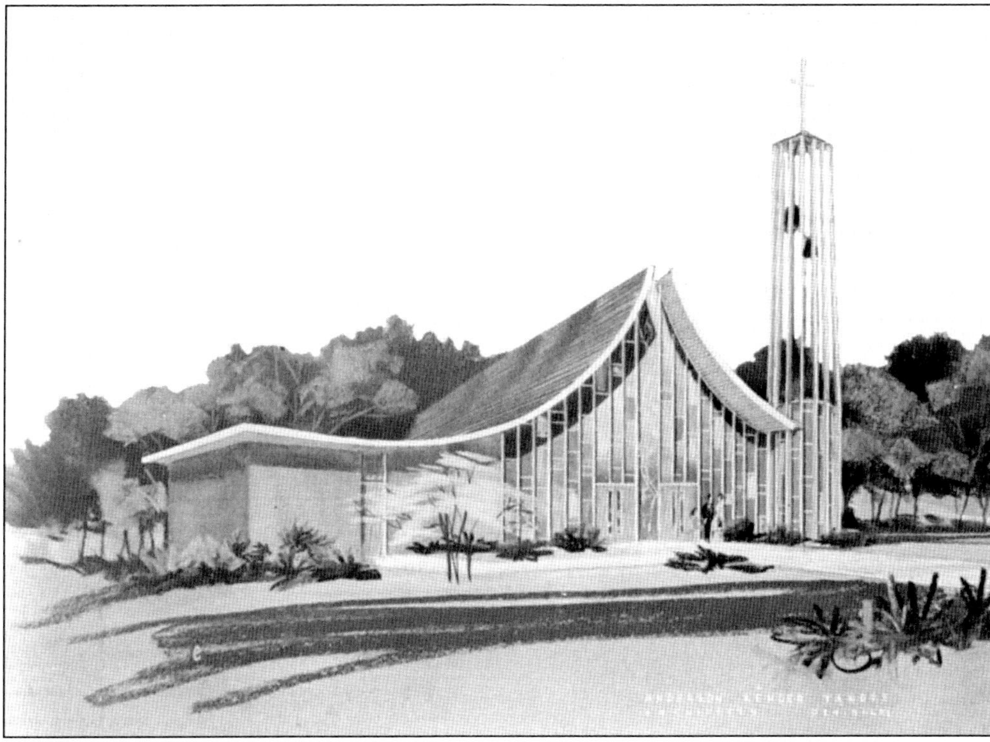

July 5, 1964 marked the beginning of a new era for the Immanuel Evangelical Lutheran Church congregation. This is the day that church members dedicated their new church building on Devon Avenue in Bartlett. Construction was made possible through the Kenneth Hansing Building Fund, Ladies Aid dinners, rummage sales, and donations from church members and friends. The five-acre church site was donated by Mr. and Mrs. William Leiseberg.

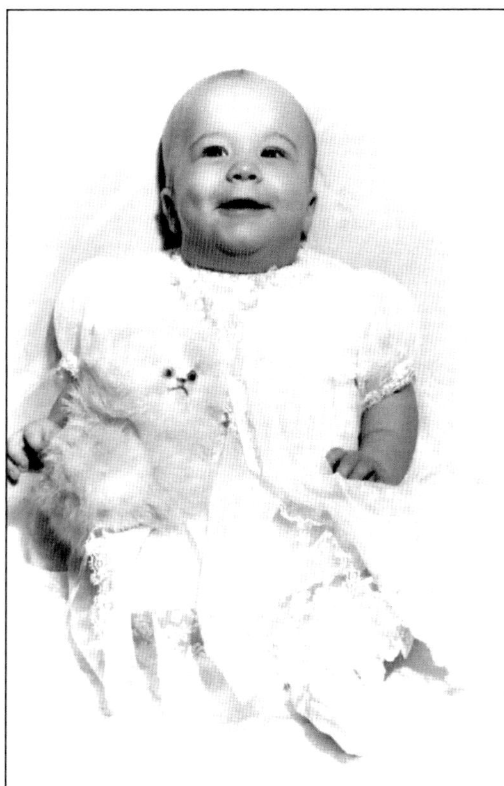

On July 12, 1964, Sandra Lynn Meyer Rice was the first child baptized in the new sanctuary of Immanuel Evangelical Lutheran Church and the fourth generation of the family to celebrate a major life event in the church. Sandra was also confirmed at Immanuel and married there on May 21, 1978.

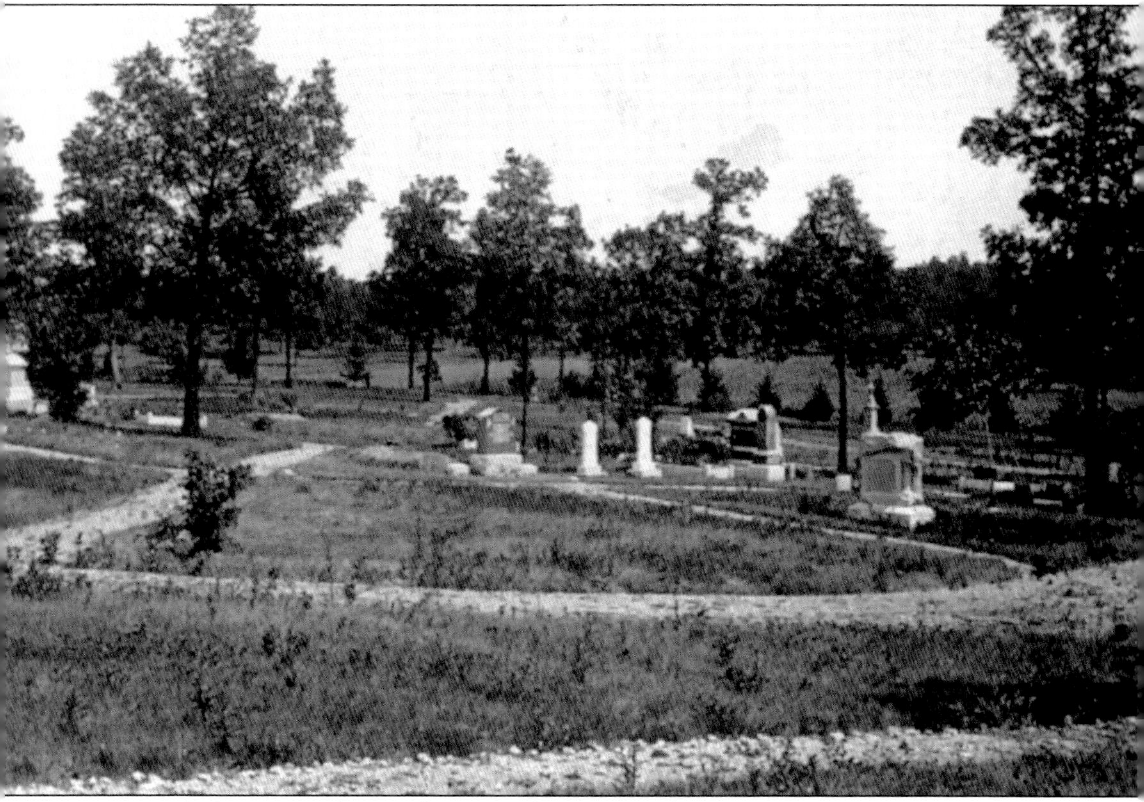

In April of 1892, Bartlett residents voted 35 to 4 in favor of purchasing land for a municipal cemetery. The Village Board immediately began taking steps to procure a suitable piece of property. After careful examination and investigation of several locations a board committee consisting of Chairman August Schick, Charles F. Schultz, and John C. Carr recommended a six-acre tract at the end of North Avenue belonging to Bartlett shopkeeper and former Village Trustee Henry Waterman. An ordinance adopted on May 9, 1892 directed the Board to issue $100 bonds with an interest rate of 6 percent and totaling $1,000 to complete the purchase.

The cemetery was laid out in a concentric pattern of blocks, with a Potter's Field at the eastern edge. Early cemetery records show that by 1900, four people had been buried in the Potter's Field.

According to the Elgin Advocate of Saturday, October 29, 1892, "the new cemetery was dedicated with appropriate services last Thursday. Union services were held by the German and Congregational churches. The cemetery is nicely located on a rise of ground just west of town."

On October 5, 1892, the cemetery committee reported to the Village Board that they had platted the cemetery land and had set lot prices according to size, ranging from $5 to as high as $30. The deed shown here is for a lot purchased in 1898 by Christ Hoffman and William Garrelts for the burial of Hoffman's infant son.

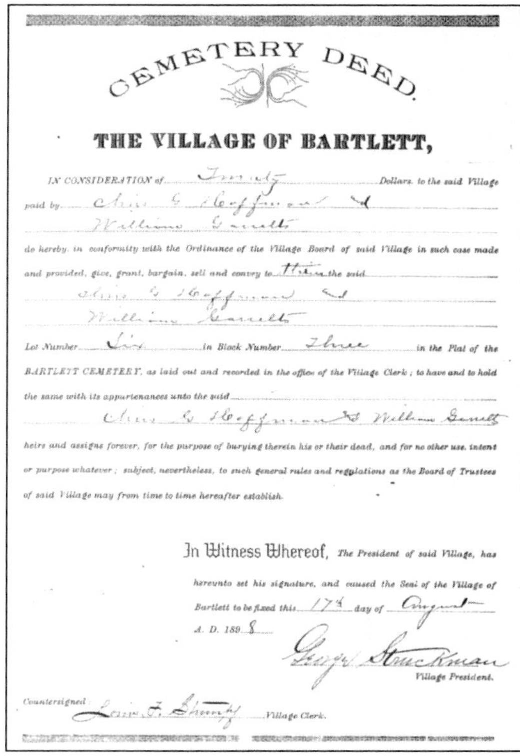

CEMETERY DEED.

THE VILLAGE OF BARTLETT,

IN CONSIDERATION of Twenty Dollars, to the said Village paid by Chris G. Hoffman & William Garrelts

do hereby, in conformity with the Ordinance of the Village Board of said Village in such case made and provided, give, grant, bargain, sell and convey to them the said Chris G. Hoffman & William Garrelts

Lot Number Six in Block Number Three in the Plat of the BARTLETT CEMETERY, as laid out and recorded in the office of the Village Clerk; to have and to hold the same with its appurtenances unto the said Chris G. Hoffman & William Garrelts heirs and assigns forever, for the purpose of burying therein his or their dead, and for no other use, intent or purpose whatever; subject, nevertheless, to such general rules and regulations as the Board of Trustees of said Village may from time to time hereafter establish.

In Witness Whereof, The President of said Village, has hereunto set his signature, and caused the Seal of the Village of Bartlett to be fixed this 17th day of August A. D. 1898

George Struckman
Village President.

Countersigned: Louis F. Schmidt Village Clerk.

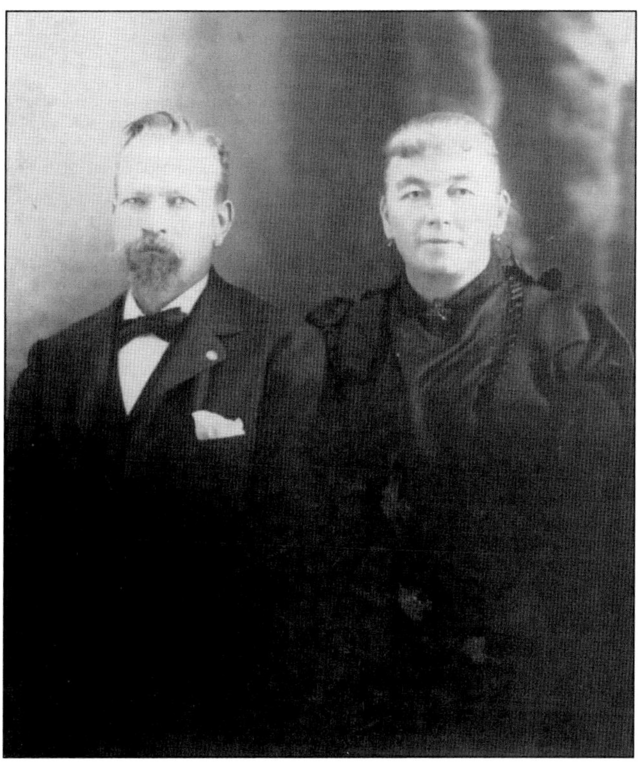

In the course of their business, Franz and Margarethe Hesse dealt in the goods and services for daily living as well as the routine matters of death. Primarily dealers in furniture, woodenware, window glass, and toys, the couple also served as the local undertakers and furnished coffins and hearses "on short notice" to local families who suffered the death of a loved one. Margarethe died at the age of 49 in 1894 and was the 16th person buried in Bartlett Cemetery.

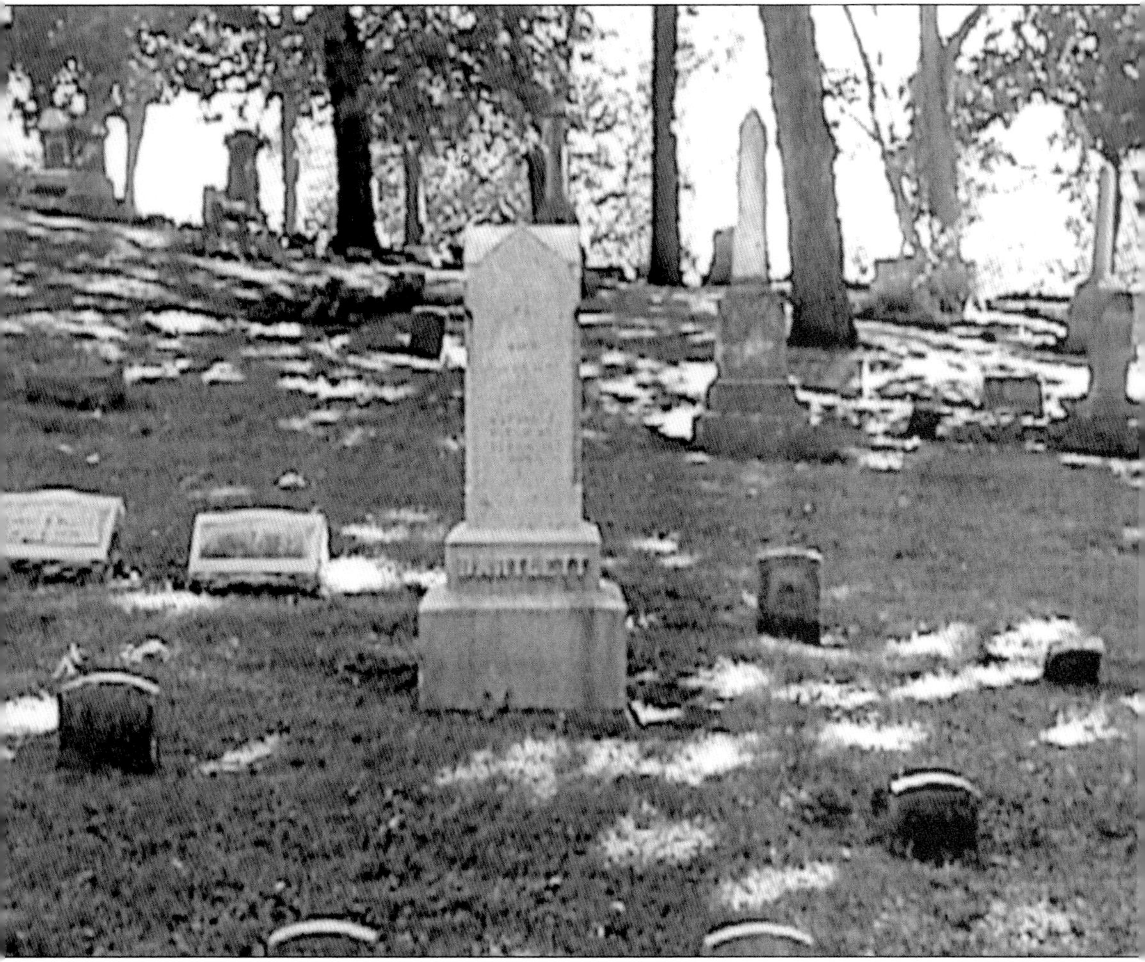

Village founder Luther Bartlett died on June 25, 1882 and was laid to rest in Wayne. In 1904, Luther's remains and those of several other family members were moved to this new family plot at Bluff City Cemetery in Elgin. A lifelong Democrat, Luther served as Wayne Township Supervisor and was highly respected in the community. Upon his death he was remembered as always upright and honest in all his dealings with his fellowman.